PLAYING AS OTHERS

PLAYING AS OTHERS
Theology and Ethical Responsibility
in Video Games

BENJAMIN J. CHICKA

BAYLOR UNIVERSITY PRESS

© 2021 by Baylor University Press
Waco, Texas 76798

All Rights Reserved. No part of this publication may be reproduced, stored in a retrieval system, or transmitted, in any form or by any means, electronic, mechanical, photocopying, recording, or otherwise, without the prior permission in writing of Baylor University Press.

Cover and book design by Kasey McBeath

Library of Congress Cataloging-in-Publication Data
Names: Chicka, Benjamin J., author.
Title: Playing as others : theology and ethical responsibility in video games / Benjamin J. Chicka.
Description: Waco : Baylor University Press, 2021. | Includes bibliographical references and index. | Summary: "Draws on the theology and ethics of Tillich and Levinas to explore how nontraditional video games can foster empathy and moral formation"-- Provided by publisher.
Identifiers: LCCN 2021025050 (print) | LCCN 2021025051 (ebook) | ISBN 9781481315463 (hardcover) | ISBN 9781481316675 (pdf) | ISBN 9781481315487 (epub)
Subjects: LCSH: Tillich, Paul, 1886-1965. | Levinas, Emmanuel. | Video games--Religious aspects. | Video games--Social aspects.
Classification: LCC GV1469.34.R45 C55 2021 (print) | LCC GV1469.34.R45 (ebook) | DDC 794.8--dc23
LC record available at https://lccn.loc.gov/2021025050
LC ebook record available at https://lccn.loc.gov/2021025051

Printed in the United States of America on acid-free paper with a minimum of thirty percent recycled content.

To Dave and Judy Chicka

For bringing video games into our home
instead of pushing them out

Main Menu

Loading... ix
Developed by xiii

Tutorial 1

Level One 19
Tillich and a Theology of Pop Culture

Level Two 41
Turning to the Other in Video Games

Level Three 63
Boss Fight: Philosophical Theology and Science

Level Four 79
Nontraditional Video Games and LGBTQ+ Others

Level Five 95
Face to Face with Immigrant Others

Level Six 109
Other Races and Religions in Protest

Level Seven 127
Economic and Social Polarities

Remaining Missions 143

Source Code 161
Credits 191
Fast Travel 211

```
┌─────────────────────────────────────────────────┐
│                                                 │
│   Loading...                                    │
│                                                 │
└─────────────────────────────────────────────────┘
```

Some of my earliest memories are of playing the Atari 2600 with my father on a massive RCA wooden console television. I am happy to report that very same Atari 2600 still works to this day. I have since converted the console television that introduced me to video games into a novel dry bar and wine rack, but my fascination with video games has lived on and even grown. While primitive by today's graphical standards, in the 1980s the moving rectangular pixels produced by the Atari were captivating. Controlling their behavior on screen by moving a joystick and pressing buttons seemed like magic to my child's mind, and that magical feeling has never waned.

Each technological leap forward has brought new video game consoles possessing new abilities that seemed impossible to surpass at the time. If a time traveler showed my Atari-playing self the Nintendo Entertainment System or Sega Genesis, younger me probably would have proclaimed the games on those systems to be impossible, produced by some sort of illusion. When Sony released the original PlayStation to North America in 1995, I was convinced at the time that its fully three-dimensional polygonal graphics would never be surpassed. Surely that console was proof the industry had come the closest it ever would to photorealistically recreating our world in video games. What an embarrassing claim in retrospect. The PlayStation 5, Xbox Series X, and computers built for gaming can now render graphics on screen that are hard to distinguish from real life, unlike the rudimentary polygons I took for the peak of graphical possibility in the 90s. There is a reason video games are so popular. They are captivating and engrossing. The advances that come with new generations of video game systems feel like they coincide with the unlocking of the creative potential of humanity.

If you think the previous sentence is a wild overstatement, consider some numbers. Video games have earned more gross income than the movie industry since 2008.¹ Since that time they have overtaken the movie and music industries combined. Gross revenue for the industry in 2019 topped $150 billion.² These numbers should not be assumed to indicate video games are nothing but a financially successful children's hobby either. While a high percentage of young people certainly play games, I am around the average age of video game players as I write these words (thirty-six years old), and 53 percent of men and women between the ages of thirty and forty-nine played games as of 2017.³ However, the games I will be describing as full of theological depth and ethical lessons are not exactly within the mainstream of the industry. I doubt readers who only know about video games through television and internet advertisements will have heard of many games mentioned in these pages. I suspect I will even be introducing those who play a decent number of video games to some new titles. Just as some movies are sheer entertainment, but not much more than that, many popular first-person shooters and action-adventure games are not very meaningful. They sure are fun though, and that is fine. The video game industry is in its infancy compared to the film industry, which has had many decades to experiment, mature, and carefully deal with important subjects. However, the video game industry is beginning to branch out, explore increasingly diverse subject matter, and mature.

A note about the style of writing that follows is in order before moving on to the main argument. While some look down on the inclusion of personal anecdotes in academic discourse, such is necessary in this book. To echo Paul Tillich and foreshadow why the theological argument in this book is focused on seemingly nontheological subject matter, the ultimate meaning shining forth through video games is most evident to those directly involved in the industry and the culture surrounding it. If a theologian is concerned with the meaning of God in the world today, that meaning can only be unpacked if the theologian is *vitally* connected with and capable of speaking to contemporary culture.⁴ To locate myself in relation to the video game industry and avoid giving an artificial view from nowhere, it is important to describe how I have interacted with video game developers and fans. Important evidence in support of the argument that follows also comes in the form of reactions I have received from those same developers and fans, which can only be conveyed through personal stories.

A note about the kind of theology informing my argument is also necessary. I am a philosophical theologian focused on truth wherever it is found, which entails not setting doctrinal limits on what is theologically relevant. I concur with Robert Neville that theology should be understood as a fallible form of human inquiry in the business of continuously improving through self-correction.⁵ Such correction is achieved through engaging and learning from other disciplines, religious traditions, and even video games. While some view Neville's approach to theology as too radical, this perspective on theology should be acceptable even to those embracing a rather traditional Augustinian or Anselmian theological method. Faith cannot *actually* seek understanding if arbitrary limits are set and some doctrines are made immune from criticism. Confessional narrative-based theology can be very celebratory and lively, but never actually questions that narrative or looks beyond its walls. Narrative theologians may analyze and enliven the story with critical tools, perhaps stripping it of sexist elements or better understanding its psychological impact, but questioning the veracity of the narrative is something that will simply never arise.⁶ Philosophical theology as I engage in it is not a confessionally focused form of theology because anything confessed must be treated as a hypothesis to be tested over sustained engagement with domains some might regard as beyond the proper scope of theology. My theology, like Neville's, is informed by Charles S. Peirce's argument that all thought is fallible, though that does not mean all thought is false. It is theology not in the mode of witness to something supposedly true, but in the mode of inquiry as to whether theological claims are true through seeking feedback from any and all relevant sources.

Informed by this philosophical form of theology, art can express theological ideas in new ways. What is ultimate can be engaged independent of church structures and authority.⁷ For example, Christian theology cannot be insular in terms of refusing to engage with the best thinking from other religious traditions, but neither can it disassociate itself from secular culture. Pop culture is an obvious fit for this theological approach, and some readers may be surprised to learn I find some secular video game fans to be more religious than self-described religious devotees. In the same way this form of philosophical theology might exist outside the mainstream of theology, the video games that are the focus of this book exist largely outside the mainstream big-budget focus of the industry. New things happening outside those mainstream walls can be surprising and are the focus of this book.

Developed by

So many people have played a part in helping me navigate the video game industry and find relevant fan and developer audiences to engage in philosophical and theological conversation that I will inevitably fail to acknowledge someone. While I have done my best to chronicle everyone who has significantly touched this project in some way through the years, I hope those missing know their contributions are nonetheless appreciated.

The germ of the idea for this book was probably a collaboration with my theological colleague Andrew Tripp at PAX East 2015. We gave a talk titled "The Science of Online Bullying: A Lesson in Diversity," and would go on to produce and host the *TheoNerd Podcast* together for a few years. Many branches grew out of that podcast, which gave me opportunities to speak with people in the video game industry. Anna Megill, a video game writer, was one of the first guests on the *TheoNerd Podcast* and introduced me to Aleen Simms, who invited me to speak about the importance of diversity on her podcast *Less Than or Equal*. Veteran video game press member Ken Gagne was also a guest on our podcast and in turn invited me to have a discussion with him about philosophy, theology, and the importance of diversity on his podcast *Polygamer*. Rami Ismail, whose arguments about the treatment of Muslims in the video game industry appear at length later in this book, was gracious enough to make time for a long *TheoNerd Podcast* interview in which he introduced me to a number of games that also made their way into these pages. Andrew Tripp's friend Audra Jamai was also featured on our podcast and introduced us to the Boston-based convention Arisia, where I have spoken on panels every year since 2017. All these conversations were vital, as it is important to me that my philosophical theological argument also makes sense to fans of video games and the people making those games.

Having mentioned conventions, I owe thanks to numerous groups in the Boston area who have welcomed my perspective rather than treating me like an outsider. Arisia and PAX East are large fan conventions, but I have also had the opportunity to engage professional video game developers at a number of conferences. Boston GameLoop is a user-generated conference, meaning attendees pitch and vote on what sessions will occur each year. I thank those present in 2015 and 2016 for voting in my talks about philosophy and religion at their conference focused on learning about making games. Adri Mills, Shae Rossi, Brian Liberge, Janine Dong, and Christina Qi co-organize Women in Games Boston. I met Adri through Arisia, which became my connection to this group, and I thank them for letting me give the first formal public presentation of my initial thoughts about Emmanuel Levinas and video games at one of their 2017 meetings. Surprisingly, not all my engagements with the video game industry have involved developers tolerating my philosophical and theological intrusions. Rik Eberhardt invited me to speak about Martin Luther at a Game Jam cosponsored by the MIT Game Lab and the Goethe-Institut Boston on the occasion of the five hundredth anniversary of the Protestant Reformation. I owe thanks to all the students in my Philosophy in Pop Culture class at Curry College for being the test subjects for the full argument of this book during the fall of 2019. I also thank Rob Smid, the Chair of the Humanities Department at the time, for enthusiastically approving my request to modify that course to include video games. Special thanks are also due to Cade Jarrell at Baylor University Press, not only for enthusiastically embracing a project that could have been met with suspicion, but also for his excellent work as my editor throughout the publication process. As is the case for all of my professional achievements, I cannot express enough thanks to my wife, Jessica, for her support. As she graciously does for just about everything I write, she read through this entire manuscript and found numerous typos and errors. More importantly, given that her Ph.D. from Boston University is in theological ethics, I am glad she did not throw out the whole thing in disgust upon reading it. Many of her suggestions on how my argument could be improved appear throughout this book. I must also thank our cat, Igby, who easily spent more time with me than any other living creature during the writing of this book. The importance of such companionship, especially during late nights, cannot be overstated.

I have dedicated this book to my parents. At minimum I owe them thanks for never tossing video games out of our house or deeming them a hindrance to my development, as some parents are wont to do. If anything, they fostered my interest once they realized it was present. I already mentioned my father and the Atari 2600 (which he was *much* better at playing than me), but I also clearly recall my mother picking me up from school on October 26, 2000, with the PlayStation 2 in the car. I saved up my own money for the console, but she dutifully waited in launch-day lines to pick up my preorder so I would be able to use it as soon as possible. When I was eight years old, my parents also had the good combination of sense and fortune to move us to a neighborhood with three other children all within a year of my age. Between the four of us, I think we had access to every video game console that existed until we all moved away for college. My parents also encouraged me to get to know the slightly older children in the neighborhood, and the Mirandas directly next door effectively became my free rental store for Sega Genesis games. I doubt my mother and father expected a professional accomplishment decades later to result from all of this, but I do not know if this book would exist if all these facets of my upbringing had been different.

Tutorial

The argument of this book is not only that video games are full of theological depth and ethical possibilities, but also that the works of Paul Tillich and Emmanuel Levinas, which upon first glance might seem diametrically opposed, can be brought together through video games. Tillich's theology of culture remains possibly the most sustained engagement with culture by any theologian to this day. Given that video games are now the largest grossing entertainment industry in the world, it makes perfect sense to engage them through the lens of Tillich's theology of culture. However, the most theologically salient aspects of the video games that will be described are the virtual encounters with others they provide, making Levinas a natural resource for considering the ethical aspects of such games.[1] The argument is not a critical analysis of gender, race, or other more specific themes that appear in some of the video games discussed, though such an argument is possible and much needed. Rather, the argument is concerned with ultimate reality, or God, and how to live best in light of that reality. It is an investigation, from many angles, of how video games as a form of art illustrate two large-scale theses: (1) God is encountered through video games, in culture and not apart from it, as the ground-of-being; (2) Responsibility to others is *the* crucial aspect of how the divine is so manifest through this mode of pop culture. Morality in this framework is not obedience to God, for there is no list of commands formed in the divine mind to which one could be obedient. Rather, it is a matter of courageously living one's own life and helping others do the same in the midst of all that is unknown about the future.

Given that awareness of God in video games occurs through interacting with others in those games, the different projects of Tillich and Levinas are brought side by side, where differences remain and yet similar sensibilities emerge. More important than resolving Tillich's use of ontology and phenomenological critiques of ontology is the fact that these two thinkers share sensibilities on ultimate matters, especially regarding the inability to neatly contain what ultimately matters about life in concepts and language in general. Tillich and Levinas provide strong arguments regarding why God cannot be *a being*. As interdisciplinary philosophical inquiry into such theological issues, neuroscience is also brought into the argument as an important dialogue partner to both support and correct some of the ideas from Tillich and Levinas (chapter 3). The result of this dialogue with science is a more limited, yet effective, form of ethical responsibility than the one developed by Levinas.[2] Video games can play an important role in helping people live up to such responsibilities toward others, but more than just their import, the meaning they convey as pieces of art must be recognized as effective in that endeavor. While Tillich focused exclusively on the theological import of art in his engagement with culture, all his categories of form, content, and import are brought to bear on video games. With such necessary modifications in place, it will be possible to show how the polarizations of life and various ways people are estranged from themselves and one another can be addressed through meeting others in video games.

Video games display the promises and perils of culture. They depict the polar tensions of life that cause anxiety and struggle among different individuals and groups, as well as the ethical failures and success stories of those individuals and groups responding to one another's pleas. This is especially true for various marginalized groups in society. Some games and the communities they foster have latched onto one pole in life and wielded it as a weapon against those they consider outsiders. This is exhibited in the angry reaction of some people to greater representation of nonmale and nonwhite characters in video games, for example. In a way that resembles the rise of white nationalism across the world right now, individuals and groups doing the most damage hold on to their distorted understanding of culture as if others trying to participate in it were trying to take the most precious ultimate reality away from them.[3] Such quasi-religious devotion to a distorted understanding of video game culture culminated in Gamergate. Initially a series of interrelated events, Gamergate eventually launched a movement that grew into a full-blown culture war. It was, in many ways, the canary in the coal mine for the current polarized political climate in the United States. Right-wing figurehead Milo Yiannopoulos has admitted as much, crediting the movement for helping him cut his teeth in a way that would eventually land him a job at the conservative website Breitbart.[4] However, other reactions to Gamergate have been perfect examples of how culture can be the form of religion and religion the substance of culture, as Tillich would phrase things.

Various marginalized individuals and groups attacked in Gamergate have been able to assert their importance through different types of video games developed in the wake of Gamergate. As game developers increased diversity both among the ranks of those they employ and the characters in their games, nonmarginalized players were given opportunities to encounter virtual others they may be segregated from in daily life, others they might even actively reject in society. As new styles of games emerged that allowed players to encounter and respond to people too often ignored as "the other" in society, some video game communities started showing more care and love in their responses to one another. Seeing and playing characters representing minorities, and controlling those characters as their lives are fulfilled, is an interactive experience unlike those available in other mediums. It is an experience that gives people the courage to be themselves in the world in the face of adversity. For nonmarginalized players, the virtual encounters provided by these games are opportunities to learn about the importance of embracing the other, and to carry that lesson into the real world.

An Industry Changed Forever

Video games do not just change when technology allows for new, impressive hardware to be developed. Politics entered into and forever changed the video game industry in the form of Gamergate.

Gamergate began in August 2014 when rumors spread that independent game developer Zoë Quinn received special treatment from games press and preferential coverage of her game *Depression Quest*, released the year prior, because they had had a sexual relationship with a member of the press. The rumors originated on 4chan, and later spread to 8chan. These are the terrible parts of the internet that actually exist and are part of what people mean when referencing the "dark web." Some of the worst human ideas and behaviors are openly discussed and encouraged on these sites. In the case of the discussions that would lead to Gamergate, Quinn's ex-boyfriend, Eron Gjoni, spread rumors that Quinn struck a deal to sleep with a journalist for the website Kotaku in exchange for preferential treatment by the outlet. The accusations were lies.[5] Quinn and the Kotaku staff member Nathan Grayson only dated briefly prior to *Depression Quest* being released, and Grayson had nothing to do with the way Kotaku covered *Depression Quest*. In fact, the only story he wrote for the website that dealt with Quinn related to their involvement in a failed reality TV show, not their game.[6] Kotaku did run a story about *Depression Quest* and how Quinn was trying to spread awareness about depression by providing an interactive window into their own experience of suffering through it, but Grayson was not involved in that story.[7] Regardless, the damage was done.

Kotaku is one of the most popular and widely visited websites about video games, and those who believed Gjoni's lies looked to Gamergate as a cause defending professionalism in games journalism. The rallying cry of Gamergate supporters was sticking up for ethics in games journalism, but their behavior was anything but ethical. The resulting situation created by Gamergate led to Quinn having personal information leaked onto 4chan and 8chan. They received detailed death threats and had to flee their home. Brianna Wu, another independent video game developer, defended Quinn against the false accusations, and she too received targeted death threats. Both developers were located in Boston at the time, which became ground zero for Gamergate. Just like think pieces supporting right-wing politicians as defenders of something supposedly pure, and usually white, articles popped up online bemoaning the death of "real" gamer identity and blaming these developers for trying to destroy "real" games by making their experimental alternatives.

Such dogmatic zeal was backed up by the movement's misbegotten notion that it was standing up for professional ethics through threats of violence. Wu ended her company's presence at one of the video game industry's largest annual conventions due to such continued harassment.[8] Video game critic Anita Sarkeesian became enmeshed in Gamergate due to the video series *Tropes vs. Women in Video Games* that she launched on her website, Feminist Frequency.[9] In those videos Sarkeesian breaks down the sexism inherent in many tropes frequently included within video games. For example, she questioned why it is that in so many fantasy games, the male characters are wearing heavy armor but the female characters are wearing what can only be described as chainmail bikinis. Bikinis are not armor, and Sarkeesian is happy to point out that such tropes exist for no other reason than to objectify women in games.[10] Once the videos went live, she received death threats as well, all in the name of supposedly defending ethics.

Gamergate's campaign of targeted harassment against Quinn and women in the video game industry rose alongside spikes in toxic masculinity and white nationalism, all aligned against minorities. Those who criticized Gamergate and supported the victims were called liars and whining social justice warriors, and were generally discredited. The situation is disturbingly similar to the trend of dismissing as "fake news" anything clearly true that one nonetheless finds unpleasant. Those who became part of the Gamergate movement reacted the same way homophobic individuals often react to LGBTQ+ individuals and their allies, by denying their homophobia is damaging in any way and blaming the victim instead. One academic researcher who studied Gamergate and was not a white man even experienced a targeted campaign of harassment like the one directed against Quinn.[11]

The events that led to and became Gamergate took place in 2014, but the bullying, harassment, and general mistreatment of minorities remains a problem in the industry.[12] In 2018, 59 percent of US teenagers reported experiencing online bullying and harassment. A massive 90 percent of teens in the same survey stated they believe online harassment is a problem greatly affecting people their age. Furthermore, nonmales remain the prime targets. While close to equal percentages of young boys and girls reported experiencing harassment, girls were 13 percent more likely to endure false rumors capable of doing more long-term damage.[13] Gamergate is not only morally problematic, its supporters are statistically out of touch with the demographics of modern video game communities. As of 2017, 48 percent of Hispanic adults and 44 percent of Black adults, compared to 41 percent of their white counterparts, frequently played video games. More adult men play games than women, but about 40 percent of adult women play, and almost 25 percent of Americans over the age of 65 play games.[14] According to a 2015 Pew survey, well over half of the US population plays video games, and women constitute roughly half of the gaming population. However, 73 percent of players reported witnessing threats or harassment, 40 percent reported experiencing such threats and harassment, and when compared to all online spaces, only 3 percent of respondents claimed video games were welcoming to women.[15]

This entire story is unfortunate not just due to its violent features but because it is based on a misunderstanding of history. Women have always worked in the industry. While the Atari 2600 home console was not the first, it was that piece of hardware that ushered video games into mainstream culture. From the earliest days of its success, women were crucial to the developments at Atari. Carol Shaw was a designer for the Atari 2600 in the 1970s. Joyce Weisbecker made games for the RCA Studio console, a less popular video game system that was a contemporary of the Atari 2600. While women now form roughly half of the gaming population, they have always been part of the industry's story. However, in the wake of Gamergate and everything terrible it unleashed, historically marginalized voices have become louder and alternative gaming experiences such as the one created by Quinn have become easier to find. Women and other groups treated as unwelcome minorities by Gamergate defenders have started making and supporting games that reflect their experiences, rather than caving in to Gamergate pressure that the industry cater only to a sort of white male power fantasy. From its origins in spreading lies about one developer as justification for harassing them, Gamergate became a culture war over what video games should be about. However, the video game industry noticeably changed in response to the situation Gamergate created.

The Penny Arcade Expo (PAX) is held yearly in Boston (PAX East), Seattle (PAX West), and San Antonio (PAX South). It is the largest gaming convention held in the United States. Attendance for each PAX event has exceeded 70,000 since 2011.[16] ReedPop, the company that currently runs PAX, no longer releases attendance figures. However, based on continued popularity and the addition of an extra day to each convention, it is safe to assume those numbers have been exceeded in recent years. Why do such numbers matter? After Gamergate, PAX was under pressure to respond in some form, and respond it did. In 2014 the convention organizers introduced the first ever Diversity Lounge at PAX East in Boston.[17] The initiative was not without problems, as some criticized the name for implying diversity in gaming was to be relegated to a small room.[18] But after an initially rough rollout, the Diversity Lounge has become a safe place to hang out, support LGBTQ+ merchants, and learn more about issues marginalized voices face in the industry. At that same PAX East, TakeThis.org began hosting AFK (away from keyboard) rooms at all PAX conventions.[19] They are quiet safe spaces staffed by volunteers who are present to help conference attendees overwhelmed by the size or culture of PAX.

While the main draw bringing attendees to PAX conventions is the show floor, where people can play previews of video games that have not been released and chat with the people responsible for making those games, there are also panels running back-to-back in dozens of rooms throughout each day. Since Gamergate, there have been more panels at each PAX about the experiences of those historically marginalized within the industry—panels about being a woman working in the industry or being a transgender gamer, for example. In the wake of Gamergate, people were noticeably interested in talking about video games differently, even at some of the industry's largest events. For example, not only did PAX East accept a panel I proposed with practical theologian Andrew Tripp in 2015 about the science behind online bullying and why diversity matters, but there were roughly 600 people in attendance at the talk.[20]

Spurred on by the interest in our PAX East panel, I hosted and produced the *TheoNerd Podcast* in collaboration with Tripp from 2015 to 2018. Over the course of fifty-four episodes, besides conversations between Tripp and myself, we interviewed people on topics that touched upon the diversity of reactions to Gamergate.[21] Comic book author A. David Lewis spoke about Muslim superheroes and representation of Muslims in games. Conversations were had with women in video games as well as other tech industries about their positive and negative work-related experiences. Interviews from PAX East featured games that contribute to climate change research, a cofounder of TakeThis.org discussing mental health and video games, and a member of the AbleGamers Charity, which makes games accessible to disabled individuals. The podcast featured a PAX East panel about the healing power of video games and an interview with an ethicist about the genuine moral potential of games, as opposed to the distorted view of ethics proliferated by Gamergate supporters. Amid all these discussions, theological connections became obvious. Large groups of people were beginning to see the potential depth of meaning in video games for the first time and were seeking to actively develop that potential. Those targeted by Gamergate have become part of creating communities that are spaces for affirming and celebrating marginalized identities.

Different Kinds of Gaming Communities

After presenting at PAX East seeded the initial idea for this book, pieces of the argument were tested in front of smaller gaming communities that allowed for more intimate feedback and conversation than conventions attended by over eighty thousand people would allow. The following highlights from such conversations are presented as further proof that the video game industry, and the communities that develop around it, really are changing due to a hunger for fostering meaning through games.

The connection between Levinas and video games was first presented at a July 2017 meeting of Women in Games Boston. Women in Games is a nonprofit organization with chapters in cities throughout the world. All local meetings are open to anyone, but leadership is composed of women in the industry, and programming often relates to pushing the video game industry toward equal treatment and eliminating discrimination.[22] My talk was enthusiastically received. The reason for such a reception certainly had nothing to do with me personally. Only two people in attendance were friends who came to offer support. The bulk of the remaining audience members were independent video game developers who did not know me and had no interest in religion. Rather, the political and moral potential of video games seems obvious to many within the industry. Besides this trial run of my work, the public forum where I most thoroughly presented and received feedback on pieces of the argument in this book is Arisia.

Arisia is a four-day catch-all convention for science fiction and fantasy in all forms of media, including video games, that takes place every January in Boston. Organizers proudly present Arisia as being "New England's Largest, Most Diverse Sci-Fi & Fantasy Convention."[23] Such diversity initially meant welcoming "soft" science fiction as appropriate for the event when a competing convention in Boston started defining itself around a strict "hard" definition of science fiction, which only promoted programming directly, or at least plausibly, tied to current scientific knowledge and advances in technology. As Arisia welcomed diverse styles of writing and more panels about all sorts of topics related to science fiction and fantasy writing, television shows, and movies, the convention grew in size until it became Boston's largest local convention on such topics. Over five thousand people now attend it each year. As a more diverse group of people attended Arisia each year, the organizers worked to make the event as welcoming and accommodating as possible for attendees.

Arisia requires all speakers, panelists, and attendees to sign a code of conduct containing typical agreements to refrain from harassment, but also requiring consent for some activities not considered potentially invasive by other conventions. Permission must be asked for and granted to take pictures of those in attendance, as well as any video or audio recording.[24] PAX does not take such privacy concerns into consideration. Some bathrooms in the hotel where Arisia is held are converted to gender neutral bathrooms for the duration of the convention. Programming runs twenty-four hours a day during the four days of Arisia, and organizers convert several conference rooms into chapels for religious services every year. When allegations of rape were brought against a now-former president of Arisia, the organization immediately announced an investigation, the president willingly stepped down, and conversations among leadership were made open to the public. All steps have been well documented in an effort to help ensure similar acts do not occur in the future.[25] Such care for others is also extended beyond those directly involved with the convention. In 2019, when hotel employees were on strike at the usual convention location, the Westin Boston Waterfront, organizers moved Arisia to the Boston Park Plaza, refusing to cross picket lines in support of the Westin employees. Westin sued Arisia for canceling their reservation, and a judge ruled in the hotel's favor. The ruling was devasting for the nonprofit volunteer-run convention, as the initial ruling required them to pay over $150,000. That number has since been reduced to over $40,000.[26] Fundraising from the diverse community that Arisia supports every year has already supported Arisia in turn by raising the full $40,000 for settling this legal matter. More money is still being raised to cover extraneous expenses related to the legal battle.

Beyond Arisia's work to make the structure of the convention welcoming and accommodating, a small sampling of titles for featured panel sessions should indicate how seriously the organizers take issues related to diversity: "Don't Feed the Trolls" Doesn't Work; Dealing with Day-to-Day Isms in Game Culture; How to be Inclusive; Toxic Fandom Behavior Online; Gaming as a Way of Exploring Identity; Playing the Other. Panels from 2019 and 2020 about exploring identity through games and playing as the other stand out as especially relevant to a theological embrace of the other. During the panel on exploring identity, there was a discussion about character creation in the *Mass Effect* video game franchise. In that series of games, players get to choose between a male or female version of the main character, Commander Shepard. Playing with a female lead character, known as "FemShep" by fans, became *the* canonical version of the game to many players. The popularity of FemShep can in part be attributed to personal protests against the lack of diversity in the industry, expressions of personal frustration along the lines of, "If you refuse to create games explicitly featuring non-male leads, I will choose an alternative whenever presented with the option." Beyond an increase in gender diversity, some males playing as a female lead character experienced the breaking down of binaries. Beyond learning that playing as a nonmale character can be fun (the games were incredibly popular), there was expressed on the panel the realization of sexuality as a spectrum. In the game, players can "romance" other characters through dialogue choices in conversations, giving gifts, and going on dates. All of that can eventually lead to sexual encounters in the game. Playing as a woman attracted to a man in the game led to some "aha!" moments in which players realized genuinely attractive characteristics in that male character. It is not as if the straight cis male players now thought they were gay, whereas they had previously been straight. Rather, the game helped usher in some awareness about the spectrum of sexual orientation and expression.

Such decisions to play as the other are potentially rewarding, though not without potential pitfalls. A male playing as FemShep may just prefer to look at a three-dimensional female character for dozens upon dozens of hours of gameplay, making the female lead character an object of the male gaze rather than a genuine case of positive diversity. In tabletop roleplaying games like *Dungeons and Dragons* (D&D), choices about character creation are even more open-ended. Rather than having to choose from a set list of characters to play the male and female version of Shepard in the case of *Mass Effect*, in D&D players can create any sort of character, with any identity, gender, sexual orientation, etc. that they desire. The only limits from the game are that players must roll a set of dice to determine character skills. LQBTQ+ individuals who may feel pressure in their daily contexts to conform to societal norms, rather than fully be themselves, get the chance to let themselves flourish in such a fantasy world. And if a transgender woman playing a transgender warrior, for example, is playing the game with a transphobic individual, they can always claim to simply be playing a role; a means of deflecting and deflating criticism not always possible outside the context of a game. The same possibilities for expressing oneself and deflecting detractors are present in Massively Multiplayer Online games (MMOs), again with some pitfalls. Some straight white male players could certainly choose to play as another race or gender just to mock and make a caricature of others, but players with honest intentions who choose to play as the other also have the chance to have mistaken impressions and incorrect ideas about those others corrected if playing with a diverse group. As always, diversity matters.

Arisia panel participants, as well as audience members, have generally agreed through the years that any diversity in games is a good thing. Those marginalized, ignored, or actively hurt by society will take validation of who they are where they can get it. If nonmarginalized players living their lives at the center of what society considers acceptable happen to encounter more diversity through playing games, maybe nothing will happen, but maybe they will become more tolerant and accepting in some way. Games are genuine places of learning, after all.[27] However, the learning potential of video games has only slowly gained acceptance due to early work that viewed video games, and technology in general, either through utopian lenses or as a driving cause of real-world violence.

The Peril and Promise of Video Games

The 1990s was a decade in which it seemed every politician was concerned about violence and video games. Members of the Senate and Congress seemed locked in a contest to outdo one another in attempts to censor violence in video games due to supposed concerns over real-world violence. For those who were paying attention to video games during the end of the twentieth century, the mere mention of the *Grand Theft Auto* or *Mortal Kombat* franchises likely brings such political campaigns to mind. However, claims about a causal link between violent video games and acts of violence in the world have been refuted over and over again.[28] Instead, the link between games and violence has been traced to journalistic and political manipulation.[29] A comprehensive study of one of the favorite franchises politicians against video games love to reference, *Grand Theft Auto*, concluded there is no decisive link between playing that series of games and increases of violence in developing children.[30] Beyond such easily dismissed worries, positive arguments about the power of playing predate video games.

According to the catharsis hypothesis posed in the 1950s by Seymour Feshbach, violent games are not problematic, because the harm they cause is virtual. More importantly, they might be outlets for aggression that lead to fewer in-person confrontations.[31] Furthermore, if some people are prone to violent behavior in games and also perform violent acts outside of games, that does not prove causality. Blay Whitby has forcefully argued that some people are just motivated to perform reprehensible actions, whether virtually or physically, and no degree of relief in the form of outlets for aggression will stop such violence.[32] The Columbine High School shooters listened to Metallica, but the millions of people who have attended Metallica concerts have generally not gone on to commit murder. Rather, it is an unfortunate truth that some people do terrible things that cannot be rationally explained. When causes can be identified, studies indicate aggression and violence are cultivated more by familial and societal cultures of the same than by playing violent games.[33] Beyond this narrative about games and violence, which can be clarified with relative ease, it is worth considering how video games fit into early debates about the promises and perils of technology in general.

In terms of generally positive or negative assessments regarding the social possibilities of technology, Michael Heim has broken the debate down into the competing camps of "network idealists" and "naïve realists."[34] For one group, computers and what they can produce represent a new utopian future, while the other emphasizes a "Big Brother is watching" world in which those in power will use technology for societal monitoring and control. Derek Stanovsky has drawn the same battle lines in relation to virtual reality technology, which is now being deployed within video games as well.[35] Andrew Calcutt presents a list of polar oppositions in technology that should raise the attention of any Tillich scholar: anarchy/authority, community/alienation, play/work, subject/object, universal/particular, gates/anti-gates, free/fee, etc.[36] However, as will be shown in the next chapter, Tillich would locate the answer to such oppositions beyond choosing one side over the other. To return to those in the idealistic camp, some have even given technical advances religious overtones. Michael Benedikt claimed computers offer a hope for redemption once assigned to the "Heavenly City" but now available here on Earth.[37] It is as if freedom from our human limitations, once left for God to achieve, is now capable of being delivered by computers in the hands of talented engineers and programmers. Those who offer a "realistic" warning to such optimism about the potential of technology have a longer tradition to which they can point in their defense.

Thamus, in Plato's *Phaedrus*, warned against writing because it could destroy human thinking, eliminate something that is essential to what it means to be human. Conversations were regarded as genuine and true, while writing was deemed a fabrication.[38] Neil Postman explicitly references this point in his critique of cultures overly reliant on technology, *Technopoly*. Such cultures supposedly lose their creative and critical thinking abilities in proportion to their reliance on machines solving problems for them, problems such a hypothetical society will be unable to solve if the machines fail, as that society's cognitive abilities will have been so diminished.[39] Such words of caution are fair. It is not likely that anyone will truly grasp the points of this book, or of Tillich and Levinas, just by playing the video games mentioned in these pages. Convincing someone with a deep hatred of homosexuality to play video games featuring gay and lesbian main characters will not automatically turn them into a supporter of gay rights. There is still a role for philosophers and theologians that cannot be usurped by video games. Reading and being taught some Tillich and Levinas might pave the way for ultimate truths in games to be revealed to players. However, some technological realists take their warnings too far. Mark Slouka, for example, bemoans a "growing separation from reality" brought on by technological advances.[40] Such a worry is misguided. Just about anyone who plays online video games will tell you the way they are treated online matters to their physical selves. If you want proof, go online and search for stories about married couples who met in an MMO or about funerals held in game for online friends who passed away. As will be shown in chapter 3, there is even growing evidence that our brains online respond like they would to similar interactions in person. It would only make sense if playing video games made similar real impressions upon players. Besides, graphical technology is now so advanced that it would be more difficult to argue that it is unlikely our brains are triggered by games than the opposite. If animated movies like *Toy Story 3* and *Up* can touch core human emotions and elicit tears, so can *Gone Home, Journey, Brothers: A Tale of Two Sons, What Remains of Edith Finch*, and many more games.

Additionally, the video games that will be described in this book let players come to their own conclusions. They offer the opportunity for learning, rather than dictating what is true to players. In these video games players encounter characters that are different, and characters that tell the player their difference has worth. Still, players can loathe the others they encounter in video games. The main story of *Gone Home* is about learning what happened to the lesbian sibling of the character that players control. It is entirely possible for a player to leave the game despising that fictional sister. Yet because players have to interact with the other in video games, rather than discuss them abstractly, the serious difficulty of exclusionary choices is brought to the forefront, making such video games real resources for imparting progressive ethical lessons. Both Tillich and Levinas agree that the transcendence of God has to do with reaching beyond personal limitations to realize oneself in that which is other than oneself yet nonetheless responsible for it. As audience members at numerous gaming conventions and conferences have told me, finding themselves realized in something other than themselves is precisely what happens when they play certain video games, the sorts of games discussed in chapters 4 through 7. When players not marginalized by society play games in which they encounter others who are irresponsibly neglected and mistreated, those players are better equipped to act responsibly when they actually meet those whom society has discarded as the other.

Video Games and Theology After Tragedy

It is informative to observe how tragedy alters ways of thinking about and being in the world.[41] Tillich was at the core of German intellectual culture leading into World War II. The work of German academics represented the true, good, and the beautiful for him. His respect for that tradition had been strained, but not broken, during World War I, when he served as a chaplain in the German Army and spent most of his active-duty days pulling dead bodies out of the mud instead of ministering to the spiritual needs of living people. Once he saw what "high" German culture did to people like almost every member of Levinas' family, Tillich's German culture fell from the pedestal on which he had placed it. He had to rethink God, and the way God is understood to relate to human culture, without reverting to forms of supernaturalism that absolutely separate the two.

The failures of the Holocaust also led to Levinas suggesting a revision, that philosophers first ask what is good rather than what is true. Rather than prioritize supposedly true concepts, a focus which did nothing to impede the tragedies of World War II, his alternative was a philosophy that makes personal ethical responsibility to others the starting point and primary focus of philosophy. Levinas' "first philosophy" is not even truly ethics, if ethics is taken to mean rational rules for behavior or the calculation of virtue. Instead, he describes the face-to-face encounter, being called by another and responding to that other. Others encounter us like nothing else—like ourselves yet different than ourselves—and like each of us they call out to respect their existence, prior to our obtaining any conceptual content about them. Levinas' work describes lived experiences and encounters, not codes of conduct, making video games about meaningful experiences that result from encountering others a perfect match for his philosophy. Just as Levinas did not want to propose strict ethical rules as much as highlight the need to be good to others, the games considered in this book do not always offer strict rules of gameplay to the player. Rather, the player encounters other characters in game and responds as they see fit. Experiencing the other and reacting to them is sometimes the sole goal of playing such games. Levinas argued ethics precedes ontology, and in what I call nontraditional games, emotional and ethically charged experiences can take precedence over winning or losing the game.

Responses to Gamergate have also inverted traditional structures. In the games described in the second half of this book, different sorts of gameplay prioritize meaningful experiences over reflex time and skillful play. Challenging gameplay and trying to win are minimized or even eliminated in favor of experiencing the weight, even ethical importance, of a situation. In short, part of the experience of playing video games now involves cultivating empathy. The interactivity of video games is a gateway into the lives of other people, creating potential learning environments on topics ranging from the plight of immigrants, or the challenges faced by the economically disadvantaged, to how members of other religions pray. Just as Levinas and Tillich argued philosophical theology must change in the wake of worldwide upheaval, the video games examined in this book challenge the status quo.

My shorthand for the games referenced in this book is "nontraditional" games, because they are rather unlike the action-packed games focused on war and conflict you are likely to see advertised more frequently. Those action-packed games are comparable to summer blockbuster movies and are referred to as AAA games within the video game industry. Such games have massive budgets in the tens to hundreds of millions of dollars, partially funded by equally massive publishing companies, and can be made by several development teams composed of hundreds of people at once. Independent, or indie, games are the alternative. They are games made by teams of a handful of people, sometimes even a single person. Such games are often self-published, rather than with the aid of an external publishing company. However, because some indie games have been among the biggest financial successes in any given year, and there are now publishers that specialize in helping such small development studios bring their games to market, the "indie" terminology is losing some favor. Aside from shifting business realities, such games are referred to as nontraditional in order to reflect the variety of different experiences they offer compared to AAA games. Such nontraditional games are where the theologically meaningful reaction to Gamergate has been most pronounced. Quick reflexes and skill do not so much dictate how players experience these games; instead, they tend to be a little slower and allow players to explore a virtual world and immerse themselves in an experience. Many offer story-based experiences in which violence is almost, or even entirely, absent. Some still offer challenging gameplay but couple that challenge with emotionally engaging and ethically charged storytelling. In some games there are not even conditions for winning or losing the game. Rather, playing the game becomes about making interesting choices and seeing how those choices impact the virtual environment, or simply interacting with characters and experiencing their lives and stories. Such different styles of gameplay reinforce how these nontraditional games can bring players face to face with others and reveal the meaningful depths of human life.

It could be argued that the logic of Christianity and Judaism presented by Tillich and Levinas is ex-centric and centered on others, while video games are individualized and focused on the player. Besides the fact that some of today's biggest games are multiplayer and social, even some nontraditional single player games are focusing on encounters with others. As mentioned regarding the changes conventions like PAX have enacted since Gamergate, when communities who love these nontraditional games come together at conventions, their love is openly expressed to one another, not restricted to adoration for their favorite form of digital entertainment. If you attend PAX, you will find many people waiting in long lines to play video games, but you will also see lots of people spending their time in perhaps unexpected ways. Large groups will gather together, sharing meals, engaging in conversation, and generally enjoying and lifting up the unique irreducible value of different community members. If these activities sound vaguely religious, that is because such people are engaged in cultivating empathy and ethical responsibility. The interactivity of video games, combined with the subject matter and style of nontraditional video games, creates a gateway into the lives of other people. This gateway allows players to interact with and experience the life of a lesbian teen facing rejection (chapter 4), immigrants and potentially sympathetic or ironfisted bureaucrats (chapter 5), Muslims finding solace in their religion during times of political protest and social disruption (chapter 6), and the economically disadvantaged struggling to flourish when faced with biased systems (chapter 7). Some of these nontraditional games, and the cutting-edge technology they are embracing, may even have therapeutic benefits for those who have lived through trauma (conclusion).

Why bring Tillich and Levinas together and apply their thoughts to such video games? Responsibility to the other is not just important if one is interested in ethics. Rather, the other ultimately matters, and video games can help remind players of this point (chapter 2). Similar to Tillich's argument that any theology restricted to the walls of the church that refuses to engage culture is doomed to irrelevance (chapter 1), this book is an account of why theologians should engage in their true calling by embracing what might be deemed completely outside their purview, video games. It is an open invitation to theologians in the hope that more will leave confessional limitations behind and embrace philosophical theology. Nothing is, in principle, irrelevant to philosophical theology, and the argument of this book pays close attention to one aspect of culture that has been especially neglected up to now. There are many people today who are not lost, not simply waiting for the right preacher to come along and help them realize they were a mainline protestant Christian all along. Rather, there are transgender, nonbinary, racially diverse, and other game players who know who they are with confidence, but with identities generally viewed with some degree of suspicion within society. They know who they are, and are just waiting to be accepted. Tillich and Levinas have the resources to show them, through the very playing of the games they love, that they can accept that they are accepted. Those very same video games can help others do the same.

A Prolegomena to Theological Engagement with Video Games

The argument of this book is not the only one in the academic world relating *religion* and video games, but it is an argument that makes up for a near total lack of *theological* engagement with video games.[42] Initial academic work about the relation between religion and video games is embarrassing now and should have been deemed as such at the time. However, the situation has improved, and the academic work has matured. Still, as far as academics touching upon religion and video games go, the dominant method has been informed by religious studies, not theology, much less philosophical theology.

Some of the very first academic treatments of video games and religion reflected scholars having to grasp what it meant to play a game, how to control characters with a controller in the game world. Given this hurdle some academics had to overcome, there were studies focusing on controlling a character in a game and the similarities to controlling one's own body in religious rituals. There are performative aspects to both video games and religious ceremonies, and playing a game could mirror the performative structure of such ceremonies.[43] The next step forward in the scholarship was when MMO games entered the picture. Scholars loved writing about games like *World of Warcraft* and *Second Life*, because in MMOs players can bring their personal interests into the virtual environment.[44] Through chat functionality in these games, players can discuss religious topics and current events. Sociological methods can be readily applied to such games. Early religious studies scholarship focused on searching for and writing about phenomena resembling real-world religions within virtual environments. Did players discuss religion within the game? Did players engage in ritual actions together? In line with such studies that tended to be observation-based, some early articles from Christians about video games noted that choices can be made in games between good and evil. Players can control characters and choose whether they perform good or bad actions within the game itself. This observation has relevance in that Christians are also concerned about good and bad, which actions are right and wrong, but articles did not dig deeper into the potential for games to transform players. They were content with observing the appearance of moral choices in games.[45] However, like the technology impacting game development, the academic stance toward video games and religion has become more nuanced and mature.

Religious scholars started looking for less overt and obvious expressions of religion in games. Rachel Wagner's *Godwired* was a landmark work in this regard, arguing for similarities in the way game culture develops around certain titles and the way religions develop.[46] Religious studies scholars became more serious about their methods and moving beyond investigating literal and obvious representations of religious phenomena in video games.[47] Still, *Godwired* and books with a similar focus that followed in its wake are still works within religious studies. I note that focus because the lack of theologians taking notice of video games is striking. Kevin Schut's *Of Games and God: A Christian Exploration of Video Games* is a title that gives the appearance of possibly filling the theological gap, but the book is focused on what Christian parents should and should not allow when it comes to their children playing video games.[48] His plea to conservative Christians is to not ban games from their lives, unless they are also prepared to stop reading non-Christian books and stop watching non-Christian movies.

Another exception to such theological neglect is J. Sage Elwell, though his argument is overwhelmingly negative. The title of his book tells the story: *Crisis of Transcendence*. The text argues that digital culture is chipping away at religion and diminishing the felt need for transcendence among people today.[49] Jaco J. Hamman's *Growing Down* and George Pattison's *Thinking about God in an Age of Technology* are closer to positive theological assessments of technology. However, in each book, video games are only a small piece of larger arguments about developing mature human beings and interpersonal relationships without rejecting technological advances.[50] Technology is not derided by Hamman, though it is still viewed as a challenge to overcome in efforts to achieve meaningful human connections, which are contrasted to virtual connections that lack such meaning. Perhaps the standout example of a theological embrace of video games is Frank G. Bosman's *Gaming and the Divine*.[51] However, the argument of that book is focused on doctrinal issues in Catholic theology and depictions of religion and religiously important themes in video games insofar as they can illuminate doctrine.[52] It is an excellent representation of how classic systematic Catholic theology can be brought in touch with the modern world, but its restriction to what in games is relevant to existing doctrine is also its limitation. Such a focus limits the ability of video games to challenge theology and hinders the theologian from learning unexpected truths from video games. As things currently stand, while the field of religious studies has shown increasing interest in video games, theologians are largely suspicious of the industry, and philosophical theology is completely absent. This book aims to remedy that situation.

Level One

Tillich and a Theology of Pop Culture

> Never consider the secular realm Godless just because it does not speak of God. To speak of a realm of divine creation and providence as Godless is Godless. It denies God's power over the world. It would force God to confine Godself to religion and church.[1]

In the wake of two world wars, Paul Tillich's philosophical and theological tradition died, in a certain sense. Tillich served Germany as a chaplain in the trenches during World War I from 1914 to 1918. However, his sermons consisted mostly of muttering prayers to dying comrades as he dragged them out of the mud. He witnessed class divisions that militaries continue to leverage and take advantage of to this day, as he watched the German working class being sent to slaughter. He received the Iron Cross, awarded for bravery in battle and other special contributions on the battlefield, but Tillich was not left with a sense of valor and honor. Tillich's war experience shook his faith in the status quo:

> We suddenly realized that if Hitler can be produced by German culture, something must be wrong with this culture. This prepared our emigration to this country and our openness to the new reality it represents. Neither my friends nor I myself dared for a long time to point to what was great in the Germany of our past. If Hitler is the outcome of what we believed to be true philosophy and the only theology, both must be false.[2]

Tillich did not pull punches regarding what must now, without question, be regarded as false. The idea of a supernatural God with definite characteristics like power and love should be dead to a world which did not experience that love and power put into action, which did not experience God saving the world from the immense suffering of war. God is not going to intervene to solve the ethical problems of humanity. If God is to mean anything within human culture moving forward, God must be that which empowers human activity, which gives courage to act in the face of threats and invests people with the assurance they can realize who they are amid the forces of the world that try to crush such a task.

The turn from a God independent from the world and supposedly dominating that world toward one inseparable from the world and empowering its freedom started after World War I and was maintained as a consistent theme up through the completion of Tillich's *Systematic Theology*. Perhaps surprisingly, in the wake of such worldwide destruction, Tillich identified a general spirit of love pervading the ethos of the time in which he lived. The personal horrors he witnessed as a member of the German military were followed up by the failures of his home country in World War II. Rather than these events resulting in cynicism and pessimism, Tillich thought history had created a sort of sacred void, which he viewed with optimism. The combined wars left the whole world facing a *kairos*, a special time during which political, religiously pluralistic, and humanistic forces were colliding for genuine spiritual renewal.[3] "There is something immovable, unchangeable, unshakeable, eternal, which becomes manifest in our passing and the crumbling of our world."[4] While tragedy is unfortunate, it also tears down facades and helps people remember ultimate truths that may have been covered up and forgotten.

In *My Search for Absolutes* Tillich claimed that when he came to America in 1933, after Adolf Hitler became chancellor, he brought with him a debt to Friedrich Schelling and Friedrich Schleiermacher and his antagonism to the Ritschlians, whom he chastised for accepting and propping up Germany's political and cultural establishment during the wars. They uncritically supported all German chancellors and never once showed an inkling of support for Tillich's hope of a Democratic Christian Socialism. Once he arrived in America, Tillich associated Ritschlianism with American Calvinism and Puritanism.[5] Despite arguing throughout their careers, Karl Barth agreed with Tillich's negative assessment of the Ritschlians. Both theologians saw the potential for demonic distortions of culture, but Barth, in light of such potential for distortion, tried to divorce theology from anything having to do with human culture.

Barth's theology is supernatural, with the narrative of the life, death, and resurrection of Jesus Christ setting the parameters for what God will do to the entire world. There is nothing humans or their cultural productions can contribute to understanding such a narrative. Everyone is simply left to either believe in what will be supernaturally imposed on the world or ignore it at their own peril. In line with such an outright rejection of culture, conservative Christians are more likely to view video games and the communities that support them with suspicion. Tillich refused to accept such a clean and easy split between God and the world, however, and would come to view theology and culture as inseparable from one another. In his alternative understanding of the proper scope of theology, neither mystical escape from reality nor supernatural impositions upon reality are possible. Instead, his turn away from supernatural theology entailed an embrace of everything related to human culture. "That transcending power, which is the ultimate power of being, is not achieved by departing from the here and now, but by resisting in it, by arriving in its tensions, by being seized by historical destiny. Faith and realism belong together."[6] We arrive at the deepest truths about who we are by participating in history, not fleeing or waiting to be released from it. A theology like Barth's that explicitly rejects culture also has little to no power to change that culture. It is a form of theology that may be invigorating for those who already buy into its claims, but due to the way it defines its core task, it is necessarily alienating for those standing outside the theological circle or having a crisis of faith. Conversely, Tillich explicitly rejected such supernatural thinking in philosophy and theology, arguing instead that both should embrace everything about the reality in which we are enmeshed as within their purview.[7]

Tillich sided with Luther in asserting that finite reality is capable of bearing or carrying infinite reality. Everything finite, under its free autonomous powers, is capable of mediating God to this world. That such a possibility can occur through the free choices of individuals is important, because Tillich rejected heteronomy, that truth could be forced on the world by God or church authorities. In Tillich's way of thinking, we are necessarily cut off from a supernatural God. None of us can see beyond the natural world, and yet we are supposed to "see" God somewhere else in such a framework. There is in fact no object labeled "God" to be found outside us somewhere else. Tillich does not provide a cosmological proof for God in which God supposedly explains the existence of the cosmos. Rather, when ultimate truth breaks through within the autonomous activities of a given culture, Tillich claims this is actually the case of a theonomous culture, autonomy united with its own depths. Theonomy is, in principle, possible anytime and anywhere, because God is the depth of reality to which any piece of finite reality can be directed.[8] Despite our contingency and being constantly faced with the threat of nonbeing and death, God as the ground-of-being allows us to affirm the worth of who we are despite life's uncertainties. The culture in which we live is part of that affirmation. If Tillich were alive today, he would likely see the potential for empowerment and revelation in video games, just as he saw it in culture and art during his lifetime. The largest danger in that endeavor is the potential for distortion that comes with uniting autonomy and God. People and cultures can freely choose to become opaque to their divine depths, rather than letting ultimate truth shine through.

Paradoxical Transcendence in Immanence: God as the Ground-of-Being

Tillich associated the supernatural God he rejected with cosmological attempts to supposedly prove God's existence. In such arguments, God is not a given but is instead sought after. The problem with this method is that beginning with inquiry in the world and then trying to find God is the kind of inquiry that may never find what it is seeking.[9] The destruction of war Tillich experienced, not to mention tragedies such as Gamergate and the killing of unarmed people of color by police that continue uninterrupted by divine power, makes a positive outcome to such a cosmological search all the more unlikely. Tillich's alternative understanding of how God relates to the world is one in which everything finite is related to something from which it can never actually be separated, God as the ground-of-being. God is the basis of everything that exists, making them what they are, meaning that anyone not living their best life and realizing who they truly are in this world is merely estranged from God as the depth of their being, not truly separated from God.[10] This God cannot be deduced from a set of premises about the world. Rather, God is the precondition for asking questions about God. Nothing would be without God as the ground or power of being, which means asking questions about how to find God already implies God supporting the existence of the one asking such questions.[11] Therefore, if anyone feels existential angst and ultimate meaninglessness, that is only a matter of mistaken estrangement from their divine essence from which they can never truly be separated. God is the unconditioned ground supporting every bit of this conditioned reality in which we live and move and have our being.

Tillich uses several terms interchangeably to refer to this unconditional God in his writing: God is ultimate reality, being itself, ground-of-being, and the power of being.[12] Regardless of which terms Tillich uses and where he uses them, James Luther Adams helpfully lays out the following features of God that help interpret the meaning of Tillich's somewhat iconoclastic terms.[13] God (1) is not an entity, another being among beings, even if conceived of as an ultimate transcendent being; and (2) is not the direct opposite of this conditioned finite reality in the sense of being unrelated or disconnected from it. Rather, God is exactly the opposite, the ultimate meaning that bursts forth in the world here and now; and (3) is unconditioned in that we cannot manipulate God like we manipulate tools. Instead, we can only aim and hope that our actions do not hinder the emergence of divine meaning in this world; and (4) God is symbolic language for the ground of all being, for nothing finite can capture and fully contain this reality, unconditioned as it is; and (5) God must be accompanied by an apophatic awareness that none of these meanings of God are, in the end, quite adequate. Awareness of the God marked by these features is not cognitive. It is also not an experience in which some external reality is made present to a perceiving subject, as if God were an existing person.

> Neither "The Unconditioned" nor "something unconditional," is meant as a being, not even the highest being, not even God. God is unconditioned, that makes him God; but "the unconditional" is not God. The word "God" is filled with the concrete symbols in which mankind has expressed its ultimate concern—its being grasped by something unconditional. And this "something" is not just a thing, but the power of being in which every being participates.[14]

Awareness of God is awareness of the presence of a power and a demand, not a being with properties.[15] The religious life consists of realizing our lives are supported and already realized in the divine depths, and, based on such assurance, acting with courage to help others flourish and realize themselves in this world.

As Adams describes proper religious consciousness of God in the situation proposed by Tillich, it is always a matter of affirmation and denial, always saying no even when you say yes to the ultimate meaning of anything. "Confronting the Unconditioned it is conscious of alienation as well as kinship."[16] Without the no, the yes becomes impossible. If theological meaning is bestowed, but never qualified, that bestowal of meaning turns into its very denial. Therefore, Tillich explicitly describes God as the ground-of-being and rejects any understanding of God as *a being* in order to avoid idolatry. The result is that all everyday talk of God must be symbolic, capable of being the means through which God is encountered, just like everything conditioned and finite, but not to be turned into the exclusive means by which this encounter is made possible. "We must always say two things about him [God]: we must say that there is a non-symbolic element in our image of God—namely, that he is ultimate reality, being itself, ground of being, power of being; and the other, that he is the highest being in which everything that we have does exist in the most perfect way."[17]

Thus, God is and is not a symbol. The symbolic expressions of a highest perfect being likely to be used in some religious ceremonies are symbols for that which is not symbolic, God as the ground-of-being. Symbols that personalize God are necessary because nobody can personally relate to the purely unconditional. However, transforming personal symbols about God into literal statements about God having definite properties and intentions also severs relations with that unconditioned God. In such elevation, religious symbols are transformed from windows through which God can shine into closed doors, leaving us on our own to deal with the world without divine grounding. To return to how Adams phrases this situation, in religion "one is confronted with the ultimate seriousness of existence, its support and threat and promise: the support of (intimacy and community with) an infinite and inexhaustible reality, the threat of the blindness that comes from the [*hubris*] or blasphemy of claiming absolute truth, and the promise of new, concrete, meaningful fulfillment."[18] God is not a being but the reality present in all beings, the unconditioned ground-of-being of all conditioned beings. This understanding of God entails that religion, as an experience of this unconditioned ultimate reality, is not a special cultural sphere but something found in the depths of all cultural creations.

If God is understood as a separate being alongside the world, it would be possible to understand God as the basis and perhaps ultimate meaning of culture, but that God would never be able to break through within culture without destroying it. Conversely, for Tillich there are no specifically religious forms necessary for expressing God, given that God does not exist as a thing and, as the unconditioned ground-of-being, can be directly experienced though not rationally comprehended: "Whereas religion is intentionally directed toward the unconditional or ultimate meaning-reality, culture is so substantially, but not intentionally."[19] In this situation we should not wait for God to come into the world and do something for us, as that would imply a separation from God that does not exist. Rather, God is waiting, so to speak, for our openness and creativity in order to be realized here and now. With God understood as the ever-present ontological grounding of this reality, God becomes recognizable everywhere, in explicitly religious activities, but also in nature and nonreligious culture as well: "Thus reality can become the bearer of a meaning that unconditionally transcends it."[20] Tillich's point is that within all cultural creations, whether related to the seriousness of politics or moments of pure play, "an ultimate concern is expressed, and that it is possible to recognize the unconscious theological character of it."[21] Importantly, Tillich argues we can trace the unconditional aspect of reality, the presence of God, to instances of great creativity more than static forms meant to stand in for that divine presence.

Adams provides an illuminating comment on Tillich's apparent love of reflecting at the edge of the ocean that wonderfully captures the unsevered connection between us and our ground-of-being, as well as how creative work relates to that connection: "In the waves can be seen the motion of the depths disturbing the faces of the waters. Here is the symbol of the infinite bordering on the finite and of the infinite depths touching the finite surfaces."[22] Or, as Tillich himself recalled, "of the Unconditioned as both ground and abyss of dynamic truth, and of the religious essence as the eruption of the eternal into finiteness, the sea supplied the imaginative element needed for these insights."[23] For Tillich, omnipotence is not about overriding power, about divine control that overrules our freedom. Rather, omnipotence has to do with the final inability of any power to remove us from our ultimate source, to eliminate the possibility of realizing our essence. We are all in ships upon the ocean, but sometimes we forget about the water and become overly impressed with the ocean-faring technology we built to keep ourselves afloat. When we so forget, creative disruptions of the status quo, in their destructive activity, pave the way for us to realize our depths of meaning once again.

Estrangement and Culture as the Form of Religion

Tillich did not simply embrace culture as the key to saving theology from its historical failures. All of human culture should, in principle, be theologically embraced, but culture truly becomes theologically meaningful when it is transparent to divine depths of meaning. Such transparency is not always the case. Three terms are important for understanding Tillich's simultaneous critique and embrace of culture: heteronomy, autonomy, and theonomy. Heteronomy relates to domination and control by outside forces. Supernatural forms of religion are heteronomous, forcing their concept of God on the world whether that world wants it or not. Autonomy is the opposite of heteronomy, the acceptance of individual and collective freedoms. However, a theological stance that merely embraces cultural autonomy and accepts the world as it is, without investigating it with a critical eye, has failed in its role, has lost its critical edge. In more traditional theological language, heteronomy is about divine transcendence that dominates the world while autonomy is concerned with immanence, asserting that no transcendent source of meaning is necessary. Theonomy is Tillich's paradoxical embrace of both positions. "Theonomy is autonomous reason united to its own depth."[24] Theonomy affirms God's transcendent immanence in the world.

Tillich did not think the relation of religion to culture was essentially about morality, knowledge, or aesthetics either. A culture might tolerate religious morality or art for a while, but tastes change, as do the issues considered morally pressing. Religion might be considered a storehouse of knowledge for a while, but propping up religious institutions and theological systems as such is how theologians have gotten themselves into tension or outright conflict with advances in knowledge from various disciplines throughout the years. Rather, Tillich's point about the relation between theology and culture is understood once one realizes that religion does not need to defend a special place for itself. "It is at home everywhere, namely, in the depth of all functions of man's spiritual life. Religion is the dimension of depth in all of them. . . . What does the metaphor *depth* mean? It means that the religious aspect points to that which is ultimate, infinite, unconditional in man's spiritual life."[25] Neither secular culture, including pieces of it largely meant for entertainment (such as video games), nor religion can actually separate themselves from one another. Following someone like Barth in believing such separation is real is actually a mistaken impression of reality and itself a sign of estrangement from God, an estrangement that can and should be overcome.

The concept of theonomy that embraces cultural autonomy is directly related to Tillich's position that God is the ground-of-being. A ground is a support, that which gives meaning to everything it supports, and which upholds that meaning. Therefore, God as the ground-of-being is not found in some other heavenly realm, but in the depths of reality here and now: "All culture is actualized religion, and all religion is actualized as culture."[26] There is nothing essentially wrong with the finite world. God does not need to destroy it and replace it with something else for the divine reality to be made manifest. Lack of theonomy is dangerous not because there is anything necessarily bad about an autonomous culture, but because an autonomous culture will tend to slip toward dangerous forms of heteronomy, as Raymond Bulman notes: "The difficulty with a *self-sufficient* or *purely secular* autonomy is that it has lost the dimension of depth, and must eventually fill the resulting void by attributing ultimacy to something finite and limited—the very essence of idolatry."[27] People will eventually set up something as a focus of their ultimate concern, and without theonomous depth, the objects of their focus could result in very dangerous forms of devotion, as was the case with

Gamergate. The same potential danger lurking within self-sufficiency can lead good theological projects to slip into heteronomy.

The generic form of the problem is when the piece of reality in which God is encountered is elevated to an ultimate status, turning God from the ground-of-being into a finite being, the problem of idolatry. Religious symbols need a transcendent *import* that goes beyond their materiality and an immanent *form* which allows divine truth to be encountered by finite humans. However, Tillich peppered his writings with his various non-symbolic names for God—"ultimate reality, being itself, ground of being, power of being; and the other, that he is the highest being in which everything that we have does exist in the most perfect way"[28]—as reminders to maintain the theonomous balance that always says both yes and no to finding God in culture. Theonomy is a positive enthusiastic affirmation of ultimate meaning at any given moment, but that affirmation should not be confused with a complete and final revelation of God's meaning. Such a mistake, eliding such a necessary qualification on all affirmations, is a mistake which then robs God of the power to empower all moments. While it should now be clear why engaging culture should matter to theologians, it may not yet be obvious why any of this theology should matter to people living in any given culture.

Theonomy is important to Tillich's understanding of how theology relates to culture because it is a concept that represents the potential for overcoming estrangement. As already noted, when God is understood as the ground-of-being, our true nature is also found there, as something that is therefore always already realized. Feelings of estrangement, of our existing lives being different than what they should be, are always feelings that can be overcome. While conditions that produce anxiety are real, the separation between existence and essence is not.[29] "In every religion the experience of the holy is mediated by some piece of finite reality. Everything can become a medium of revelation, a bearer of divine power."[30] Estrangement can be overcome because God, and this is Tillich's insight taken from Schelling, embraces both the divine self and all else, everything for which God is the ground-of-being. "The ultimate can become actual only through the concrete, through that which is preliminary and transitory."[31] The way to overcome estrangement is to realize God is already present. Once that awareness dawns, it becomes possible to step into the world, with all its potentials for distortion, with courage.

Estrangement is found in cultural life in the form of polar opposites, dividing life in the world into exclusive options and forcing a supposed need to choose one or the other, but never both. Binary categories such as individual and society, self and other, and freedom and destiny are examples. As Adams describes it, estrangement is a problem created when anyone "attempts to place himself at the depth or the center of being rather than relate himself to it; when man, who is dependent upon the primal 'given' creativity of being, sets up his own creaturely and conditioned character as unconditioned."[32] Heteronomy relates to estrangement when one choice is regarded as exclusive of another, a choice often foisted upon others by religious institutions. When Christians who are gay, lesbian, and transgender are told by churches that being Christian and LGBTQ+ are exclusive options, that is a case of heteronomy and estrangement in action. When estranged, when forced to live as something other than who we essentially are, that experience can be accompanied by guilt and meaninglessness, even if such feelings arose unnecessarily due to policies imposed by institutionalized religion.[33] Autonomy is a natural reaction to such a false choice, one seen in atheistic reactions to such harmful work performed by religious institutions. Theonomy, on the other hand, supports cultural autonomy. People are allowed to be themselves—gay, lesbian, or transgender in this case—while also understood as fulfilled ultimately due to their relation to the ground-of-being. The result of relating autonomy to God is a theonomy in which supposedly mutually exclusive options are actually deemed mutually supportive. Instead of creating opposition, a collective society should be the sort of place where individuals are allowed to develop, partly from protections and freedom granted by that society. Instead of being transgender only outside the church, someone could come to realize who they are because the church affirms the essential identities of *all* people.

Gamergate defined video games as being for "gamers" in such a way as to restrict their subject matter to little more than violent sexual male power fantasies. The movement created a moblike mentality among its defenders, who employed such a limited definition of gamer to automatically discredit different groups and individuals.[34] That limited definition of gamer created polar tensions in this world, as it was used as a weapon to legitimize hostility toward those creating and enjoying alternative experiences in video games. However, instead of video games being only of a certain violent style for only certain people, a theonomous approach to the industry can highlight how women and other minorities are supporting the strength of the entire industry by creating alternative experiences that broaden the potential audience for video games. In these alternative games we have human creations intimately tied to their ultimate depth, culture being the manifestation of religion and religion being the meaning of culture. Such games will not eliminate the existence of or detract from the enjoyment had in playing certain mainstream games. Both things can be true, just as the movie industry has come to embrace frivolous action-packed movies and serious dramas.

Estrangement and its theonomous cure can be manifest in individual lives, but they can also define entire societies. A theonomous society is one in which groups of people will not create binary choices as means of preventing some from fully participating in society. Nazi Germany was heteronomous, a society that created an absolute split between being German and Jewish, Slavic, or Romanian, between being German and a person with a disability, or between being German and a gay man or lesbian woman. The same is true of Gamergate which, though not a society, was a community with a large backing that tried to reduce marginalized people into objects to be used and manipulated at will, starting with women in the video game industry. Unfortunately, just like the personal transformation that comes from a divine encounter, heteronomous distortions also demand unconditional adherence, which is why Tillich referred to them as demonic. They are not demonic in some literal sense of being movements controlled by evil creatures, but in that they halt the realization of a theonomous situation in which God's reality is made manifest due to the way they use their power to twist and pervert that situation for their own gain. One of the roles of churches and theologians is to set that situation straight, to critique perversions of culture wherever they are found so that their divine depths will shine through once again.[35]

Theology of Pop Culture

Just as Tillich formed his thought in the wake of two world wars, Gamergate has made the political and ethical significance of video games undeniable. The events in 2014 became a movement that extended beyond video games into politics and a general culture war between those who would limit who gets to matter in society and those seeking inclusion and flourishing for all. Such unfortunate events, from Tillich's time to today, put pressure on any theology divorced from culture. It should be increasingly difficult for any theologian to deny one of Tillich's basic points, that the truth of religion should embrace and be found in the entire world. "Religion is the substance of culture, culture is the form of religion."[36] Some will surely follow Barth in completely cleaving theology from the world, and then offering their supernatural solutions to the world, though it is unclear why they think the world would have any reason to accept their offering. A theology that is going to be accepted and embraced by someone must be capable of being accepted as true *for them*.

Tillich notes that revelation must be received for it to be revelation. That reception is how we get religion, and it is always concrete, specific, and historical. Thus, "revelation and the reception of revelation are inseparably united."³⁷ The personal aspects of religion come from the fact that any genuine revelation of the ultimate must be received by humans. As such, there is no way to put arbitrary limits on what can or cannot be a vehicle of such truth. "In every religion the experience of the holy is mediated by some piece of finite reality. Everything can become a medium of revelation, a bearer of divine power."³⁸ However, the act of reception puts its own twist on revelation. Consider God speaking to prophets in the Bible. God did not give them a new alien language of the divine, but tore down the curtain so that existing facts were now known in light of ultimate meaning. Bushes become personal when they mediate the divine to us (and Moses).³⁹ Personality emerges in relation with another. This fact puts pressure on ontological elements of Tillich's system, a pressure of which he was aware. "Man can experience the holy in and through everything, but, as holy, it cannot be less than he is; it cannot be a-personal. Nothing less than we, nothing that encounters less than the center of our personality, can be of ultimate concern for us."⁴⁰ Understandings of God as personal express the reality of this encounter, but they clash with the fact that such revelatory encounters are universal and can happen anywhere through anything.

If a theological message is simply a rejection of someone's ideas and beliefs about who they are in the world, a rejection that expects them to embrace a completely unrelated alternative set of claims about who they are, such theological claims will almost never be embraced.⁴¹ Rather, following Tillich, theology should engage culture in two dimensions, the vertical and the horizontal. The vertical dimension is critical, judging all standpoints, even religious ones, and calling them to accountability. It reflects the critical eye of the theologian, making sure no genuine affirmation of the ground-of-being breaking through within and changing this world is incorrectly turned into a dogmatic idol. Verticality is a reminder to avoid idolatry and not mistakenly turn something revelatory of God into that which hinders understanding. The horizontal dimension is welcoming and inviting, reflecting Tillich's insistence that theology must embrace all human culture and affirm God's presence everywhere, including within popular culture.

It is well known that Tillich engaged the arts extensively during his career. Tillich's *Theology of Culture*, as well as some of the foundational texts commenting on that theology, are full of references to artists and works like Raphael, Dürer, "The School of Athens," Grant Wood's "American Gothic," Michelangelo, Shakespeare, Kafka, and Goethe, just to name a few.⁴² While this list certainly reflects high culture, it can be easy to forget that these figures and the art they produced were also popular in their own day, both reflecting and influencing their societies. Since many of the pieces of art

Tillich engaged are now considered classics, it can also be easy to forget the great changes happening in the art world during Tillich's lifetime. Impressionism and expressionism were taking off as new, important movements, and popular forms of art were gaining respect.[43] Given Tillich's insistence that theology must engage all that human culture has to offer, as well as his own interest in the arts, it should not be surprising that his theology provides more than adequate resources for dealing with the most popular piece of popular culture today—video games.[44]

FORM, CONTENT, AND IMPORT

The categories from Tillich's theology of culture that make sense to apply to video games are form, content, and import. From Tillich's perspective, the content of any piece of art does not actually matter. Non-religious art can convey theological meaning even better than religious paintings, for example.[45] The key issue is whether different cultural forms have divine import, whether they point beyond themselves to the ultimate meaning manifest within them. If the answer is yes, then that is a case of theonomous art capable of challenging false ways of viewing the world and cracking them open to truth once again, a case of God's transcendence immanent in a cultural creation. Consider how Tillich described the difference between someone being struck by religious versus secular art:

> If a person who had been deeply moved by the mosaics of Ravenna, the ceiling paintings of the Sistine Chapel, or the portraits of the older Rembrandt, were asked whether his experience had been religious or cultural, he would find the question difficult to answer. It might be correct to say that the experience is cultural in form and religious in substance. It is cultural because it is not attached to a specific ritual act; but it is religious because it touches on the question of the Absolute and the limits of human existence.[46]

As noted in the introduction to this chapter, Tillich had no interest in conservative religious positions that would reject all advances in culture, often without knowing anything about such stances. Tillich was deeply interested in whatever products happened to emerge from culture, because any piece of culture, including popular culture, can in principle be imbued with ultimate importance. However, it is widely acknowledged by Tillich scholars who focus on his relation to art that import, or style, not form or content, is the most important element of art when it comes to theological engagement.[47]

A focus on import, or the spirit of a piece of art, allows any cultural product, any piece of art, to become transparent to its divine depths regardless of its subject matter. As Tillich put it, "the more *Form*, the more autonomy; the more *Gehalt*, the more theonomy."⁴⁸ However, video games place some pressure on this emphasis. There is a debate among video game scholars regarding whether game world and story are crucial to motivating players to engage and move through games, or whether interesting gameplay is all that matters.⁴⁹ Just a decade ago, the following could be presented as a statement of fact: "Players will not play a game just because it has a good story, and a good story cannot make up for boring or otherwise poor game play. Games are not only about the virtual characters in their stories, but also about the player."⁵⁰ The industry has changed so much in a decade, but just three years after that statement was published, the game *Gone Home* was released. It created a new genre of games known as walking simulators, which is a genre defined by seemingly boring gameplay. All players do in terms of controlling a character in such games is move them back, forward, left, and right in the game world. There is no exciting gameplay, no challenging battles. However, many people who love video games love this genre for the interesting experiences it allows players to have and the moving stories it allows them to experience. Chapter 4 is focused on the theological depth of such games. James Gee and Elisabeth Hayes, the same authors of that poorly aged quote, went on to claim video games are incapable of simulating experiences like living in poverty, given that video games are commercial products designed and created with the goal of making money.⁵¹ *Cart Life*, a game highlighted in chapter 7, shows their claim is demonstrably wrong. These games also require a shift in Tillich's focus. It is not the case that import, spirit, or *Gehalt* are the exclusive means by which art ultimately matters, as all of form, content, and import can convey ultimate meaning when it comes to video games.

Developers can choose to emphasize any component among form, content, or import when creating a game. If their goal is to create a challenging first-person shooter, the form of the game will dominate and need to be crafted with great precision. Many smaller independent developers focus on content and telling interesting stories through video games. In such cases, form may not matter much at all. Emotional stories have been told in games with both realistic graphics and simplistic pixel art that looks like it belongs on the original Nintendo Entertainment System. While games emphasizing form and content can have theological import, some of the most nontraditional games have emphasized conveying a certain spirit above all else. Playing some of these games is comparable to Tillich's form-shattering experience of engaging expressionist art.

Flower is a highly experimental video game released in 2009 that garnered controversy over to what extent it even qualified as a game. To play *Flower*, players hold a motion-sensing controller and simply wave it around while flower petals on screen fly through the air and mimic the movements of the controller. When the petals soar near other petals in the environment, those petals join the growing flock flying through the air. When enough petals are under the player's control, arid areas of the game world can be repopulated with beautiful plant life. Such simple gameplay, combined with a beautiful art style and impressive graphics, elicited strong emotions from many players. It raised questions within the industry about untapped potential in video games and what sorts of experiences and emotions they make possible.

All of this is true when it comes to people who play video games as well. Some players who do not care about story in video games were among those who thought *Flower* did not count as a game. Such people tend to enjoy fast-paced and heavily skill-based games emphasizing form. Players who enjoy interesting experiences and might be intimidated by challenging gameplay can enjoy the content of alternative, nontraditional games. They might enjoy walking simulators like *Gone Home* that emphasize story content first and foremost. Again, neither preference should be thought of as opposed to theological import, as theonomy is impossible without embodiment in concrete pieces of culture. However, video games are different than other art forms in that they are an interactive form that engages the person beyond the mere act of interpreting art. The interactivity of the video game art form matters, and that form can emphasize the form itself, the content conveyed by the form, or form-shattering spirit or import of novel styles of video games. For these reasons, Tillich's almost utter neglect of form and content must be challenged when engaging video games with his theology.

The implication of Tillich's approach to culture in general, and art in particular, is that form and import/style/spirit cannot exist in pure versions apart from one another, just as religion and culture are crucially interrelated. That being said, Tillich still located more theological importance in styles of art in which spirit, or *Gehalt*, is dominant. For example, he complained that Cézanne was only concerned with realistic landscapes,[52] but praised Van Gogh for peeling back the surface and getting into the depth of things.[53] He referred to art focused on realism above all else as "self-sufficient finitude."[54] He associated all genuinely religious art with expressionism.[55] Among those artists receiving his praise were Grünewald, Dürer, Bosch, Breughel, Goya, and Michelangelo, as well as several of Tillich's contemporaries, such as Erich Heckel, Emil Nolde, Karl Schmidt-Rottluff, Edvard Munch, and Franz Marc. Tillich greatly preferred expressionism to impressionism and realism. Even though this exclusive emphasis requires modification, it should be noted that just as Tillich criticized naturalism and impressionism for providing a sense of self-sufficiency, content with accurately capturing the features of subjects rather than breaking through to the unconditioned meaning of reality,[56] there has been a recent turn away from realistic graphics in many video games toward a vast array of stylized graphics. Tillich's praise of expressionism could have been written about such games: "The individual forms of things were dissolved, not in favor of subjective impressions but in favor of objective metaphysical expressions. The abyss of being was to be evoked in lines, colors, and plastic forms."[57] Tillich would have likely praised *Flower* if he were alive and reviewing video games in 2009. However, even though a theological assessment of art that rests content with approval of only expressionism and spirit needs to be rethought in light of video games, a broadening of Tillich's theology beyond the confines of expressionist art is in line with the trajectory of his life.

After emigrating to the United States, Tillich apologized for his provincialism and identification of all great cultural artifacts with Germany. The failures of his home country during World War II only solidified his new perspective. Tillich's limitations are also natural to some degree. There is only so much one individual can do in a lifetime to engage theology and art deeply, and preferences in both realms will impact what material is engaged. Tillich could not have anticipated the development and popularity of video games. If his preference for art that prioritizes style and spirit over form and content is not perfectly suited to the form of art that is video games, that is just evidence that further theological engagement with culture and art is necessary. However, Kelton Cobb is also correct that Tillich's neglect of popular culture also reveals a theological limitation. As Cobb notes, "much can be learned about the total situation of a culture's deeper allegiances from an examination of its magazines, television viewing habits, popular novels, fashions, lawncare, broadcast news media, car industry, billboard hits, cinema, favorite leisure destinations, and state-of-the-art technologies."[58] However, while Cobb argues Tillich's approach to culture is essentially elitist and incapable of coming to terms with popular culture, as opposed to high European culture, without some serious revision, Tillich's approach actually just needs a shift in emphasis.

Russell Re Manning has noted two consequences of Tillich's undue focus on expressionism and spirit in art: his inability to find anything of positive religious value and theological substance in other styles of art, and his similar inability to do the same when it came to more traditional religious iconography.[59] Some of Tillich's own statements on form and content in art border on ignorance and outright insult, such as "the more form, the more autonomy; the more import, the more theonomy."[60] Re Manning's conclusion should be a warning to theologians who would follow Tillich in engaging culture and art without broadening their view of both: "rather than discerning the future of religious art in the expressionistic style, he has been taken in by Expressionism as the Trojan Horse of a secular and nihilistic aesthetic alternative to religion."[61] If all religion takes on cultural forms, and no culture is incapable of conveying ultimate meaning and disrupting a polarized estranged situation, a limited appreciation for the sort of art that actually achieves such breakthrough is simply unacceptable. Beyond this challenge, one more reason that relating his theology of culture to video games might have troubled Tillich should be noted.

HETERONOMY AND TECHNOLOGY

Bertrand Russell supposedly once said people in sailboats have less trouble believing in God than people in motorboats. The implication is that when technology provides everything people need, God is no longer necessary. Tillich was wary of an overly technological society for straightforward reasons. He believed the expansion of technology would lead to dehumanization. He even expressed his concern as a sort of formula sometimes.[62] Advances in natural science that increase the ability to understand reality, when combined with mechanical techniques to master that reality and an insatiable capitalist drive, spell disaster. He viewed his theology in touch with culture as a means of revitalizing the human element and avoiding such a future.[63] He worried that the more we learn to control the world around us, the more that world will lose its ability to become transparent to God.[64] But what should be made of these concerns when the posthuman is already a real phenomenon?[65] As technological advances enhance our ability to control the world around us, do the thirst for transcendence and a role for God truly wither? Like all human achievements, technological advances are ambiguous. In order to be meaningful, such advances just need to be free of potentially harmful distortions.[66] Arguably nothing in popular culture could be more technologically based than video games, and yet the games investigated in this book do not materialize Tillich's concerns. Just as Tillich thought he had correctly identified the human-shaped hole in an increasingly technological society and sought to provide a new theological answer, a world shaped by video games and Gamergate also needs a new answer appropriate to that virtual interactive culture.

To take a step back and give Tillich some credit, Gamergate did make his predictions about technology prescient, at least in part. As will be discussed at greater length in chapter 3, humans have mirror neurons that help us learn empathy as part of interacting with others. When we see others experiencing joy or pain, we also experience a bit of the same. This is how many people learn to draw the line between silly pranks and outright cruelty as part of adolescence. While the instigators of Gamergate were fueled by hate to such a degree that empathy formed by mirror neurons may not have stopped them, the sort of face-to-face feedback concerning pleasure and pain experienced by others is missing on the internet.[67] Furthermore, video games are certainly only possible, especially with the advanced graphics in so many of them today, due to the technological society Tillich feared. But not all games turn people into objects among objects. *Gone Home, 1979 Revolution, Cart Life*, and the other video games that will be highlighted in further chapters actually heighten the human experience and express the depths of human meaning. As will be shown in the next chapter, encountering the faces of others in such games never reduces those others to mere objects in a game either. The meaningful call found in the face is prior to anything objective learned about the other, in person or in game.

POP CULTURE, TRAGEDY, AND OPENINGS TO MEANING

Tillich paved the way for a theological appreciation of any cultural form understood in relation to the ultimate, including popular culture and video games. Viewing those pieces of culture in relation to God means they should not merely be taken at face value, appreciated for being beautiful or entertaining and nothing more. Rather, video games and the communities they have fostered have been both demonic distortions and shocking revelations of their depth of meaning. For most of its existence, the video game industry was viewed as, and presented itself as, providing a frivolous hobby. Gamergate created a novel, destructive situation within the industry, and ultimate truth in such situations is found in both the damage done and the responses to the damage.[68] As Adams emphasizes, tragic disruptions of culture can be related to a sense of right timing, *kairos* moments when God will both use and destroy cultural forms. Such moments eliminate the damage done by actually bringing the destruction to completion in favor of something new and true.[69] "Kairos is fulfilled time, the moment of time which is invaded by eternity. But Kairos is not perfect completion in time."[70] We wait, and we act, but there is no final end to wait for, just a reality present now to which we respond. This means theology is engaged in the risky, ambiguous, never-assured business of meaningful living, helping everyone and anyone realize who they are meant to be in this world. Tillich warns theologians that they cannot retreat to lists of dogmatic statements as solutions to the world's problems but must engage tumultuous situations with unknown resolutions: "Intellectual and spiritual life, no matter how vital it may be, is doomed to fruitlessness and emptiness if it does not receive new impulses from the actual social situation and the challenges which it presents."[71] Tillich could not have conceived of video games playing a role in revealing ultimate depths of meaning that are at the core of his theology, especially given his suspicions regarding technology. Nonetheless, as Tillich asserted when it comes to any cultural product, those divine depths can be discovered in the work of video game developers as with all other autonomous cultural creations. The inverse is also true, as Gamergate and its defenders deprived video games of such deeper potential meaning.

Gamergate was an attempt to pit culture against culture, one free, albeit hateful, autonomous group against all others. The result was the demonic distortion of both culture and how meaning is found in culture. Such a situation can create anxiety for those experiencing the fullness of their lives being threatened by others. Rather than being a woman *and* a game developer, or transgender *and* a fan of video games, Gamergate attempted to create a polarized culture in which both-and was replaced with either-or. In such situations, anxiety and courage hover over every choice. When a movement like Gamergate emphasizes polarization that creates estrangement, it is natural to draw within, tighten boundaries, and seek protection rather than act with courage. "*Neurotic anxiety* is a result of failing to take this ontological anxiety upon oneself—the anxiety in which we all are one, which is identical with our finitude. When related to the present, ontological anxiety becomes the *will to security*, which gives rise to aggression against threats of every kind."[72] Anxiety without courage can lead to all sorts of political problems, and Tillich credited World War I for opening his eyes to the dangers of separating politics from theology.[73] From that point forward, Tillich admitted political reform was a permanent fixture of his thought. Theology and hope for social revolution against authoritarianism should go hand-in-hand.[74] The election of Donald Trump to the office of President of the United States in 2016, his creation of border walls, and decision to place children in cages within Immigration and Customs Enforcement camps are modern examples of anxiety without courage. Gamergate is a prime example of the same phenomenon. Such cowardly anxiety can result in the creation of the very thing it seeks to avoid, just as the unprovoked invasion of Iraq by the United States in the name of national security emboldened terrorists. It created political destabilization which led to the subsequent empowerment of the Islamic State of Iraq and Syria (ISIS), and bolstered their recruiting efforts, as ISIS could point to an unjust invasion that demanded a response.

Courage, on the other hand, is the willingness to give up what have been securities of the past and view the anxiety-inducing problems of the present as reason to boldly step into the future. When seen through Tillich's understanding of both the horizontal and vertical dimensions of life, in light of the ground-of-being that embraces culture instead of dominating it, tragic disruptive situations can become sources of positive hope for the future:

> Courage, and that in faith which is courage, affirms the ultimate prevalence of being over non-being. It affirms the presence of the infinite in everything finite. Theology which is based on such a courage tries to show that just as non-being is dependent on the being it negates, so the awareness of finitude presupposes a place above finite from which the finite is seen as such.[75]

There are no universal independent norms to guide us in attempts to live the good life. Sometimes strength, other times social standing, revolutionary tides, violence, or merely who happens to be in power will determinate cultural norms of what is right and wrong. But whenever such heteronomous forces take control, that rise to power can also be understood as a sign that there is still a thirst for transcendence and infinite meaning, and that it must be found in something new. If a culture has become opaque to its ultimate meaning and the source of that meaning, some form of upheaval can become the opportunity for that culture to become self-transcending once again.

Tillich was correct that threats, ambiguity, estrangement, and risk are ever present, even amid breakthrough of ultimate meaning. The average age of a person who plays video games in 2021 makes them a millennial. Broadly, millennials are facing the prospects of gigs instead of careers, losing social rights, never owning a home, and increasing healthcare costs with less money to cover them. Millennials facing all this and more know and feel Tillich's points, at least implicitly. They might even feel these things so deeply as to accept the symbol of this world as fallen. But they can also experience moments of grace, to use another traditional symbol, as happened when communities responded to Gamergate by creating places where everyone can be accepted. When video game communities did the hard work to support minorities who were being excluded and hurt by actually creating structures for support—structures such as the AFK rooms now available at all PAX conventions—that work broke the business-as-usual approach within the industry. The dangerous heteronomy of Gamergate led to autonomous reactions against and rejections of that cultural force, and some of those reactions were also theonomous.

This chapter will close by returning to its beginning, noting how Tillich was able to view social upheaval, the tragedies of history, and general disappointments of life optimistically. Part of what attracted Tillich to existential philosophy was its continual pointing to the need for such disruption, for its reminder that dogmatic systems can extinguish the flame of life.[76] On the one hand, a detached, unchanging concept of the eternal cannot be the block on which all concrete issues of justice are judged (e.g., theological dogma), but neither can the holy be simply equated with taking particular stances (e.g., churches that equate following God with rejecting LGBTQ+ individuals). The proper view is *kairos*, the right moment. It is not a specific prediction, nor a hoped-for ideal that is beyond and unlike everything in the present historical situation. Rather, for Tillich, "it signifies a moment of time filled with unconditioned meaning and demand. . . . Kairos is the fulfilled moment of time in which the present and the future, the holy that is given and the holy that is demanded meet, and from whose concrete tensions the new creation proceeds in which sacred import is realized in necessary form."[77] Consider the message of Mark 1:15 in light of Tillich's concept of *kairos*: "Now after John was arrested, Jesus came to Galilee, proclaiming the good news of God, and saying, 'The time is fulfilled, and the kingdom of God has come near; repent, and believe in the good news.'" Out of unfortunate events, good news can spread.

Level Two

Turning to the Other in Video Games

> You know, one often speaks of ethics to describe what I do, but what really interests me in the end is not ethics, not ethics alone, but the holy, the holiness of the holy.[1]

It is probably no coincidence that Emmanuel Levinas geographically moved so much in his life and also developed an ethical philosophy in which all others should be respected and helped, regardless of their similarities or differences to oneself.[2] He was born on January 12, 1906, in Kaunas, Lithuania. He had orthodox Jewish parents and learned to read the Bible in Hebrew but, given that Kaunas was part of the Russian Empire before it gained independence (the city was known as Kovno prior to independence), Levinas was educated in and spoke Russian.[3] What a wonderful blessing to grow up reading great Russian writers like Dostoyevsky and Tolstoy in their native language instead of encountering them as an adult through translations. However, the blessings Levinas enjoyed did not last long. During World War I, Jewish people were forced out of Lithuania. Levinas and his family moved to Kharkov, Ukraine, only to return to Lithuania in 1920. In 1923 Levinas took advantage of the opportunity to move to Strasbourg, France, where he studied philosophy and began a lifelong friendship with Maurice Blanchot. From there, he would attend the University of Freiburg in Germany to take courses with Husserl and Heidegger from 1928 to 1929.[4] In 1930 he became a French citizen, and in

1939, was drafted into the French army as an interpreter. Levinas' meandering upbringing and familiarity with several different languages was fortunate for him when he was captured as a prisoner of war in 1940. However, as a French officer, he was sent to the military prison camp Stalag 1492 instead of a concentration camp. As Michael Morgan summarizes the world through which Levinas lived and to which he was responding in his work, it was one in need of some means of embracing those rejected and marginalized as the other: "It is a world where the victors and the victims are mirror images of one another, in which indeed there are no victors, only victims."[5] Given that the present argument involves a comparison of the ways Tillich and Levinas, Christian and Jewish philosophers, responded to tragedy in novel ways, one more relevant example will be provided. There is something about being unable to escape life's upheavals that seems to bring ethics to the forefront of theological reflection with urgency, as opposed to being a topic that can be ignored in favor of more abstract matters.

Christian monk Thomas Merton had an upbringing that would take him around the world, which, combined with intense and early encounters with death, would lead him to a rather liberal stance toward non-Christians even before the Second Vatican Council made that a more acceptable position for Catholics. Merton was born in Prades, France, in 1915. When his mother died when Merton was six years old, his artist father moved Merton around the world to follow artistic pursuits. They traveled to Bermuda, New York, back to France, and then to England. Sometimes Merton was in school, and sometimes he was not. Sometimes he was living with his father, other times with his grandparents or family friends. When his father died of a malignant brain tumor when Merton was sixteen, Merton's grandparents and family friends became his family. By 1937, when his grandparents were both dead, Merton was left effectively alone. It is not surprising that his tumultuous and rootless upbringing led him to find solace and peace in the Abbey of Gethsemani in Kentucky, which he joined in 1941.[6] Merton also must have known Levinas' ethical point about the other intuitively, having had to rely on so many different people to raise and help him during his life, which never featured a stable family or living situation prior to life in the abbey. Such intuitive affinity with Levinas is evidenced by the fact that just before Merton died in 1968 of accidental electrocution from faulty wiring, he was touring Asia and speaking to Buddhists and fellow Christians about pitting one's own religion against others as a relic of the past.[7] It is not necessary to live through the Holocaust, the death of one's entire family at a young age, or Gamergate in order to discover truths about how humans should relate to one another. However, sometimes the circumstances of trying times hastens the discovery.

The placement of Gamergate, both world wars, and the Holocaust alongside each other is not without reason.[8] Consider how Levinas dedicated *Otherwise Than Being*: "To the memory of those who were closest among the six million assassinated by the National Socialists, and the millions of all confessions and all nations, victims of the same hatred of the other man, the same anti-semitism."[9] As Michael Purcell notes, this dedication is followed by a more personal one, written in Hebrew, in which Levinas lists his father, mother, brothers, father-in-law, and mother-in-law. All of them were killed in the Holocaust.[10] Morgan, noting this personal aspect of Levinas' work, asks the following question in the early pages of *Discovering Levinas*, a practical question framing the more abstract philosophical thoughts that follow: "What does Auschwitz tell us about the crisis of the modern world?"[11] The failure of political systems and religious institutions prompted both Tillich and Levinas to offer new ways of thinking about philosophy and religion. Similarly, Gamergate is a modern failure that revealed flaws in the status quo within the video game industry. In all cases, fundamental problems in need of new answers were revealed. New sorts of video games that emerged in the wake of Gamergate are ripe for dialogue with Levinas and his new way of thinking. After several hundred pages of excellent exposition on Levinas, Morgan returns to the question of what to do after the Holocaust with the following summation: "To do what we always should have been doing, in a situation in which it is more urgent and more 'difficult': to be compassionate to others and to make primary in our personal and social lives our obligation of responsibility to others, to relieve suffering and pain, to oppose persecution and oppression and injustice."[12] Persecution, suffering, and tragedy are at the heart of each story in this book, be they stories of Christian and Jewish philosophers or of creators and fans of secular video games. All these events revealing deep failures of the modern world are also waiting for new answers that face such problematic situations with responsibility and care.

Given that Levinas developed his thoughts about ethical responsibility, the other, and how both relate to God in the wake of tragedy, his work also has special relevance for video games after Gamergate. Do not kill me. Respect my difference. Such calls from the other can be located in post-Gamergate video games as readily as they can be found in Levinas and those influenced by his work. In each case, responses to great human failures inverted inherited structures of thought and patterns of behavior. As noted in the introduction, nontraditional video games provide styles of gameplay other than shooting and causing explosions, styles of gameplay that allow the experience of encountering and interacting with other characters to be the focus, and sometimes sole point, of such games. In many video games, players can lose the game by failing to overcome certain obstacles. They might fail to skillfully navigate an obstacle course in a level and fall in a pit or end up being eliminated by opposing players in various military shooter games. However, the proliferation of nontraditional games after Gamergate has resulted in games that downplay or even eliminate the need for player skill in favor of providing players with experiences that involve feeling the weight of ethically charged situations. Some of the new video game experiences that have been made available in the wake of Gamergate involve cultivating empathy in the face of the other.

Against trends toward totalization in Western philosophy, trends that eliminate difference for sake of inclusion in the sought-for totality, Levinas argued for a revolution within the philosophical tradition. Rather than broaching ethical questions about what is good only after posing logical, epistemological, and metaphysical questions about what is true, and aesthetic questions about what is beautiful, Levinas became convinced the ordering must be reversed. However, he was not calling for a simple inversion in which ethical philosophy is emphasized prior to dealing with traditional philosophical topics. Levinas called ethics first philosophy, and in *Totality and Infinity* he even associated this philosophy with metaphysics. Even though Levinas formed his ideas about ethical responsibility toward others while reflecting on in-person, face-to-face encounters, those ideas need not be restricted to such encounters. As will be shown, the interactivity of video games is a gateway into the lives of other people, creating encounters with the other that carry all the import of in-person encounters. In a world increasingly connected virtually rather than in-person, realizing the ethical call from the virtual face of the other is of crucial importance for our future on this fragile planet.

From Being to the Other and Special Ethical Responsibilities

At the core of Levinas' philosophy is the encounter of the self and the other, specifically the face of the other. No matter what activities each of us perform day to day, when we encounter others, their faces call out to us. Prior to knowledge of any facts about that other person, when we encounter them, their face calls out with a demand waiting for a response. In a reversal of Heidegger, Levinas argued others are not in the world for the sake of being-itself, however philosophers have defined and debated the meaning of being through the years. Instead, being, each of our beings, is in the world for others. Heidegger's concern was that an ontology of being would only result in self-concerned beings, but his own understanding of being functions as a totality bestowing meaning on everything else. Heidegger's being in the world pertains to someone who always sees the being of the world as disclosed for themselves, as tools at hand already colored in understanding for their usefulness. To truly avoid a philosophy that props up the primacy of self-concern, Levinas argued ethics is more fundamental than ontology.[13] For Levinas, "our consciousness and our mastery of reality through consciousness do not exhaust our relation with reality."[14] The other is the source of something we could not produce ourselves—namely, our very being.

Expressed in less technical terms, the point Levinas makes has to do with identity and difference. Each of us tends to understand what is our own as good. We know our regular surroundings, are comfortable around our family members, and are generally not threatened by that with which we are familiar. What is different, though, what appears as the unknown other, can be deemed threatening precisely because it is unknown. People are more likely to act with aggression and violence against such perceived threats, but the point Levinas is trying to convey is that such actions are irresponsible insofar as they violate a more primary feature of such encounters. Even if the other is completely unknown, in the absence of any information whatsoever their face still calls out for respect, for life, and for dignity. However, this less technical presentation is not quite correct in terms of order of priority.

According to Levinas, the face of the other calls out to each of us before we know ourselves. In fact, it is only in responding to that call from the other that the sense of self emerges. Therefore, while it is a somewhat commonsense fact that people are more likely to accept people with whom they are familiar, that is a distortion of a more basic situation. Nobody knows who they are until they have responded to the call of the face of the other. Before that response, there is no distinction between familiar and different. As Levinas puts it, "the act of saying will turn out to have been introduced here from the start as the supreme passivity of exposure to another, which is responsibility for the free initiatives of the other."[15] Thus, ignoring others who are unknown while privileging the familiar is an abnegation of ethical responsibility based on a lie. For example, white nationalism shares with Gamergate the feature of privileging those who are similar while aggressively rejecting those who differ, a false caricature of reality. There is no such thing as "similar to" prior to responding to the other. Who each of us is, who "I" am, and therefore who we could be similar to, only emerges in the response to the face of the other, prior to which we are all the other to one another.

Each and every one of us is first and foremost established as a self, as who we are, by another. Levinas refers to this situation of personal identity emerging out of a more basic situation of other encountering other as an "inversion of intentionality."[16] The self is not first subject but the object of the gaze and call of another; inverted intentionality. "The subjectivity or the very sub-jection of the subject is due to my being obsessed with responsibility for the oppressed who is other than myself."[17] As Jeffrey Kosky notes, this point entails that responsibility is the ground of human relationships: "As what supports or lies under, responsibility is thus a sort of 'ground' or condition for 'beings'—which are no longer beings insofar as they stand not in Being but on responsibility."[18] Thus, rather than searching for an understanding of being to ground and support our existence, one of the most ancient philosophical explorations, Levinas finds such support and grounding in something other than being. He finds it in ethics and responsibility in face of the other.

Just as a successful answer to the question of being would ground our existence in something other than ourselves, something assured that secures our being in this world in ways not attributable to anything limited and finite, Levinas finds such assurance in the call of the other. Like the transcendent being of God that has provided this security in many theological schemes throughout history, Levinas too finds security in something that transcends every one of us, the face of the other. As Kosky explains the way Levinas both fits into and revises thinking about the grounding of our being, "the self is first affected by others or by exteriority without finding the possibility of this affection as an intentional meaning constituted in itself."[19] Otherwise stated, we do not first appear in what we freely choose to do and think, but in how we respond to another that is more basic or primary. As Levinas would put it, each of us is grounded in the accusation of the other. We are all charged with responding to the other's call, a call that we did not create ourselves and which will never go away, a call that therefore securely grounds our being as we respond to it. To be is to be accused, to be called out by the other to whom a response must be given. A sense of self only emerges after that fact, after the encounter with the other, hearing their call and responding so as to define oneself in that response. "The way I appear is a summons. I am placed in the passivity of an undeclinable assignation, in the accusative, a self."[20] While this answer finds the ground of our being in the call of another being, not being-itself, the ethical solution provided by Levinas shares structural similarities with Tillich's ground-of-being solution.

Because the encounter with others is functionally what supports each of our senses of ourselves through the need to respond, each of us is responsible for the rest of us, for all others. Such face-to-face encounters are also apophatic in Tillich's sense. Both the subject responding and the other calling are unconditional in that they are not first known. The personal subject is first called, and no description of the other can provide adequate knowledge of the source of our being. Instead, there are only more or less adequate responses to the call. Kosky even refers to the call of the other as unconditional, using one of Tillich's preferred terms for the ground-of-being: "The accusation or responsibility in which I am summoned to appear is absolute or unconditioned because even if I refuse to heed the summons, even if I flee or evade it, I have still responded. Once the summons summons me, a response is inevitable insomuch as refusing to respond acknowledges the ego that has been summoned, if only for it to reject the summons."[21] Levinas' answer to the question of being is ethical. Only in ethical responsibility to the other is anyone's being, their sense of who they are in the world, grounded and sustained.

THE OTHER AND ETHICAL RESPONSIBILITY

The way in which Levinas disrupts traditional ontological questions and answers contains ready religious overtones. As Purcell notes, Levinas was concerned that traditional ontological answers that turn away from the ordinary things of life may obscure the meaning of that life. Levinas instead looks directly to the ordinary daily events and concerns of life for salvation: "One gives to the beggar who solicits money on the street without calculating any economic equation, or even considering whether the gift is counterfeit. . . . What Levinas does is pull phenomenological thinking back to reflect on ordinary incarnate existence and its ability to disrupt the grander schemes of thought."[22] We may turn from the beggar, or take delight in that which should provoke outrage over injustice, but such negative reactions already implicate the preceding ethical. The face of the other is nude, and that nakedness is their plea laid bare. Therefore, the basic situation of life is that we can be focused on self-interest but will always be interrupted by ethical responsibilities when called out to face them.

Tools and techniques are necessary to transform an indifferent world into one which meets our needs. Deliberate sustained effort is necessary to meet the needs of an individual, even more to meet the needs of families and entire societies. Furthermore, any one of our needs can exist in direct opposition to those of another. Imagine people who pray for sunny weather whenever they are on vacation. What do their prayers mean in relation to local farmers who are praying for rain as a drought threatens their livelihood? The world that we enjoy when it meets our needs is also a world for others, and that reminder should always be at the forefront of our thought. As Purcell notes, "my place in the sun is also an open invitation to the other than myself which invites invasion. The subjectivity which I enjoy as an ever open existential awaits the advent of a personal other, who gives the language of 'who' and 'whom', and breaks open self-enclosure."[23]

William James referred to this phenomenon as sciousness, as contrasted with *con*sciousness.[24] Like the situation of the self being called out by the other, James meant that conscious awareness is called forth from more undifferentiated indiscriminatory being in the world when startled by another that brings forth deliberate attention. You may not notice the blue and white object in your vision as anything in particular until the blue jay squawks and demands attention. Purcell finds essentially the same point in Levinas: "The emergence of the solitary 'I'—the result of a contract between existence and existent—is a work to be achieved, and not without effort, and perhaps impossible for the solitary self."[25] A solitary individual, according to Levinas, can use and enjoy the world as they please, but in such a way that never really leads them outside themselves to something truly different and separate from personal desires. "The world offers the subject participating in existing in the form of enjoyment, and consequently permits it to exist at a distance from itself. The subject is absorbed in the object it absorbs, and nevertheless keeps a distance with regard to that object. . . . It is not just the disappearance of the self, but self-forgetfulness, as a first abnegation."[26] The other provides this difference that a solitary person enjoying the world can so easily forget, because the other faces that person in the form of a demand they could not have created. When the conscious awareness of two people, as opposed to one individual, is brought out into daylight and found to be in conflict, self-affirmation does not matter above all else. Acknowledging and responding to the call of that other is now a factor that can only be ignored through self-delusion. Everyone likes to enjoy nice weather while on vacation, but the needs of farmers also matter. To describe the situation in more religiously tinged language, the most basic grounding of all reality is a situation in which we are chosen despite ourselves. We are chosen by the other through their call to us, and we ought to take up that call and embrace it as a challenge to which we are fit to respond, rather than ignoring it altogether.

Ethical responsibility is not an autonomous choice we freely initiate, according to Levinas, because it is initiated by the appeal from the face of the other. Therefore, in a weighting of terms opposite that of Tillich, responsibility is heteronomous, "prior to freedom."[27] No individual takes stock of themselves and only then makes a decision regarding how to act in the world. The face of the other is the source that initiates such a movement. The other forces a response to its call, and in responding, even if that response is to ignore that call, the personal being of the one responding is established. However, it is important to note that the usage of the terms heteronomy and autonomy is not the same in Tillich and Levinas. Levinas' sense of heteronomy is "the aspiration, especially philosophical, to move from this world to another, from the everyday to the beyond."[28] This is not what Tillich meant by heteronomy, which he associated with attempts to dominate and control. If anything, the ways Levinas defines autonomy as the attempt to domesticate everything in life according to each of our limited human purviews is more in line with Tillich's definition of heteronomy.[29] Therefore, when Levinas calls for an overturning of undue emphasis in Western thought on autonomy in favor of a turn to heteronomy and something different, such a call is actually more in line with Tillich's definition of theonomy. Heteronomous responsibility (Tillich's theonomy) makes each of us who we are. This heteronomous call of the other's face is to not kill, which certainly means not to murder the other, though it is also more than that.

IMBALANCES OF POWER AND SPECIAL ETHICAL RESPONSIBILITIES

The call, if truly heard, means we cannot ignore, exclude, discriminate, or otherwise act with hatred or indifference toward the other. The other appears in such a way that establishes an asymmetrical nonreciprocal relationship: "The Other as Other is not only an alter ego: the Other is what I myself am not. The Other is this, not because of the Other's character, or physiognomy, or psychology, but because of the Other's very alterity. The Other is, for example, the weak, the poor, 'the widow and the orphan,' whereas I am the rich or the powerful."[30] However, as Morgan rightly notes, all these other features of interpersonal encounters are involved, but only secondarily. "[E]very encounter between one person and another, is always *already* such a nexus of plea, command, and inescapable responsibility *before* it is anything else—which it always is."[31] In other words, Morgan is trying to note that prior to helping someone because they are a widow or because they are an orphan, their call for help should be given a response because a call from the other and the response of the self is the most basic feature of interpersonal reality.

Morgan is trying to highlight a certain amount of indifference as important in the situation described by Levinas, a means of hedging against the natural human tendency to fraternize only with those like ourselves. "To be sure, in everyday affairs our relationship is also defined and shaped by a host of rules, regularized patterns, and principles of conduct—social, moral, legal, and otherwise. But it is Levinas's point that all of these 'derive' from the encounter with the face, which is particular and determinative."[32] This is more a matter of emphasis, though, than disagreement between Levinas and Morgan. Levinas can be found agreeing with Morgan in various formulations of ethical responsibility: "It is my responsibility before a face looking at me as absolutely foreign that constitutes the original fact of fraternity."[33] Before responding to special obligations to others created by various socioeconomic forces, the most basic philosophical situation is a level playing field in which everyone is responsible to everyone else. We do not choose to be in this condition but are instead placed in this situation by the other. This condition is even more basic than any commitment we *choose* to make toward the other.[34] We exist in a passive state of solidarity before we choose what we are going to do about it. As Roger Burggraeve summarizes, "in spite of myself, the being and well-being of the other concerns me. I am involved with the other even before I can involve myself with the other out of one or the other preference or 'liking', benevolence or magnanimity."[35] Before we actively decide whether or how to relate to another, we are in fact already related to the other. This fact, if realized, would help prevent people from actively deciding against entering into responsible relationships with others whose race, religion, etc. happens to not motivate ethical relations, because such relations are already real and primary.[36] As Levinas remarks, "no one is good voluntarily" because we are always already primordially connected to the good.[37] Before voluntarily choosing to do all the bad things to the other that humans have in fact chosen throughout history, we first exist in something like a state of innocence in which the other relates to us and reveals us in an unsullied state of being.

Morgan is technically correct that every personal encounter is other meeting other, the call of one bringing forth the being of the other and vice versa. Burggraeve agrees with Morgan that we are first and foremost all the other to each other: "Precisely because the alterity of the other is not based on his difference—the difference in qualities, character, social and cultural differentiations—but on his irreducible separatedness and infinite distance, the face of the other refers to all others."[38] However, Levinas added nuance to this basic philosophical situation. He was all too aware that societal factors make for an inequality in both the call and response that emerge in face-to-face meetings between others. His ideas were developed after surviving the Holocaust while most of his family did not. Acknowledging the importance of biography, that Tillich, Levinas, and the current arguments surrounding video games all relate to tragic events, helps highlight how responsibilities are not equitable in practice. While it is possible to bring up the well-known passage, on which Levinas frequently dwells, from Vasily Grossman's *Life and Fate* in which a woman gives a German soldier a piece of bread rather than hitting him with a brick,[39] such possibly irrational yet honorable acts of everyday kindness do not eliminate real imbalances of power in such situations.

This point is just as relevant for modern politics. There is not much a wealthy politician pushing for the building of a border wall needs or can demand of a poor immigrant, despite their pleas of need related to such wall building, but the inverse is not true. Some demands require more of our active attention.

The aspect of indifference Morgan highlights in face-to-face encounters is meant to address this problem. When otherness is not indifferent and instead is defined in terms of properties that make others unlike "myself" or "us" (involving physical, religious, national, and a host of other factors), all sorts of exclusions based on prejudice related to those differences can result. History is certainly a testament to this fact. However, interestingly, Tillich agrees with Levinas on imbalances of power entailing imbalances of ethical responsibility.

Phenomenologically, Tillich describes power as involving possible conflict and tension when people with different degrees of power meet. While meetings of people and groups unequal in power can result in abuse of that power and injustice, such meetings also provide opportunities for cooperative extensions of power to achieve justice. If balanced correctly, the result can be loving, though abuse of power is always a possibility. "One transforms the resisting powers or one adapts oneself to them. One is absorbed by them and loses one's own power of being, one grows together with them and increases their and one's own power of being."[40] As great as cooperation is, it involves its own tensions. Cooperating with friends and family can creatively and productively extend power beyond one individual's limits, but it can also limit individuality and the full realization of one's own being. Tillich therefore raises a potential problem with associating love with power: "If power needs force and compulsion for its actualization, does it exclude love?"[41] He answers in the negative. "Love is the foundation, not the negation, of power."[42] If love is to be effective, rather than at the mercy of powers that would prevent or destroy its work, it must in turn exert its own power. "In order to destroy what is against love, love must be united with power, and not only with power, but also with compulsory power."[43] Tillich's solution for achieving justice and avoiding abuse of power is akin to a preferential option for the poor and marginalized in which power should be directed to help those in need, necessarily at the expense of those who need little to nothing. For example, a white supremacist rally took place in Charlottesville, Virginia, in August 2017, during which Ku Klux Klan members and neo-Nazis carrying torches chanted, "Jews will not replace us," and one of their supporters, James Alex Fields Jr., drove his car into counterprotesters and murdered Heather Danielle Heyer. The President of the United States at the time, Donald Trump, referred to both sides present that day as having good people, instead of condemning violent racists.

The alternative way Tillich would assess the situation should be clear. The answer is not to claim all sides are full of good people and then ask everyone to sit around a table, talk, and respect one another's differences. It is sometimes necessary to condemn in no uncertain terms and use power against people who try to use their own power to prevent love from being extended to others—other races and religions in this case. Such condemnation and action do not mean one is unfairly biased, but rather display one's love of justice in action against hate. Use of compulsion is only problematic if it hinders the final aim of love and justice. Similarly, for Levinas, justice limits the otherwise infinite responsibility brought forth in the encounter of others: "I separate myself from the idea of nonresistance to evil."[44] Nazi Schutzstaffel (SS) officers killing innocent prisoners could, practically speaking, demand nothing of their powerless prisoners during World War II, while each prisoner's most basic call to be allowed to live could have been met through a different use of power. Concrete and particular requirements of justice, helping those suffering in specific situations, outweigh general metaphysical responsibilities in the abstract.

THE PRIVILEGED POSITION OF THE MARGINALIZED

Levinas knew imbalances of power impact face-to-face encounters. Sometimes a pressing existential need to defend oneself or one's family can, and should, take precedence over the ethical ideal of responding responsibly to all others.[45] In order to return to the state of indifferent neutrality described by Morgan, Levinas described forgiveness as necessary:

> There are two conditions for forgiveness: the good will of the offended party and the full awareness of the offender. But the offender is in essence unaware. The aggressiveness of the offender is perhaps his very unconsciousness. Aggression is the lack of attention *par excellence*. In essence, forgiveness would be impossible.[46]

Therefore, Levinas' position is as follows: The basic fact of reality is that the other calls forth each of us with a demand to which we respond. However, in some situations there is a great asymmetry between what can be demanded and how one can respond. Thus, calls from the marginalized other take precedence over calls from the powerful other who cannot, in reality, call out for much. This imbalance of ethical responsibility can return to a balanced indifferent situation, but only if transgressors genuinely apologize for their abuses of power. Unfortunately, aggression toward the other and violation of ethical responsibility indicates a de facto lack of awareness. Thus, when apologies still reflect unawareness, forgiveness will not be given, and the marginalized should continue to receive special aid given the continued imbalance of love, power, and justice in such situations.

In short, some can violate their ethical responsibilities to such a degree that they are not to be embraced. Heidegger arguably falls into this camp, knowingly embracing the Nazis as he did, fully aware of the atrocities they were committing.[47] One could be similarly suspicious of "apologies" from some violent police officers and their departments across the United States, given that they continue to deliver violence and death to innocent people of color with alarming frequency. In face-to-face encounters, the other addresses those they encounter out of a state of need. Given their symbolic and literal power, police officers can demand little to nothing from those communities they have violated, and lack of structural change in light of apologies by those officers and their departments indicates a lack of awareness regarding how police brutality violates the call of the other. Their false apologies are simply further indication that Levinas was correct. We bear special responsibilities to the marginalized until balance is restored to a given situation.

This section ends on the privileged position of the marginalized because that is precisely where Levinas' thoughts on responsibility and the other connect with God and more traditional concerns within philosophy of religion. Levinas cannot accept the idea of a God whose sacrifice would redeem us, a God that would remove our responsibilities from our shoulders: "The idea of the hostage, of expiation of me for the Other, in which relations based on the exact proportionality between wrongdoing and punishment, between freedom and responsibility (relations which transform collectivities into societies with limited responsibility) are overturned, cannot be extended outside me."[48] Redemption is up to us, but there is a trace of God in the encounter between the self and the other.[49] In face-to-face encounters,

> God is drawn out of objectivity, presence and being. He is neither an object nor an interlocutor. His absolute remoteness, his transcendence, turns into my responsibility—non-erotic par excellence—for the other. And this analysis implies that God is not simply the "first other," the "other par excellence," or the "absolutely other," but other than the other, other otherwise, other with an alterity of the other, prior to the ethical bond with another and different from every neighbor, transcendent to the point of absence, to the point of possible confusion with the stirring of the *there is*.[50]

Just as the other is a different answer to traditional ontological questions than answers provided by philosophers who focus on being, Levinas argues that ethical responsibility provides a different and even more powerful sense of God's transcendence than a God who is identified as a supernatural being.

The Other and God

Some caveats about this section should be stated up front. While the present argument places a Christian and a Jewish philosopher in dialogue, this book is not primarily a piece of comparative theology. Furthermore, I am not Jewish and have no expertise to bear on Levinas' Jewish commentaries. The point of this dialogue is to shed light on the full theological depth of video games, which happens to involve insights from two rather untraditional thinkers from two different traditions. Given the focus of the argument on philosophical theology and ethics, not the philosophy of Levinas in general, this section will focus on the main theological commentaries of Kosky, Morgan, and Purcell exclusively, favoring theological depth over nontheological philosophical breadth in my interlocutors.

Kosky has convincingly shown that there are not two versions of Levinas, the earlier philosophical and later religious versions, to be cleanly separated. Rather, "the analysis of responsibility opens onto a philosophical articulation of religious notions and thus makes possible something like a philosophy of religion."[51] Morgan has also shown, with his excellent treatment of Levinas and philosophical theology, that Levinas was in fact remarkably consistent with his thoughts about God and transcendence throughout the "two phases" in which some argue he changed.[52] Ethical responsibility shown to the other is exactly where ethical philosophy and philosophical theology meet as one. Kosky's book on Levinas and philosophy of religion starts by arguing there is "no religion without responsibility" and ends with the claim that there is "no responsibility without religion."[53] The philosophy of Levinas emerges as a kind of responsibility that, without changing in character, also becomes how divine transcendence is revealed. However, as for Tillich, such revelation takes a paradoxical form. God is revealed in God's concealing and found in the traces of God more than in direct revelation per se.

REVIVING TRANSCENDENCE AFTER THE DEATH OF GOD

Friedrich Nietzsche supposedly put an end to transcendence. Metaphysical thought about being and being-itself is all misplaced will to power, human fantasy but not reality. Philosophy should instead turn its gaze to the immanent plane and away from supposedly transcendent beings. The problem for those who follow this advice but continue thinking of God is that accepting Nietzsche's parameters on what is and is not allowed eliminates genuine transcendence. As Levinas summarizes, "the Transcendent, or the Absolute, or the One, cannot enter into relation with the soul without beginning within it; but by doing so it ceases to justify its transcendence. The One can do nothing but resists knowledge. Not only sensory intuition, but all forms of thematization: concept, idea, symbol."[54] The problem with accepting this new situation for philosophy of religion and theology is that it seems to create an impossible situation by definition. God must be transcendent yet immanent, infinite and yet intimately known, fully rational yet beyond rational comprehension. Kosky nicely summarizes the theological dilemma: "Isn't it a willed servitude to claim to have an idea of a thing but not to accomplish fully the thought of it?"[55] The answer provided by Levinas is that we are not, in fact, fully rational in this arena, that knowledge of God is not exhausted in conscious awareness. However, the responsible ethical subject is one to whom the infinite can still make sense.

Similar to his remarks about problems inherent in solitary enjoyment of the world, Levinas equates isolation, resting content with oneself, with atheism. However, Purcell notes that such an atheistic isolated situation is presented by Levinas as the condition for the possibility of transcendence: "The withdrawal of the subject into itself is the possibility of transcendence, for transcendence presupposes separation."[56] Out of individual isolation, the other becomes the source of transcendence. The appearance of the other, which also brings forth the appearance of the self, is the route out of self-isolation to that which transcends the self. Recall that for Levinas, we cannot usher ourselves into being. Rather, our characteristics appear in responding to the call of the other, with the call taking the primary place in the series. Therefore, not only is a solitary atheistic situation actually good news for the philosophical theologian, but it is the necessary condition for transcendence, just as the self is insufficient without the other. As Levinas put it, "the idea of infinity, revealed in the face, does not only require a separated being; the light of the face is necessary for separation."[57] However, when true transcendence is encountered, when God appears, that divine revelation is also a disappearing. Just as the face of the other is prior to, and therefore only covered by, empirical descriptions of the concrete person that emerges only after their face first appears and calls to us, a truly transcendent God also eludes encapsulation in face-to-face encounters.

The metaphor Levinas chose for expressing the encounter with transcendence from such a solitary starting point is height. The height is the authority that is attached to the call from such an apparently lowly place of need in the face of the other. "The absolute nakedness of a face, the absolutely defenseless face, without covering, clothing or mask, is what opposes my power over it, my violence, and opposes it in an absolute way, with an opposition that is opposition itself. The being that expresses itself, that faces me, says no to me by his very expression."[58] The face of the other pleads to each of us out of a vulnerable place, is naked in laying its needs bare, but also has height in the sense that such vulnerability has power to command. God is the ground of this height, but not through the imposition of the divine in ethical demands, since God is not a being. As Morgan summarizes, "God is *revealed in* the *height* of the face. God is not revealed by that height; it is revealed in it."[59] God is neither the face nor its height, but that feature of such encounters that calls attention to the height of the face of the other. It makes sense to refer to God here because the ethical call revealed in the encounter with the other is both transcendent, in that it is a universal feature of all face-to-face encounters, and immanent, in that it is particular to each other we happen to encounter. Just as Tillich indicates that paying attention to our ultimate grounding is the way of moving forward amid life's uncertainties, speaking of God for Levinas is the means of acknowledging the ultimate importance of the ethical encounter with the other.

While each used a different metaphor, and metaphors moving in different directions at that, it is interesting that Tillich and Levinas both referred to God in terms of dimensionality and its extension. Tillich found God in the sacred depths of reality. For Levinas transcendence is a matter of height. "The Other is the very locus of metaphysical truth, and is indispensable for my relation with God. He does not play the role of a mediator. The Other is not the incarnation of God, but precisely by his face, in which he is disincarnate, is the manifestation of the height in which God is revealed."[60] The other is not a direct sign of God, but the other is the only means by which God is accessible. Just as Tillich's God must be both affirmed and denied as transcendence present in immanence, the other makes God accessible in God's absence. God is not equal to the other but made accessible by the other, much as Tillich's God is present in the conditioned world precisely by not being reduced to any part of that world. Precisely because God is not a being, and is more associated with absence than a dictatorial ruler, we must develop societies and rules for justice when we encounter others. Realizing the right sort of relation with God frees us to be responsible rather than passing the buck to a supposed divine overlord. In each case, whether you prefer the framework of Tillich or Levinas, God has not been heard if our lives and the way we behave have not been transformed by God's presence, and absence, in experience.

Both Tillich and Levinas, in embracing such a divine paradox, agree theologically that the concept of God as a being is a myth that should be rejected. Just as Tillich's God is the ground-of-being, not *a being* with comprehensible properties, Levinas employs the language of height to clarify that God is not reducible to the other or even personal in any literal sense.[61] As Morgan summarizes the point, "the language of God—of the divine, the sacred, and the holy—is a theological way of expressing that height, of calling attention to it and acknowledging it."[62] For both Tillich and Levinas, we can relate to a real and transcendent God, yet that God is not a real being. For each philosopher, our relation to the transcendent God is asymmetrical, coming to us and to which we must respond. Even more, both employ their chosen metaphors, height and depth, as moral concepts to highlight personal transformation that should result from an encounter with the transcendent nonpersonal God. Height refers to the inescapable force with which subjects encounter moral responsibility toward the other.[63] As myths taken literally, talk of God dwelling in either the heights or depths abnegates human responsibility and passes it on to a God who will supposedly perform our jobs for us—but this never will occur, because that God is not real. But as mythical or symbolic language that is known as such, as words incapable of grasping and encapsulating the meaning of God's transcendence, Tillich would agree with the way Levinas expresses the power of such personal language. "A face is not an appearance or sign of some reality, which would be personal like it is . . . A face does not function in proximity as a sign of a hidden God who would impose the neighbor on me."[64] Rather than rationally encapsulating God with a set of concepts and a list of divine properties, real encounters with God end with acting instead of thinking, changing rather than schematizing. The practical implications of encountering God are how it is known that God was really encountered, as opposed to a fiction of our own creation.

Levinas also shares with Tillich a form of apophatic negative theology, though few have recognized this point, possibly because of connections between apophatic theology and the trajectory of thought against which Levinas was reacting. Regardless of the reasons, both Tillich and Levinas paradoxically affirm and deny God is in the world, transcendent yet not so transcendent as to be disconnected. Morgan, however, has latched on to this connection, quoted here at length.

> In traditional theology and philosophical thinking about God, God is conceived as infinite, omnipotent, and overwhelming. Such thinking can seem to be confronted with a paradox about how the human can confront the divine, the finite the infinite, and still survive, indeed about how the finite can encounter the divine and respond to it. The reason for the paradox is that if divine power is unlimited and infinite, it leaves no room for finite freedom, and yet the latter exists. . . . But Levinas sees things differently. It is as if there are moments in human existence when the divine encounters the human and yet "departs" at the same instant, and in departing, the divine leaves behind a "trace" of itself. That trace resides in the face of the other person to whom we are related; it is a trace of a divine presence that is in

fact a divine absence, an *illeity*, and its effect is to leave behind a residue of its overwhelming power, of its infinity, a residue that is manifest in the other person's face, her vulnerability that in virtue of being the site of the divine trace is also her demandingness.[65]

Levinas connects the divine trace, the absence, to the empowering of ethical responsibility in light of the face of the other. However, in connecting this alternative understanding of divine transcendence with ethics, he resists associating God with strict immutable moral codes. While some, especially conservative theists, might bemoan the lack of robust, clear conceptual content associated with God's mode of appearing, it could be argued that identifying divine presence with absence is exactly what provides human empowerment.[66]

Levinas and Tillich are comfortable with a form of theology and ethics that is risky and a little uncertain in terms of what it specifically means for the future. In the sense that God is not a being or thing that can be unambiguously present in our reality, both Tillich and Levinas agree that atheism helps overcome incorrect understandings of God, stumbling blocks that hinder people from embracing their alternative, nontraditional models of divine transcendence. As Morgan notes, reiterating the connection between this God that is no thing and ethics, "[t]he theistic God is a 'myth,' Levinas says, whereas the God who 'speaks' to us does so through the other person, the *real* transcendent, who engages me as the stranger, the widow, and the orphan. . . ."[67] As Tillich would say, God breaks through in this finite world, or shines forth in the face of the other, if you prefer Levinas' expression, without being reducible to that reality—paradoxically transcendent and immanent. Language of divine presence is meant to direct attention to a possibility always present, yet often not realized, which must retreat the moment its truth is realized, lest it get in its own way and become just another idol that hinders impactful personal transformation. Levinas describes this connection between ethics and God's transcendent presence in absence in the passage below.

> Ethics is not the corollary of the vision of God, it is that very vision. Ethics is an optic, such that everything I know of God and everything I can hear of His word and reasonably say to Him must find an ethical expression. In the Holy Ark from which the voice of God is heard by Moses, there are only the tablets of the Law. The knowledge of God which we can have and which is expressed, according to Maimonides, in the form of negative attributes, receives a positive meaning from the moral "God is merciful," which means: "Be merciful like Him." The attributes of God are given not in the indicative, but in the imperative. The knowledge of God comes to us like a commandment, like a *Mitzvah*. To know God is to know what must be done.[68]

GOD'S TRANSCENDENCE AND SPECIAL RESPONSIBILITY TOWARD THE MARGINALIZED

Not being reachable or rationally comprehensible, God directs us otherwise than God, to the other. The God that believers desire to encounter turns such desire in another direction. To ask a question like if and how God is good is actually to turn that question upon oneself. How does Levinas respond to questions about the ways in which God is good? "He is good in this very precise, eminent sense: He does not fill me with goods, but compels me to goodness, which is better than to receive goods."[69] Just like Tillich's unconditional God is found in the conditional world but does not give any specific set of commandments when so found, the encounter with divine transcendence should fill us with the courage to be responsible toward others in the world.

Pointless suffering like the Holocaust and the subsequent death of God do not, in fact, amount to a complete refutation of God's reality. Rather, the supernatural God is dead so that we may make God living. Suffering, tragedy, and irresponsible behavior are openings through which genuine encounters with God can challenge and empower ethical activity once again. With the temptation to obtain knowledge of God removed, the ability to respond to God is made possible.[70] The absence of God's presence means there is no excuse available for people to renounce their ethical responsibilities. "It is certainly a great glory for the creator to have set up a being capable of atheism, a being which without having been *causa sui*, has an independent view and word and is at home with itself."[71] Along with Levinas and Tillich, we should all thank God for this specific sort of atheism, for God's own sake.

Virtual Others Calling Forth Responsibility

The current argument about theological depth within and ethical responsibility brought forth by video games is breaking new ground, but it is not entirely unprecedented. In *Thinking Otherwise*, David Gunkel extends the thoughts of Levinas in developing the concept of ethical responsibility toward artificially intelligent others.[72] Interactions in online video games are also amenable to the thought of Levinas because, while many things about identity can be changed online, even into nonhuman identities, players know that behind it all is another person.

Levinas is ready to be both applied to and exemplified by video games for three additional reasons. First, his concept of *illeity*, or absence, relates to how ambiguity is always present in the way face-to-face encounters unfold. Game developers must be comfortable with this idea, as making a game full of ethical encounters that leave the player with options for response also entails leaving those choices up to players, for better or for worse. The ethical call of the other is always present, but the form of the response is uncertain. Second, the face itself is nonphenomenal. The encounter of the face of the other is prior to ontology, which means prior to the study of existing beings in this world. It is therefore prior to any normal everyday encounter of things other than ourselves like birds and trees or specific people.[73] Its function is to bring forth the sense of self before any concrete knowledge of the other manifesting that face is obtained. As a fundamental aspect of how reality is experienced before it is overtly the face of this or that person, the face of the other need not even be the "face" of a human, just the direct encounter of an ethical call demanding a response. Given that the face is not literally the appearance of another person, but the conveying of a plea that demands a response, there is no prima facie reason to deny that the face of the other can be encountered in video games. In fact, affirming this can and does happen is the more logical conclusion to draw from Levinas. Before anyone knows anything at all about the other, their physical features, beliefs, desires, or anything else, the other is faced in the form of a demand. There is no reason to doubt such demands could be present in fully formed characters encountered in video games, even in single-player games in which only others behaving according to their programming are encountered.

Finally, and perhaps most importantly, the philosophy of Levinas is ultimately not as concerned with clarifying terms as it is with the actual encounter of the other. Levinas was certainly an excellent philosopher who carefully specified how both God and the other can be encountered and responded to but not fully captured in rational thought. Having noted that point, such technical clarity was not his primary concern. There is no face-to-face encounter in reading his words, those that have filled this chapter, or any excellent book on Levinas. However, video games can allow players to experience and learn from the sorts of face-to-face encounters Levinas describes. Rather than just learning what Levinas means about the other, responsibility, and God, video games allow players to experience those lessons and put them into practice as they respond responsibly or irresponsibly to others based on their virtual encounters with the other. This final point is important and deserves some elaboration.

Because the appearance of the face of the other is not a matter of visual perception, of phenomenologically noticing features of the other that are different than mine or intellectually comprehending their thoughts and beliefs in contrast to mine, such appearances and encounters of a face can happen virtually. Consider some of Kosky's brief concluding thoughts about the difference between genuinely encountering the face of the other and obtaining factual information about the other and consider whether the face of the other can only be encountered in-person: "Since the responsible self is not only the one to whom the revelation is made but is itself the revelation, transcendence is revealed without being subject to, conditioned by, or limited by what I can hear, by what I can find as a possibility in and for consciousness."[74] There seems to be nothing about a physical encounter that is a precondition for coming face to face with the other. An ethical calling forth, the ushering of a demand to which the one being encountered must respond, can happen in fiction, even video games. In the case of video games, the player takes the place of the self called forth by the other. For players who enjoy things like straight cismarriage, the privileges of being white in America, and the economic advantages reaped by systematic oppression of poor working-class individuals, they can have those enjoyments called out and challenged by characters in video games who demand their right to enjoy those same things and stop limiting them to privileged classes.

While these topics can be discussed in books and lectures, those books and lectures necessarily miss the mark due to limitations of the medium in which they are delivered. Actual interactivity is what matters, according to Levinas. The medium really *is* the message, in large respect, to echo Marshall McLuhan: "Our conventional response to all media, namely that it is how they are used that counts, is the numb stance of the technological idiot."[75] In a way, Levinas admitted this strange but necessary limitation of putting his thoughts in print: "[E]xpression does not manifest the presence of being by referring from the sign to the signified; it presents the signifier. The signifier, he who gives the sign, is not signified. It is necessary to have already been in the society of signifiers for the sign to be able to appear as sign. Hence the signifier must present himself before every sign, by himself—present a face."[76] The face refers to itself as signified in face-to-face encounters. The problem is that words and speech about the face of the other are already removed from the encounter in which the face can do its semiotic work. Kosky basically comes to the same conclusion: "The exceptional presence of the other in the signifying face implies the absence of the other from every image, concept, or horizon within which the Same might contain or grasp it. Its exceptional presence in expression is absolute presence, in the special sense that Levinas gives absolute: ab-solute, loosened, freed, separated, or unbound—absolved from the presence it enters."[77] Video games can remind players of this point. The face of the other is not reducible to any specific characteristics of any given person, but in ethical failings people are reduced to being Black, gay, etc. and are rejected as such.[78] That is how racism and homophobia develop. When, amid our daily tasks, we forget about the primal encounter of the face and regress into behaving responsibly only toward those similar to ourselves or with whom we are familiar, the face of the other disrupts normal everyday activity and thinking and demands that its plea be recognized. Video games provide opportunities to encounter the other that can snap us out of such complacency. Some understanding of Levinas assists in ensuring such an awakening occurs, but playing a game in which others are encountered gets closer to the heart of the philosopher's points than merely reading about those points. Levinas needs video games and the video game industry needs Levinas.

The communities that have developed around the video game industry need to learn Levinas' argument about the inviolability of the other, to be reminded about the way the plea of the other is truly made manifest in experience. In light of death threats against minorities working in the industry, the industry needs to be reminded that the face of the other calls out to not be killed because the other is that which each us of can choose to kill if we do not heed their call. "The fact that the face is either killed or spoken to means that the same finds itself paralyzed before the face. The face always remains absolutely other than the same; for no possible approach to it, not even violence, can include it in the same."[79] Obviously violence is real and the calls of the other are not always heard, but when the face of the other is *truly* acknowledged, it becomes impossible to commit violence against it, because the reality of the situation is understood. Acts of intellectual or real-world physical violence occur when the other's face is either forgotten or ignored. When everyday life all too easily lets us fall back into comfortable associations about what is ours and what is other, video games can help us to never forget the deeper ethical reality of our situation.

Level Three

Boss Fight: Philosophical Theology and Science

> With diminished oxytocin and empathy, it's all too easy for the other to become The Other, and then The Enemy, and then The Inferior or The Demon. Without knowing the exact physiology, governments and armies realized thousands of years ago that the way to engage testosterone, decreasing empathy and increasing the desire to punish, is to manufacture an external threat to the group's existence.[1]

As already mentioned, the idea that would eventually lead to this book first saw the light of day at PAX East 2015. The scientific component of the presentation at that convention has not been mentioned yet, but it is crucial to understanding why the work of Tillich and Levinas should be brought together, and why video games make a pivotal difference in that endeavor. However, before jumping to that dialogue, it is worth summarizing how the differences between the "modern" Tillich, with his focus on ontology and essence, and the "postmodern" Levinas, concerned with ethics and preserving difference, have already come together. Someone deeply invested in the work of one figure might be suspicious of the work of the other, and much more so of the present argument bringing them together. However, such suspicion would be unfounded.[2] Tillich and Levinas are often lumped into the modern and postmodern camps, and members of each camp are supposedly incapable of mingling with one another, but they complement each other in a number of important ways.

The Unconditional Breaking through the Other in Video Games

Tillich's effort to transcend theism by affirming a God beyond the God of theism and rejecting supernatural forms of theology is a project not far removed from the concerns of Levinas. Tillich, like Levinas, in some ways owes a debt to Heidegger's distinction between metaphysics and fundamental ontology. Tillich, like Heidegger, aimed to avoid an ontic theology asserting God to be a particular being, and instead developed a model of God in which God is the being of beings, the power of being ushering forth in all finite beings. There is a sense in which Tillich did for theology what Heidegger did for philosophy, perform a rescue mission from an exclusive focus on particular definite beings.[3] For Tillich, being is beyond thought and resists its totalizing tendencies to conform. Nevertheless, Tillich departs from Heidegger in making some space for metaphysical theological statements. That God is being-itself is a true statement about God for Tillich, the only one possible, in fact, even though he expresses the point with a few interchangeable symbolic terms. This divine reality is also other than every being in the world. Only through making this distinction between beings in the world and the ground-of-being can anyone realize their essence.

Both Tillich and Levinas affirm a God that is a mystery and cannot be exhausted or captured in any statements about that divine reality. Tillich emphasizes the ontologically ultimate aspect of God and Levinas emphasizes the aspect of otherness and difference, but their sensibilities that led them to such conclusions do not fundamentally disagree. Levinas privileges the priority of the other and explicitly opposes that basic foundation to ontologies built upon being, but the distinction between being and being-itself is what provides the most basic distinction in Tillich's theology. Only because God is unconditional, *other than* beings in the conditioned world, does his work save theology from the traps of conceiving God as a specific being. Whether it be the face of the other or the ways in which God is other than yet present in this finite world, both Levinas and Tillich have a God that makes each of us who we are. For both, God is other than everything else that can be investigated and known in the world, yet also connected to personal experiences, and that intimate connection is how individuals realize who they are.

Because God is not a being to be captured and understood in thought and theological concepts, both argue the practical payoff of realizing God's presence is to turn us toward what is other than God. God provides the courage to be oneself and engage culture with the goal of affirming rather than destroying life. Tillich explicitly rejects the mystical desire for union with God rather than engaging concrete particulars in the world. Having a real experience of the divine breaking through and changing this world, but then referring to that experience as the only sort in which God can be found, lifting up the description of that experience as a literal encapsulation of God's nature, is the height of idolatry. Levinas asserts more straightforwardly that God is experienced in the other toward which we must responsibly behave. However, because only traces of God are found when encountering others, he agrees with Tillich that God cannot be accurately described in concepts and statement about divine properties. Rather, a God radically other than we are turns us to respond to the demands of others as a result of the divine encounter. The trace of that which is beyond being is not *that* different than Tillich's claim that the ground-of-being is present in yet different than and transcendent to everything that has being.[4] The difference is a matter of emphasis. Both have an asymmetry in which the otherness of God is what accounts for our being in this world, a dependence upon a God that remains other than us despite being necessarily and intimately connected to each of us. No amount of further probing could fully reveal the God so encountered. Asymmetrical dependence is always present. God lifts the veils from human eyes, making it possible to see oneself and the world as they truly are, but if anyone thinks that means God is fully and exclusively understood in such moments, the veil has already been replaced.

Nathan Dickman has noted that the act of questioning lies at the heart of both these projects.[5] Actually hearing questions that arise from the current situation is crucial before delivering theological answers in Tillich's engagement with culture. For Levinas, the other calls us into question, and our response simultaneously determines who the other is to us and therefore who we are ourselves. While other academic projects engaging Tillich and Levinas are virtually nonexistent, I find it no coincidence that Dickman's argument follows the current one in taking tragedy as its starting point. His argument begins by reflecting on all the assumed values the 9/11 terrorist attacks on the United States brought into question. His conclusion is that tragedy brought on by human violence brings Tillich and Levinas, existential and postmodern thinking, together as questions about truth in the wake of disaster transform into questions about how to best behave moving into the unknown future. "Meaningfulness and the enigma of the Other do not make up an exclusive disjunction, but, rather, a productive tension."[6] Considering in what ways one's essence can be realized and what actions will rise to the call of the other are not exclusive options. Both result in courageous ethical behavior in the world.

Dickman notes other potential similarities between Tillich and Levinas lying behind superficial differences. "For instance, is Levinas' concept of 'face' as that which bears the trace of the infinite a 'self-negating symbol'? Alternatively, is the 'power of being' also 'otherwise than being'?"[7] Tillich's basic ontological question is "What is being itself?"[8] Tillich elaborates on this basic ontological question as follows:

> The ontological question presupposes an asking subject and an object about which the question is asked; it presupposes the subject-object structure of being, which in turn presupposes the self-world structure as the basic articulation of being. The self having a world to which it belongs—this highly dialectical structure—logically and experientially precedes all other structures.[9]

While Levinas offers what, in Tillich's way of describing things, might be called a subject-subject structure of being, it is not clear that the differences in language are indications of deeper, more serious conflicts.[10] Tillich's most basic affirmation is God is unconditioned, the ground-of-being, something prior to subject-object distinctions about the world yet supporting all subjects and the sense of their own selves and what the world they encounter means for them. In light of these similarities, Robert Scharlemann has suggested adding a third term to Tillich's basic scheme of self and world empowered by God as the ground-of-being.

Asking a question is different than being asked a question. We cannot really put our own being into question, because we have it. But another can question our being in the form of what response we will give their questioning.[11] That is one of Levinas' central claims. Scharlemann's suggestion, in light of Dickman's focus on questioning, is that a Tillichean scheme of self, world, *and* other might make the most sense.[12] This addendum introduces a subtle shift in focus within Tillich's thought. Nothing specifically related to ontology can make us responsible to this or that person. Specific ethical demands arise from the other. The relevance of this point is evidenced by the way another philosophical theologian greatly indebted to Tillich has dealt with ethics recently.

Consider how Robert Neville construes goodness. Rather than special responsibilities toward others, his work, which is in many ways an extension of Tillich's philosophical theology and position that God is the ground-of-being, concludes *all things* are good in some sense. His position is that all determinate existing things have form and "to have form is to embody goodness."[13] Rather than judging things harshly for negative relations with others, Neville focuses on his claim that "anything with form has goodness by virtue of that form."[14] Simply stated, everything is good in itself, for the form it has achieved and the small victory over nothing that achievement amounts to, even if that form means doom and destruction for others to which it is related. Therefore, no special ethical responsibilities are entailed by Neville's position. It would be nice if the world were not so racist and sexist, but, in the end, it does not matter because everything will be good for the form it has achieved. Neville is hesitant to take a strong stand on specific social issues not so much because times and tolerances ebb and flow, but because his metaphysics necessitates calling all things good. Attempts to end racism could have unknown consequences worse than the situation they were meant to resolve, but that too would ultimately be no better or worse than a future without such unforeseen circumstances. Everything will be fine because no matter what happens, everything is good in the sense that everything that has achieved form has that achievement grounded in God and is therefore good.

It is in light of such potential inactivity that arises from a focus on being that Levinas argues the face of the other is *otherwise* than being, a move meant to ensure special ethical responsibility is registered. Though it may be surprising, given Neville's indebtedness to him, Tillich also has a resource for addressing ethical inactivity in the concept of estrangement. While Tillich and Neville are both ground-of-being theologians, estrangement allows Tillich to affirm that everything is good while simultaneously attacking distortions of that goodness.[15] Goodness and value, in the sense that anything with form has the goodness and value achieved by that form, is present in each theological position, but Neville's theory stops there. For Tillich, form is good when it does not hinder the realization of someone's essence. When hindrance is real, the form of something has become estranged from the ground-of-being. Such distortions can be personal, when someone is experiencing existential meaningless, but they can also be relational when that same person actively hinders others from such realization. Furthermore, essence need not mean an Aristotelean essence shared by everything that erases difference. Defending personal essence does not necessarily entail that all people share an essence, just that the potential of anything to be X, Y, or Z—to be anything that they might become—is an absolute truth about every being.[16] It can mean something as simple as my essence is to not be racist, or sexist, etc., so as to not prevent people of other races or genders from realizing their own essence. My essence is to not prevent others from realizing their essence. Conversely, if anyone is hindering others from being who they are, that is a good indication they have not realized their ultimate identity in the ground-of-being either. In short, for Tillich, part of realizing one's own essence should involve actively helping others make sure they can be similarly realized. To illustrate this point, Tillich compares personal moral choices with political states as persons. In totalitarian regimes, the head of state cannot be criticized. Alternatively, Tillich writes about "creative justice," in which justice applies to different people and groups differently.[17] One person's plight in life may need to be highlighted, raised up for awareness and changed, while another's may not. Such creative justice calls for far more than mere tolerance, which literally implies there is nothing to do but avoid mistreating others. Tillich's stance on morality and achieving justice is focused directly on meeting the needs of others and paying attention to difference. Particular responsibilities to others are not excluded from his system.

God empowers individuals to realize their essential selves in the world by the way they respond to others. Tillich's God is a God empowering people to overcome the anxieties of life and realize themselves here and now, despite the myriad of forces that try to prevent such realization. Postmodern readers may bristle at the language of "essence" in Tillich, but realizing who we are in relation to the divine depths is precisely how Levinas describes the infinite God. This God is not capable of full comprehension by any person, but is that which fulfills the meaning of human life. Merold Westphal goes as far as to suggest "it may be that Levinas's God is best understood as the depth dimension of each human person by virtue of which a categorical, infinite, asymmetrical call to responsibility emanates."[18] In light of these agreements, be they ontological or phenomenological and critical of ontology in nature, there is no need to assume incompatibility between Tillich and Levinas.[19] Typical postmodern insults hurled at ontology, that it necessarily excludes, are unnecessary, at least regarding Tillich.[20]

Levinas' criticism of systemizing and generalizing is not the same as apophatic theology, but aligns with its instincts—not in a rejection of modern systematic projects such as Tillich's, but in recovering much older insights about human limitations.[21] What is most important religiously is not propositional statements, but silence, or indirect invocations of God at best. As Wesley Wildman phrases the possible rapprochement between postmodern criticism and philosophical theology, both are attuned to the God "manifest in and in spite of human decisions and behavior, as that which appears in the shortcomings and breakdowns of human reason."[22] Overconfident self-assertion has led to great worldwide tragedies, and its apophatic humbling may be just what is needed. So many arbitrary constructions have been used to legitimize nothing but ideologically driven hate. Both Tillich and Levinas, in their unaffirmable affirmations about God, share Wildman's question: "Do we encounter something unquestionable, something that pushes back by questioning us?"[23] Even if there is nothing there of which we can adequately speak, no divine object, that God-shaped hole pushes back and makes us want to say something even if the best we can do is caution ourselves to avoid idolatry. Levinas and Tillich agree searching for a divine being will never adequately answer our questions.

God is the unconditional ground-of-being present everywhere in Tillich's paradoxical affirmation of transcendence in immanence. As shown in the previous chapter, this entails that such theological claims about the ground-of-being cannot be divorced from culture. Rather, all culture must be embraced: "Religion is the substance of culture, culture is the form of religion."[24] Given that popular culture is part of culture at large, this same point applies to video games. Importantly, to support my claim that Tillich and Levinas complement one another, many nontraditional video games developed after Gamergate are not about challenging gameplay but focus instead on providing digital environments in which players can encounter others. When the content of such games focuses on emotionally or ethically charged situations, the point of playing such games becomes encountering the calls from the faces of such digital others and responding to them within the game. Even though a choice to meet the needs of a struggling immigrant in a video game will not directly help immigrants crossing from Mexico into the United States, for example, video games that provide such experiences still create situations in which the player is called out and defined in how they respond to the primary call of the face of the other. Such virtual cultivation of oneself in response to the other should continue when responding to others in real life. The result of such virtual interactions is that Tillich's main point is realized in the main point of Levinas. The realization of one's essence in the ground-of-being, which occurs within cultural forms, is exemplified by the ethical response to the face of the other in video games, the most popular element of culture today. However, an established body of scientific data about interpersonal trust and distrust places some limits on the ethical responsibility that comes from encountering God in the other.[25] Fortunately, video games can help solve problems that such data creates for Levinas.[26]

A New Challenger Approaches: Oxytocin and the Importance of Video Games

As a graduate student finishing my doctoral work in Claremont, California, I worked as a researcher in Paul Zak's Center for Neuroeconomic Studies. Zak is a trained economist and neuroscientist. He coined the term "neuroeconomics" to label his effort to put some data behind attempts to describe, understand, and predict human behavior. The work of the center intersects with many topics like morality, topics once considered solely subject matter for philosophers and theologians. In particular, Zak and the center are known for their work studying the neurochemical oxytocin. Oxytocin first became widely known when high levels of it were found in breastfeeding mothers and their babies, resulting in an association between the chemical and maternal instincts to care for offspring. However, it is now known to be a more general stimulant for empathy, generosity, and trust. To learn about this and measure morality in a lab, participants take part in what are called trust games involving money that participants take home with them at the end of the experiment.[27] While there are many variations, the basic setup of such experiments is as follows.

In a trust game two participants are given the same amount of money, usually around ten dollars. One participant is given the opportunity to give any amount of that money to the other participant. That amount will be tripled, which is a signal of trust on the part of the first participant because of the next steps in the experiment. The person on the receiving end can then give back any of the tripled amount, a sign of their gratitude for the other person handing over some of their money. Of course, the person who just received a free infusion of income is also free to reciprocate nothing and keep all the money they were just given. That is not what typically happens, though. Over 90 percent of the time, people who are given money by the first participant reciprocate by giving some back in return. An average of $5.52 is sent by the first person and $6.96 is returned by the second. Oxytocin levels in the second person are also 41 percent higher, on average, indicating when a person entrusts money to a stranger, the stranger's brain motivates sharing resources with others.

The inverse was also found. In cases where the first participant gave little money, a sign of distrust, dihydrotestosterone (DHT) levels increased in the second participant. DHT inhibits oxytocin release, increases aggression, and leads to actions that are self-protective instead of generous and trusting. The impact of testosterone on oxytocin release can be understood just by comparing men and women in the trust game (men's bodies contain ten times as much testosterone as women's).[28] The average amount reciprocated by men is 25 percent, 42 percent for women, and 24 percent of men return nothing, while only 7 percent of women are similarly callous. And when men had increased levels of testosterone artificially induced, they were 27 percent less generous in the ultimatum game.[29] Such people are in the minority of participants in trust games.[30] However, before continuing to describe how oxytocin impacts our ability to be moral toward the other, the impact of testosterone and other stress hormones needs to be explored, as it places a real limit on Levinas' understanding of ethical responsibility.

STRESS HORMONES AND LIMITED YET EFFECTIVE RESPONSIBILITY

Scientific evidence indicates that Levinas' claim that responsibility is limitless requires modification. The other and oneself do not exist independently, but only become so in an interpersonal interaction. The face is nude. The other's needs are laid bare as they call each of us forth through the authority or power of weakness, simultaneously being in the position of authority to give an ethical command and being in need.[31] However, Levinas goes at least one step too far in asserting we are responsible for the responsibility of others, that we should always care about *all* others without limitation. Given that each of us is also the other to everyone we encounter, we are each responsible for the freedom of others as they are responsible for ours, as well as their responsibility toward others besides ourselves.[32] We are not only responsible for how we respond to someone's plea, but for how that response impacts that other's response to other people they meet. "Man answers for more than his freely chosen acts. He is the hostage of the universe. Extraordinary dignity. Unlimited responsibility. Man does not belong to a society which bestows limited responsibility upon its members. He is the member of a society of unlimited responsibility."[33] Taken at face value, the lesson seems to be that everyone should sacrifice everything they have for others. This might come across as a nice sentiment, but is it true?

We will inherently fail to live up to such infinite responsibility. In part, that inevitability of failure is Levinas' point. We are not free to choose whether to respond to the pleas of others. They always accuse us, and in doing so define who we are. But is it really my fault as a teacher if my students do wildly irresponsible things with what they are taught? Only in a minimal sense, if I taught them poorly, but surely not in the sense of being responsible for their free choices. Roger Burggraeve, on the other hand, claims I would indeed be responsible for their errors.

> This does not mean that we ourselves would be the origin of those failures and mistakes, but rather that we should not abandon the other, in his failings and irresponsible actions, in his evildoings, to his fate. Without our even having made one mistake, we stand in guilt with the others. . . . we do not renounce our solidarity with the other, even though the other acts in error. This concretely means making sure that the other is not crushed by his failings and guilt, but on the contrary is 'assisted' as such that he can take up and bear his responsibility towards himself and others.[34]

But when do specifics about the other who is failing matter enough to change the picture painted by Burggraeve? What if their failure is becoming a Nazi or a Klu Klux Klan member? Is there a point when someone is so far gone as to be beyond hope? Perhaps more importantly, when does helping such another morph from ethical responsibility to beating your head against the wall to the point that you are exhausted and incapable of helping those who would have benefited more from that expenditure of energy? At some point, is it not just allowable but actually the right thing to do to let someone go and focus on more effective work that can be performed in aid of specific people rather than *all* people?[35] Time and energy are not limitless resources that can be devoted to helping others endlessly without qualification, as Zak's work has shown.

Testosterone and stress inhibit oxytocin release. The unlimited neverending demand to behave responsibly in the face of the other is exactly the sort of situation that would be likely to induce chronic stress.[36] In stressful situations, epinephrine initially moves us to action and to do something about the stress-inducing phenomenon. Cortisol will also be released, which brings about an acceleration of blood pressure, breathing, and heart rate—all the things you would expect to occur in your body while dealing with prolonged stress. Both chemicals inhibit oxytocin release which, as Zak describes, makes evolutionary sense: "The evolutionary logic here is the same as the rationale behind those airline safety instructions that tell you to put on your own oxygen mask before trying to help your child. When you're struggling to survive the next sixty seconds, a high degree of altruism, or even a refined sense of moral scruple, may not be the best way to go."[37] Zak goes on to connect such struggles in life with constant access to news and the societal pressure to get involved in current events, even if that just means more stress-inducing social media arguments:

> New media is an incredibly potent force that has the potential to foster understanding throughout our society, and among all societies. But it needs to be wielded with care, and as in all things, the criterion for success is the extent to which what goes on actually widens, rather than narrows, the virtuous cycle. Is it oxytocin-driven or is it testosterone-driven? Does the communication foster human connection or does it foster anonymity and abstraction to the point that it cuts off empathy?[38]

The situation we are faced with is one in which there is an absolute moral imperative, and an infinite obligation to fulfill it, and yet we have limited individual capacity to fulfill such obligation. Unlimited responsibility can cause burnout.

Think of this sort of social stress in relation to Gamergate. Perceived or real, a group of people felt they were losing their place within the sphere of their favorite hobby, a hobby they thought was secure even when jobs, school, relationships, and other aspirations were not going their way. Such perceived loss of status set an unfortunate series of events in motion.[39] Losing that security blanket, even if the sense of loss was completely fabricated, removed the final plank preventing a constant stream of stress from inhibiting oxytocin release.[40] Gamergate started over matters of defining in-groups and out-groups and became a dihydrotestosterone-fueled movement of hostility. As the point could be expressed to Levinas, we need to say no sometimes, for ourselves and for the sake of the other—because an ineffective helper can sometimes be worse than an enemy.[41] However, the solution is not that simple, as there is an additional problem for Levinas. The empirical evidence for in-group bias and out-group hostility is that initial offerings of trust are much higher toward in-group members and lower for those belonging to the out-group.[42] It seems oxytocin, like God, can inspire both compassion and violence. Fortunately, video games possess the means to nudge us toward Levinas and responsibility rather than hate.

OXYTOCIN VERSUS THE VIRTUAL OTHER

Importantly for an argument about the ethical freight of video games, there is also data that literal face-to-face in-person interactions are not necessary for levels of oxytocin to increase. It *is* the human element that matters when it comes to the release of oxytocin, but that human element can come into play even when another person is not physically present. When setting up trust experiments, the initial transfer of money can be initiated by a human choice or dictated by a computer drawing random numbers. When participants are informed of the different setups, people who received money as a sign of trust from humans had oxytocin levels 50 percent higher than those who received money by random draw. The amount they returned was also 41 percent of their new total, versus 21 percent for those who knew they received money due to a random draw.[43] There is also anecdotal evidence that social media triggers these same results. While speaking with a news reporter for a story,[44] Zak drew the reporter's blood before and after fifteen minutes of using Twitter and found the following: "His oxytocin level increased by 13 percent, and his stress hormone ACTH decreased by fifteen percent. It appears that even this most casual form of technologically mediated interaction—what psychologist Wendi Gardner calls 'social snacking'—can have significant positive effects."[45]

If such spikes from social media truly happen with regularity,[46] it would be more foolish to ardently deny they could occur through video games than to suggest they most likely happen there as well. This suggestion has force because the Twitter example is quite mild compared with instances of people falling in love through playing online games together, traveling thousands of miles to live together based on that love, and joining each other in marriage.[47] The conclusion supported by these contributing sources is that morality, rather than solely depending on rational control through philosophy or religion, is already a part of our physiology and how it functions daily in our interactions. While we do not always succeed in being responsible to the other, the concern at the core of Levinas' work is also at the core of how our bodies physically respond to one another.[48]

Beyond oxytocin, anyone with standard functioning mirror neurons in their brain winces to some extent when they see another person in pain. Just how badly they wince and what degree of pain causes the reaction varies from person to person, but the underlying principle is consistent. The inverse is also true. When someone sees another person experiencing great joy and happiness, they also experience some degree of pleasure.[49] Consider a typical story of kids growing up. Bullying is real. Children pick on other children all around the world. Part of children playing involves playing at causing pain. However, as they mature, children experience shame and even disgust at their actions. As mirror neurons fire and sensations are also experienced by the one inflicting them, limits between play and cruelty are learned. The absence of such feedback is part of what leads to clinical psychopaths, who are unable to distinguish between pain and pleasure. For the vast majority of people, a feedback loop formed by mirror neurons and the impact of their behavior on others is part of how empathy is cultivated.[50] However, technology has created a problem when it comes to cultivating such empathy in the twenty-first century.

This feedback loop fed by mirror neurons is missing on the internet, especially when anyone can hide behind fake names and never show their real face. Zak chose to highlight a positive example of the impact the internet has on our bodies with the anecdotal evidence about Twitter, but the inverse also applies. If positive online interactions release oxytocin, harsh interactions on social media can inhibit oxytocin release and raise levels of stress hormones, inhibiting oxytocin release and making cooperation less likely. Gamergate can easily happen, and perhaps should have been expected. Levinas makes what is in some ways a simple point that is difficult to enact in an increasingly virtual world. So, what can be done to cultivate empathy and responsibility toward the other in the absence of the face of the other? As will be shown in the following chapters, which describe the many ways video games put players in the position of either helping or harming others, video games can help.[51] In the absence of in-person interactions that trigger biological pathways to cooperation, video games can fill the gap in the same way that the physical presence of another person is not necessary to increase oxytocin levels and interpersonal cooperation in trust game experiments.[52] This point is crucial, because there is a dark side to oxytocin that leads to an in-group/out-group problem.

There are solid evolutionary reasons why our species might be suspicious of those whose physical appearances or behaviors are different. For many thousands of years, individuals lived in social worlds limited to their village or tribe. With food, shelter, and safety from predators all less secure than they are today, outsiders were, for understandable reasons, considered threats until proven otherwise. Such situations that may have aided the survival of the species are largely irrelevant to the modern world, however. Today a great number of people no longer struggle just to survive day-to-day. With exposure and education, in-group bias and suspicion of outsiders can fade. However, a study from the University of Amsterdam led by psychologist Carsten de Dreu tells a different story.

In their study, De Dreu's team created a tailored version of the trolley problem. In the trolley problem, a train is out of control on the tracks and cannot stop. It is headed straight for, and will kill, some number of people (usually five) stuck on the tracks ahead. However, someone at the switch controlling the tracks can transfer the out-of-control train onto another set of tracks where it will only kill one person. The thought experiment can be adjusted with different numbers and sorts of people, as well as different parameters such as the ability to sacrifice oneself to stop the train. In all cases it is a rather straightforward way to test utilitarian ethics. Will participants choose to kill one person to save five, or the opposite? In the experiment out of Amsterdam, two versions of the trolley problem were used. In one, the single person to be sacrificed to save five had a Dutch last name. In the other, they had a common Arabic name. The participants in the study were Dutch college students, and when induced with high levels of oxytocin and faced with the option to kill one person with a Dutch name to save five others, they chose to save the one person like them and kill five others more often. De Dreu's team concluded the effects of oxytocin described by Zak and his lab are real, but only for someone's in-group at the expense of out-groups.[53] De Dreu's takeaway from the team's results is striking. "Ethnocentrism is a very basic part of humans, and it's not something we can change by education."[54] However, there were problems with this study, especially related to the lack of a control group among participants and a similarly biased setup of the trolley problem that never presented participants with a more neutral, placebo-like version of the ethical dilemma.[55] However, other scientists have since corrected some of those flaws, and their results have also supported the concept of a dark underside to oxytocin.[56] While the data is convincing, De Dreu's bleak conclusion that a binary us/them culture war is inevitable does not stand, though knocking it down does seem to require some work.

It is possible to ignore the appeals of others, and as a species we seem quite adept at doing so, but for Levinas that tendency represents a fall from a more basic situation. Failure to act responsibly when confronted with the call of the other is only proof that the call was already heard before it was ignored. However, this point by Levinas does not address biological tendencies manifest in the majority rejecting others due to difference (e.g., crackdowns on immigration), or assimilating those who are different and reducing their uniqueness (e.g., bi, transgender, and other queer-identifying individuals being often ignored in discussions of LGBTQ+ rights in favor of gay and lesbian issues). Burggraeve thinks such a problem is precisely why Levinas is needed, as Levinas provided a means of preventing ethical responsibility from being extended only to others who are like us. In a sense, this point of view developed by Levinas is just as natural as biological bonds. "One can rise above it, or rather one is ethically called to rise above it, towards every different other. And this calling is made possible by the fact that the human person is in 'essence' already ethical in nature, that is to say, already attuned to every different other, already opened up and involved, in spite of oneself, to the fate and the well-being of the other."[57] However, while this argument seems solid, it is important to engage philosophy and theology with science because the reality is not so simple. Moral behavior can be extended to the other, but doing so requires regularly experiencing a sort of forced encounter that shocks us out of our natural proclivities toward similarity until responsibly attending to the call of the other also becomes natural.

Levinas has a powerful argument about responsibility to others, but impediments to its realization are part of human biology. Video games can help address this matter. Diversity of representation can break down the barrier of what is considered in or out. The scientific data suggests the importance of a worldview in which exposure to diverse people prevents the creation of a dihydrotestosterone-fueled case of harassment. When boosts of oxytocin from interacting with all sorts of different people are a regular part of someone's online and offline life, they should function as a natural barrier for inclinations to hate the other.[58] Even if there is a disagreement of opinion, that disagreement is less likely to result in a culture war when people of various races, religions, and genders are considered part of one's in-group. When people are constantly surrounded by better representation, respectful and well-intentioned discussion can happen instead of exclusion and violence. Exposure to different people engenders trust in different people, while a group that self-identifies homogenously is more likely to attack anyone unlike it. People exposed to a diversity of representations will be more likely to trust those represented and, in turn, do a better job of responding to the others they meet, which induces further oxytocin release and helps continue a virtuous circle of online behavior.[59] If people naturally trend toward socialization only with others they consider part of their in-group, video games can help provoke responsible ethical behavior by creating encounters with virtual others until the in-group has been so expanded that there is no longer any out-group.[60] If we follow Levinas' advice when accosted by the face of the other, and when our sense of an in-group is diverse enough, a self-reinforcing cycle will result—one lowering natural human inhibition to show the same responsibility we exhibit to those like us toward others who are different.[61]

Even more relevant for the current argument that video games are a source of oxytocin release and responsible behavior is that Zak was once overcome with emotion while watching a movie on a flight. This experience led to a sort of "eureka!" moment in which he decided to investigate how videos can induce oxytocin release. The setup for the experiment was taking a fundraising video for Saint Jude's Children's Research Hospital and editing it into two versions, one simply showing a father walking through a zoo with his child who had cancer, and the other showing the dramatic tear-jerking scenes in which the parents discover their child has cancer.[62] When participants in experiments viewed both videos, the zoo video was apparently boring enough that it dropped oxytocin levels by 20 percent, but the emotional video increased levels by 47 percent over baseline.[63] Increased empathy and moral behavior toward others, even strangers unlike ourselves, can happen through encountering the plea that comes with a face-to-face encounter, even when than encounter is virtual rather than a physical flesh and blood meeting.

Zak takes away a somewhat religious lesson from all these studies: "This means that when a situation we see or learn about causes us to 'do unto others as we would have them do unto us,' it is in part because we are *literally* experiencing another person's pleasure or pain as if it *were* our own."[64] A problem for this religious-esque situation is that the testosterone issue still lingers. When testosterone levels are elevated, pleasure is still had, but *at the expense of* others instead of *through the experience of responding ethically toward* others. It is here that Levinas and video games can help find a solution to this scientific dilemma. His philosophy is a means of understanding all interpersonal encounters as having no sides other than myself and the one calling out for help and to whom I am responsible. There are no "us" and "them," just helper and helped, with the former only arising in response to the latter. The dark side of oxytocin implicated in instances of such interactions with the other going awry just makes virtual interactions even more important. Given natural biological tendencies against ethical responsibility to the other, encountering the other in video games can shock us in the same way that Tillich describes the breaking in of the unconditional within culture as an ontological shock. We cannot create this phenomenon, but we encounter it, find ourselves transformed by it, and necessarily respond by behaving differently in the world as a result. Encountering truly diverse others in video games and online communities matters even more in light of scientific data about morality—these virtual meetings are a means of avoiding this dark undercurrent of our natural tendencies and returning to responsible empathic responses to the other.

Level Four

Nontraditional Video Games and LGBTQ+ Others

To understand *Gone Home* you first need to understand the initially derisive label attached to it. The game was actually released in August 2013, before Gamergate started. However, its popularity increased as the events of Gamergate unfolded. Negative reviews of the game referred to it as a "walking simulator," a label meant to indicate the absence of what most people who play video games are used to in terms of traditional gameplay. Rather than shooting, action, and adventure, in *Gone Home* players control a character from a first-person perspective and walk that character around a house as they explore journals, notes, and other items their virtual family has left behind in the house. There is no danger to the player in the game. The game cannot be lost. Players do not battle or kill any enemies. Just like Gamergate supporters criticized Zoë Quinn and Brianna Wu for not making "real" games, *Gone Home* was labeled by many as a walking simulator to indicate it was not a real game. Fortunately, such negative voices did not ultimately get their way. Kotaku referred to the game as an "experimental exploration game."[1] That label is more accurate and, once the experiment became a success, *Gone Home* ended up launching the walking simulator genre of video games. "Walking simulator" has become a badge of honor for an entire new genre of games that prioritize storytelling and creating an immersive experience over challenging gameplay, because many people have realized there is more to video games than shooting, winning, and losing.[2] Walking simulators have been among the most critically praised video games since 2013.[3] *Gone Home* made such success possible.

Gone Home was made by the Fullbright Company, originally a four-person independent game studio cofounded by Steve Gaynor, Karla Zimonja, and Johnnemann Nordhagen, and including Kate Craig. Leading up to the release of the game, the studio announced they would not be showing *Gone Home* at the Indie MEGABOOTH showcase at PAX Prime (now called PAX West), even though the convention aligned with the release of the game. Given the size of PAX and how many potential customers could be reached by having their game on the show floor at the convention, this announcement surprised many people. When asked for their reasons, the studio cited problematic remarks from convention organizers directed against women and LGBTQ+ individuals.[4] This decision by the Fullbright Company to put people over profit is just further evidence of how the video game industry is changing. Even though the team missed that marketing opportunity, the right decision also ended up being profitable in this case. *Gone Home* was released about six months before Gamergate erupted, but became a favorite among minority fandoms in the wake of Gamergate, and was released on the Xbox One and PlayStation 4 in 2016 due in part to that popularity. Such popularity is no coincidence, when considered in relation to Gamergate. The well-realized setting, inverted game structure, and touching story of *Gone Home* create a compelling lesson in accepting those with different sexual orientations. It is also no coincidence that its story is so well realized, because it is partly autobiographical, as experiences and memories of the development team, one of whom is a lesbian, factored into the design of the game.[5]

In spite of the initial negative branding of *Gone Home* as a "walking simulator," implying it was not a "real" video game, the game was nominated for and won numerous awards from numerous outlets, including game of the year in one case.[6] Not only did it win, it did so while in competition with one of the most beloved AAA games of that generation of video game consoles, *The Last of Us*, a zombie survival-horror game with a development budget that dwarfed that of *Gone Home*.

Being a Lesbian Teenager in 1995

Gone Home takes place on the evening of June 7, 1995. Players control twenty-one-year-old Katie Greenbriar, who returns home from a college trip overseas to learn what has been happening to her family in Oregon during her absence. Her father Terry, a has-been writer who wrote a hit John F. Kennedy conspiracy novel, is struggling with the fact that he never lived up to its success again. Terry's father, a successful author, never respected his work, and now Terry makes a living reviewing home electronics. Katie's mother, Janice, is a wildlife conservationist who was recently promoted to director and finds her new coworker quite attractive. Hidden letters reveal she is considering having an affair with that coworker, and some of those notes are next to Bibles, implying she may feel a strong sense of guilt related to her Christian upbringing. However, the main storyline deals with Katie's eighteen-year-old sister Samantha, or Sam, as Katie always refers to her. Upon starting the game, the player finds the house deserted with a note on the front door from Sam imploring Katie not to investigate what happened. Ignoring that note and uncovering all these storylines is the point of playing the game.

Gameplay consists of walking around and searching the house from a first-person perspective. As players do this, they start to piece together what happened during Katie's absence. The family apparently moved to this house somewhat recently, and, after moving in, Sam found it difficult to adjust to her new high school. Eventually, and awkwardly, she became friends with another girl, Yolanda DeSoto, or Lonnie, a JROTC cadet. In addition to the diversity of centering the game's story around high-school lesbians, Lonnie's family moved to the United States from Mexico. *Gone Home* creates an excellent sense of place and time—Lonnie and Sam bonded over playing *Street Fighter*, attending punk rock concerts, and the burgeoning riot grrrl movement. Lonnie is in a band, and posters as well as cassettes of underground punk music that can be found in the house immerse players in the game's setting. One night after Sam and Lonnie sneaked off to a concert, the two became romantically involved. However, after various incidents at school, Sam's parents found out about their relationship, forbade Sam to close her bedroom door while Lonnie was over, and were generally in denial over their daughter being a lesbian. As the time neared for Lonnie to leave for basic training, Sam was distraught.

The game wonderfully captures the feeling of being a teenager living in the Pacific Northwest in the mid-1990s due in part to technological advances put in the service of storytelling rather than explosions. These stories unfold as players explore an empty house. None of Katie's family members are home when the game begins and that does not change. Rather, the voice actor playing Sam, Sarah Grayson, recorded audio tracks that play at certain key moments when players find journal entries and important objects related to each family member's story. As you hear Sam tell the story of what is happening in the family, the sense of interacting with real lives is enhanced by the game world. When Fullbright made *Gone Home*, they scanned real-world objects into the game. All the journal entries and notes found in the game are actually digitized handwritten documents. A personal favorite touch is the VHS tapes of

The X-Files recorded from episodes aired on TV, accompanied by handwritten labels.[7] Steve Gaynor also created a rule for his team that anything the player sees in the game that could be interacted with in real life must be something they could interact with in the game. This means every drawer, sink faucet, light switch, etc. found in *Gone Home* can be opened and closed or turned on and off. These objects have nothing to do with the story, and the interactivity is limited to opening and closing or turning on and off, but Gaynor said that for games like theirs that rely on immersion for the story they are telling to grip the player, anything that breaks that sense of immersion cannot be allowed.[8] So if you play the game, do not simply pay attention to the voice acting and the stories, but explore the house and try to notice these little details that create a sense of a lived-in space in the mid-90s. Such flourishes that might go unnoticed help foster the game's ability to convey to the player that they are interacting with real people's lives.

While players can explore the house indefinitely if they so desire, *Gone Home* is a story-driven game with an ending. The ending comes after Lonnie's punk band plays their final show before she is set to leave for basic training. After the concert, she and Sam spend the night together alone in the attic of Sam's house, the house players are exploring. Playing as Katie, players learn that Sam and Lonnie looked through all the photographs they had taken together and Sam, realizing that all of her good times with Lonnie were going to soon be in the past with none to follow, began to cry. Lonnie attempted to comfort her, telling her that life would move on. However, Sam did not want her life to continue without Lonnie, who also began to cry, and they eventually fell asleep in one another's arms. The next day, Lonnie departed for basic training before Sam awoke. Besides experiencing how Sam came to grips with her own sexuality, struggled with family acceptance, and was bullied, but nonetheless met the girl she loves, some vaguely worded notes in the game could be interpreted as Sam contemplating suicide or self-harm. The notes are ambiguous, and not all players came to such a conclusion, but as the story arc ends, some players will not be sure what they will find in the attic, the location where the game ends.

Beyond increasing representation of minorities in video games by focusing on a story about high-school lesbians, *Gone Home* offers an elegant alternative model for the structure of video games. It does an excellent job of inverting the "save the princess" structure of gameplay that has been with the industry since its origins and enshrined as a trope perhaps most strongly by Nintendo's *Super Mario Bros.* franchise. Picking apart the problematic nature of the "save the princess" or "damsel in distress" trope is what Anita Sarkeesian did in her video essay that led to Gamergate supporters harassing her.⁹ The basic problem with games structured around this trope is that they rob female characters of all agency. The women in such games are incapable of having their own stories. Rather, they exist only in service of helping the lead male character realize their status as hero through saving the supposedly helpless women. In *Gone Home*, at a point where players may expect to find a dead body or feel the need to help Sam, the game's ending reveals Sam is now confident in herself and spending time away with her girlfriend. The final piece of voice acting in the game reveals that Lonnie got off the bus to basic training because she could not bear to be apart from Sam. The two ran away together and are happy. Even for those aware and critical of the trope about saving women in games, players who consider themselves LGBTQ+ allies could feel the need to play the role of white knight, to step in and take credit for helping people who are often marginalized and not aided by society. I certainly experienced this feeling when I played the game. However, the game structure of *Gone Home* overcomes that patronizing tendency in video games. There is no damsel in distress. Sam and Lonnie are both fine. They do not need saving. They just need people to stop judging them and start letting them be themselves, living their lives in ways they find fulfilling.

FIG. 4-1. Hair dye spilled in a bathtub in Gone Home (2013) that tricked some players into interpreting the dye as blood and as an indication that Sam may be injured.

FIG. 4-2. The entrance to the attic where Sam and Lonnie spent what they initially thought was their final night together in Gone Home (2013).

In case there is suspicion that I am exaggerating the emotional impact of this game, I should share my experience with completing *Gone Home* for the first time. I first played *Gone Home* on my PC shortly after its release, sometime in the fall of 2014. I played it to completion in one sitting, as it only takes several hours to finish. I played at night, during a cool, rainy evening in New England. The game also takes place on a rainy night, which probably increased my sense of immersion in the world, though I do not think it is necessary to schedule this game around the weather forecast to be impacted by it. Before describing how I reacted to the ending, I should also say a little about the only experience with which I can compare my feelings upon reaching the game's ending.

I am a big sports fan. I attended Texas Tech University for my undergraduate education and was present at almost every Red Raider football and basketball home game played during my time at the school. I do not just sit and enjoy games when I am in attendance either. I shout, yell, and cheer. I am emotionally invested in the teams I cheer for in the sports I follow. I am elated when they win and feel like someone punched me in the gut when they lose. I am typing these words while sitting in my home office just outside of Boston, and also happen to be a fan of the Boston Red Sox. If you know Major League Baseball, there is no need to explain how the emotions of that fan base ebb and flow with the results on the field, especially in 2004 when the Red Sox won their first World Series Championship in eighty-six years. I provide this sketch of my love of sports because when I entered the attic at the end of *Gone Home* and realized Sam was safe and happy together with Lonnie, I leapt out of the chair I was sitting in and shouted "YES!" at the top of my lungs. It was an automatic response on my part. I was invested in Sam's ability to openly be herself and find happiness. When it happened, I was overcome with emotion. To depart from sports analogies and borrow from the Methodist tradition in which I was raised, my heart was strangely warmed by the experience of playing *Gone Home*. Video games can be deep, full of meaning and ethical import.

It is worth dwelling on my experience with *Gone Home* a little longer, because it reveals that interactivity with video games goes both ways. Tom Bissell has come to this same conclusion. In his book *Extra Lives*, he reflects on a poignant scene in *Mass Effect* in which his actions were unable to prevent the genocide of an alien species. Due to the fact that he did not complete an earlier mission in the game, one character that possibly could have been in his party was not. The result was that when he had to choose one character to die and one to live in order to complete a particularly risky mission, he was faced with a Sophie's choice. One character was a lover to his main character, but that lover had also done something terrible. The other character was almost useless in terms of skills that could help the player in the game, but innocent. In that situation, what does one do?

> You have agency, yes, but what of it? It is just a game. But when a game does this well, you lose track of your manipulation of it, and its manipulation of you, and instead feel inserted so deeply inside the game that your mind, and your feelings, become as seemingly crucial to its operation as its many million lines of code. It is the sensation that the game itself is as suddenly, unknowably alive as you are.[10]

The best video games can impact the player and control them, just as the player controls what happens within the game. Along those same lines, *Mass Effect* is notable because creating romantic relationships with other characters in the game is one of the things players can do in that digital world. However, unlike some games that cater to the male gaze and allow every female character to become an object of sexual conquest, the characters in the *Mass Effect* franchise have their own sexual orientations. Some are straight and some are bi, and the third game in the franchise introduced gay and lesbian characters for players to interact with. No matter how attractive a player may find a certain character, not everyone can be romanced, just as in the real world. The game pushes back on the desires of some players and uses its own agency upon them. The same is true of *Dragon Age: Inquisition*, which includes a transgender character among the array of characters who can be romanced but who also have their own orientations and agencies.

REPRESENTING ALL LGBTQ+ INDIVIDUALS

Some of the first steps toward better representation and diversity in the video game industry involved putting women in starring roles and focusing on stories of gay and lesbian characters. Since then, games representing the experiences of bi, transgender, and so many other individuals have become easier to find.

If Found . . . was released in 2020 by DREAMFEEL, a small development studio run by Llaura McGee. Their previous game was *CURTAIN*, a game centered on the story of two queer women in a destructive relationship and set in Glasgow, Scotland. Both *CURTAIN* and *If Found . . .* fall into a genre sometimes referred to as empathy games. They are the kinds of games frequently highlighted by the organization Games for Change, which focuses on empowering developers who make games that can lead to real societal and political changes.[11] While *Gone Home* is certainly a nontraditional game, *If Found . . .* is even more unique. It is more a visual novel than the sort of video game most people are used to playing, yet another reason theological assessment of video games cannot just focus on the style and import of these games. Content matters, even if that content is delivered in a form that resembles a print book.

If Found . . . essentially tells a queer coming-of-age story but uses the video game medium to give it a surreal science-fiction twist that conveys how strange and different that experience can be compared to the experiences of other young people. The game is available for PC, and players flip through the virtual pages using their mouse, which appears as an eraser on screen. That eraser magically removes words and scenes while uncovering new ones on each page. As words and illustrations morph on screen, they reveal the story of the main character, Kasio, a transgender woman whose mother does not understand gender identity. That lack of understanding comes across as transphobic and deeply painful for Kasio, whether her mother intends her words to be so or not. Her mother's words frequently compare a good past for Kasio with a bad present and future. Kasio's mother is curious why she cannot start a "family of her own," is concerned about "this alternative thing" (apparently, her way of referencing Kasio being a transgender woman), and generally laments that Kasio is "not the person I've known." The mother never uses Kasio's name, and even refers to her as "son" in a letter. When

Kasio confronts her mother about such hurtful language, Kasio is met with "I'm your mother," as if mothers can do no wrong toward their children. Controlling the game with an eraser icon conveys how hearing such words can make someone feel like they are being erased. Images in the game also play with the enormity of space to convey how important these words are to Kasio. For a transgender individual, words are not just words; they can feel like drifting into a black hole or embarking on an exhilarating journey accompanied by others. Around one hour into the game, another character uses Kasio's name for the first time and Kasio's excitement is palpable. The game culminates with the tension between the mother's care for her daughter and the harm she is actively inflicting with her words coming to a head, as hurtful words and phrases from the entire experience bombard the player at once. Since the entire game is controlled with an eraser, the message that has been alluded to throughout the experience becomes clear in the game's conclusion. Sometimes, for someone to truly be who they are, it is necessary to let go. Sometimes, if people cannot accept reality as it is, including someone else's personal reality, erasing the past and moving on may be the best option.

Dating simulators are a massively popular genre of video game worldwide. Such games play a little bit like digital versions of choose-your-own-adventure books, except always focused on deciding who to become romantically engaged with among the various characters in the game. The popularity of the genre is not exactly innocent, as the vast majority of these games cater to male sexual fantasies, but more have been made recently with a female audience in mind, albeit a straight cis one. However, *Dream Daddy: A Dad Dating Simulator* bucks the trend of the whole genre. In that game players control a single father whose husband has died. He has a daughter who encourages him to go meet the other single dads in town, all of whom also have children of their own. The game is a great example of positive representation of gay men, but it also goes one step further in increasing the diversity of gay men it represents. Some dads in the game are overweight while others are thin, a rarity in video games when most characters look like ancient Greek sculptures. There are Black, white, Asian, and Hispanic dads. Some were previously married to women while others had former spouses who were male. Players also get to choose the race and body type of the dad they will be playing as, all of which amounts to an excellent source of affirmation and validation for the diversity of gay players who might play the game. As an early example of a game providing insight into gay experiences, *Coming Out Simulator* is a semi-fictional game about the experience the game's developer, Nicky Case, had when coming out to conservative Asian parents. The game centers on making multiple dialogue choices to advance the narrative, and all characters in the game remember the choices players make. While simple, that game mechanic is a reminder that words matter and commonly used terms and phrases do not match everyone's experiences. All these games provide insights into worlds players may not be familiar with, and they make those worlds relatable and accessible in a way that is not always so easy to find in our day-to-day lives.

Playing with Identity

All the games mentioned in this chapter have to do with identity, and literally playing with identity as players control and interact with characters of different gender identities and sexualities. I have spoken with people about this topic a lot over my years of speaking at video game conventions. Interesting questions have popped up during the question-and-answer sessions. Why do you choose the character you play? Do you feel different when playing a certain game or character? Video games can provide players a safe environment to express various parts of their personality and help them learn more about what they like and do not like, and ultimately who they are. Some people have conveyed that even though they are straight and cisgender, playing as and engaging with LGBTQ+ characters in video games helped tear down the sense that there is a binary of male and female, set at birth, each side only capable of being sexually attracted to the other. *Mass Effect* has been cited a few times as opening players up to the reality that sexuality is a spectrum. It is one thing to hear these concepts, or even accept them as an ally who maybe has never felt their meaning, and something else entirely to actively explore identity in an interactive medium.

Some early studies on playing with identity through the internet were rather reactionary. Various concerns boiled down to fear of the internet and other digital mediums not being the same as real life, and therefore automatically inferior. Such work cautioned that playing with multiple or false identities online could hinder the development of mature individuals, or even cultivate schizophrenic dangerous ones.[12] More recent work is more appreciative of the potential benefits that come from digitally playing with identity. Sherry Turkle, an MIT psychologist, argues in favor of role playing a sort of "second self" online: "In the course of life, we never 'graduate' from working on identity; we simply rework it with the materials at hand. From the start, the online social worlds provided new materials."[13] Turkle's statement seems to apply so much more to video games than the internet, as they allow players to step into the shoes of that second self and try it on for size. Video games provide an opportunity found in no other digital medium.

People can remake themselves in games and within gaming communities. And if they are not in the process of remaking, they can openly express parts of themselves society actively oppresses. Maybe someone never realized they could assert they were gay because such a possibility is not treated like a real one in the place where they live. Video games can help overcome real-world limitations such as that.

This point is not just theoretical, but already happening. James Paul Gee and Elisabeth Hayes interviewed a biracial woman who found greater acceptance in *Second Life*, an online roleplaying game, than in many of her real-life social circles. While in-person interactions for this woman tended to focus on race, in *Second Life* other people got to know more about what she considered her real identity as a designer, DJ, and spouse. "Here is what Jesse said about diversity in one phone interview: 'Well the way I see life is that everyone you encounter can create a learning experience for you and the more diverse group I can encounter, the more I'm going to learn. I'm surrounded by diversity just in my own family in real life, but it doesn't compare really to the amount of different points of view I've encountered here [in *Second Life*].'"[14] They also note Jesse claimed feeling more heard in such communities.[15] Does it take time and energy to maintain these alternative personas? Yes, it does. But when society does not accept someone for who they are or provide resources for them to flourish openly, time and energy spent in game might be the best means of personal development and fulfillment— LGBTQ+ individuals certainly will not find a better reception in conservative America than they will in *Gone Home*.

A Note about Heidegger

Why is Heidegger almost entirely absent in a book about products of constant technological revolution, aside from a few stray references? There is no proper place for this note, but the issue must be addressed before diving into more video game examples, given that Heidegger is constantly referenced in philosophy and theology books that deal with technology. He is almost entirely absent in this book because Heidegger was, in many ways, the culmination of a suspicion present since Kant that philosophy gets at reality while technology blocks genuine thinking. In a way, Heidegger fits in perfectly with the embarrassing words of caution about technology in previous pages and surveyed in the introduction. Technology is, for Heidegger, the mark of a society that has embraced nothingness instead of understanding being.[16] The argument up to this point has shown such a claim is incorrect. Despite real lingering problems in the world, technological development and the ability to control what may indeed be "natural" has brought our species closer to the realization of many human ideals. Just because poverty and death remain real problems around the world does not mean we should not acknowledge that technology has helped decrease poverty and lengthen life spans. As Mark Dooley notes, rather than a sign of profundity, Heidegger's extreme protest against technology is more indicative of someone with gravely misplaced priorities. Most of the world could be happy and healthy, and Heidegger would be still protesting in the streets that everyone forgot the question of being.

> But only a philosopher who thinks that there is something more essential to bow down before would suggest that universal health and happiness are symptoms of a time of ultimate despair. For Heidegger, however, the task of thinking must take priority over the political task of ensuring that as many people start out with equal chances of education, health, and happiness as possible. This remarkable suggestion is the result of the firmly held belief that nothing matters more than our retrieval of the forgotten question of being. Similar considerations drove Lenin, Mao, and all those who believed that fresh running water was a silly pursuit when compared with the bringing to fruition of the 'new man.'[17]

Against Heidegger's suspicion, the importance of technology is not something that will be leaving modern theological work any time soon. If anything, such a focus is only likely to become more prominent.

The modern version of the dialogue between religion and science within philosophy of religion and theology has been going strong for nearly six decades. Early work in the field represented high hopes and lofty goals. Theologians placed big architectonic ideas from theology and science next to one another and compared them in the process of building comprehensive metaphysical schemes.[18] However, the tenor of such conversations has undergone a slight shift in more recent years. Big ideas have not been eliminated. They have become more nuanced as prolonged engagement with scientific disciplines has revealed how difficult their successful construction is to achieve. Rather, practical technological sides of the field have been emphasized recently. The "Science, Technology, and Religion" unit of the American Academy of Religion has started to focus on the technology component of its name in its calls for papers at recent Annual Meetings.[19] Work engaging robotics, artificial intelligence, and posthumanism is becoming more common. In contrast to what Heidegger would have wanted, the shift of focus to an acceptance of technology is so solidified in contemporary theological work that even conservative Christian theologians are writing books about the inevitability of posthumanism.[20] The merger of humans and technology is already a reality from which there is no return. Wesley Wildman observed this shift and both predicted and encouraged its continuation in 2007 in his article, tellingly titled, "From Grand Dreaming to Problem Solving."[21] While it is fun to develop theories that attempt to synthesize large swaths of theology and science, such projects can easily overstep their bounds and even become irresponsible, especially when technology that can improve lives is available now and could be the topic of theological focus. Far from covering up something important, a growing theological consensus seems to be that a focus on technology might help bring about practical changes that make this world a better place. Efforts to exclude technology, for which video games are a major driving force, from theological attempts to engage the modern world will likely doom such work before it even begins.

Meaninglessness and Its Theological Discontents

Gone Home is about a young woman expressing meaning amid meaninglessness, her essential nature that includes being a woman in love with another woman amid family and societal forces that would push and pull them apart. Such an expression of being accepted in spite of other mitigating factors can be transformative for LGBTQ+ players still experiencing real-world harassment instead of acceptance. For players who are not themselves gay or lesbian, this game provides an opportunity to hear the call of the other. The same is true of *If Found . . .* and transgender individuals.[22] There is even proof that *Gone Home* is directly responsible for helping some players hear that call of the other and respond to it with love and care whereas in the past they had ignored it. Some people credit *Gone Home* for converting them from objecting to gay rights to supporting them.[23] Games in touch with such emotionally salient aspects of different people's lives align with Tillich's focus on realizing true personal identities in concrete cultural situations. While there is no way to win or lose in *Gone Home*, the stakes are high and there are consequences. The game provides a chance to make or break bonds with a virtual lesbian relative. There is no prompt within the game for players to choose what they make of Sam, but players will come to that conclusion on their own. Her face calls out and players must respond to its call. Face-to-face encounters can disrupt relations based on power, authority, and conceptual representation and instead snap awareness back to a primordial ethical calling. By encountering Sam and Lonnie, these virtual others, players can decide whether to pursue a shared abstract goal of equality or reject that responsibility in favor of exclusion. Both the ultimate importance of being fully oneself in this world and the ethical responsibility to others calling out for such recognition are points that come through with clarity while playing games like *Gone Home* and *If Found . . .* among others.

Just as Tillich and Levinas were atheists in a certain technical sense, with their "atheism" ultimately serving the purpose of preserving the reality of God's transcendence, there is something vaguely theological about identity and letting people be who they are or helping them come to a fuller self-realization if social forces are impediments to such realization. Jeffrey Kosky has called Levinas' philosophy a religion for the nonreligious,[24] which is reminiscent of how Tillich's God beyond God strikes personal theists as odd. This God is not capable of full comprehension by anyone but is that which fulfills the meaning of everyone. God is found in the depth of personality identity, of the self and the other as the self realizes itself in the other. God as the ground-of-being is not equated with the conditioned finite world, is not reduced to the human, but is that reality which we could not have created and which accounts for our true meaning. Furthermore, whether it be the responsible self in response to the other or the true essence of things in the ground-of-being, true transcendence is the core idea shaping such nontheistic concepts of God for each thinker.

Divine transcendence disrupts the given and becomes realized in something new. That new reality made possible by God is realized concretely in the present and is not something to be deferred to the future in some other realm. *If Found . . .* offers a powerful lesson about accepting people for who they are, a lesson that can bleed into the real world and help people realize why pronouns matter and calling people what they want to be called is important. For transgender players experiencing discrimination and roadblocks in life, this divine otherness breaks through the game and reveals a new possibility that is capable of being realized in the present. For players who are not transgender, and perhaps especially for those with some prejudice against transgender people, the face of the other encountered in Kasio calls that way of being and behaving into question. It is difficult to imagine how a player who pays attention can come away from the experience of playing *If Found . . .* without understanding that seemingly small words like "choice" (e.g., Kasio's mother worrying that Kasio's *choices* are going to catch up to her) can be deeply hurtful. Such an understanding should also help players understand why identity and politics are theologically relevant. A scene late in the game literally proves Tillich's point about theology, culture, and the realization of one's essence. While Kasio and her friends are at a concert (some are in the band), "High Cost of Living" by Threat plays as all these characters get to freely be themselves for a while, and do so in a manner they have not been free to express at any other point in the game. People who raise issues about identity and language are not doing so in order to play identity politics and demand political correctness, but because identity is of ultimate importance when it comes to realizing one's essence, and language has power that matters if a group, country, or religion is truly going to be for everyone.

Both Tillich and Levinas strive to overcome associations of God with one country, God of only one special space, or one special time. They want to avoid a God for this, but not that, here not there, and the violent clashes of power that almost inevitably result. Besides being metaphysically bankrupt, such conceptions of God are socially dangerous. It is in light of this focus on a God for all, and that God being for everyone here and now, that Tillich sides with Levinas against mysticism. Tillich criticizes mystical thinking for fleeing the concrete world in search of the transcendent God instead of realizing that the unconditional can only be found in concrete existence, where is it present everywhere, and within which new creations can arise because of that intimate presence.[25] What does such divine transcendence available now in concrete historical situations look like in practice? If players who struggle with pronoun usage and transgender identity play these games, struggling with such issues in the games should alleviate real-world hardship.

Video games can also help address the problems with unlimited responsibility highlighted in chapter 3. Whereas failing and nonetheless trying again to live up to one's ethical responsibility day-to-day would quickly become debilitating, video games offer a sort of opportunity to practice prior to gameday. Mothers should never have to live through years of conflict to simply use their child's name, but maybe playing *If Found . . .* can drive home that point and hasten the correct use of names and pronouns in society. In these games it is possible to locate the voice of God, so to speak, breaking into this world through the screen and reminding players to accept who they are, because God has already done the same. We just need to accept that we are accepted, on Tillich's account. God saves us from accusing and damning ourselves and calls others to similarly respect who we are in this world. For players who do not have that personal problem of acceptance, but struggle to accept or maybe even actively oppress others, that voice of God in these video games appears as the call of the other, a call which brings moral choices about identity to the forefront. The other encountered in these games accuses the player as the one having to take responsibility in face of that accusation. In that regard, sad aspects of these games also serve as needed reminders during a time in which it is becoming easier to think LGBTQ+ equality has been attained just because the United States Supreme Court made same-sex marriages legal in all fifty states in *Obergefell v. Hodges*.

The rough times Kasio lives through, with her friends but often utterly alone, are a reminder of how neglected some LGBTQ+ people still are despite legal advances. It is a little sad, and more than a little damning, that the "happy" endings in *Gone Home* and *If Found . . .* involve people running away from family to be who they truly are. As Tillich would remind in such cases, nobody should have to go anywhere else to realize themselves. It is real, right here and right now, for each of us, if only cultural forces of ignorance, prejudice, or outright hatred would not block such a truth from seeing the light of day. Not unlike Tillich's insistence that the unconditioned God capable of resolving polar tensions of life is always waiting to be realized if we live life a bit more deeply, Levinas indicates that calls and demands from the other are easily forgotten and hidden behind superficial features of daily life, but are always present nonetheless. Beyond calls from others in the form of specific characters in these games, each game, taken as a whole, functions as a call from the other to help. If players listen and respond, such games can change behavior and help develop more ethically responsible people in the world, not just in game.

Level Five
Face to Face with Immigrant Others

The topic of this chapter is not entirely discrete, and neither are those of the chapters that follow. While chapters 4 through 7 each focus on video games that deal with a certain group of marginalized people, the topics, and the games that deal with them, are interrelated and build upon one another in various ways. This can be seen in how the game that is the main subject of this chapter, *Papers, Please*, ran afoul of one retailer.

Lucas Pope is something like the Platonic form of an independent video game developer. There is nothing more independent than making games alone, which is nearly how Pope makes games. He is not part of a small indie studio composed of several other people. He works alone and only contracts out components he is not equipped to create (though this often only entails language localization services). The credits for *Papers, Please* simply credit Pope for handling design, code, art, music, and sound, listing unspecified special thanks to a handful of people, and then listing localization services. Pope's style of developing games is even more remarkable considering that he once worked for developer Naughty Dog on the *Uncharted* franchise, a series of games that represents some of the highest-budget action-packed games of all time and a development studio that consists of hundreds of people.

Part of the inspiration for *Papers, Please* came from Pope's departure from Naughty Dog. Given the freedom that comes with working for oneself, Pope moved to Japan with his wife and gained extensive experience with checkpoints and passport inspectors while traveling back and forth between Japan and the United States.[1] Pope is also not shy about noting other real-world parallels that inspired him to create *Papers, Please*, as he drew inspiration from the Berlin Wall and conflicts between East Germany and West Germany.[2] Besides the ability to draw inspiration from traveling, being a one-person development team also allows for video games produced by that person to feel like they are truly made by an auteur in the same way that some filmmakers are referred to as such. *Papers, Please* did not simply arise out of experiences from overseas travel but rather built upon Pope's previous work. *The Republia Times* was his previous game, one in which the player acts as editor in chief of a newspaper in a totalitarian state. Gameplay in that earlier game consists of reading news stories and deciding which to include, reject, or falsify in order to appease the state. Republia and its citizens appear in *Papers, Please*, and the theme of totalitarian tactics is further developed in that follow-up.

One of the auteured aspects of *Papers, Please* that was easily made possible, given that Pope only had to approve himself, was the inclusion of full body scanners. Pope included them to heighten tension in the game by bringing the morality of players regarding privacy, and their personal comfort with invasions of privacy, up against instructions in the game to scan people in an effort to catch and prevent terrorists before they act.[3] While the game's graphics are a pixelated throwback to earlier generations of video games, images of pixelated fully nude bodies revealed by the scanners are in the game. This caused Apple to reject the initial version of *Papers, Please* from its store due to "pornographic content." While the company later apologized, called the initial rejection an error, and eventually allowed the full version of *Papers, Please* in their store, there is reason to be suspicious of the genuineness of Apple's claims. Apple allowed a very graphic game from an actual porn star in their store, yet initially rejected *Papers, Please*. Pope himself admitted to Kotaku of being unsure whether Apple made an innocent mistake or caved in to pressure from negative coverage about their censorship.[4] Despite Apple's protestations, achieving such a singular vision is one of the advantages of nontraditional video game development, an advantage that is close to impossible within AAA studios comprising hundreds of people. If a game published by Microsoft or Sony needed modifications to be available on a digital storefront, they almost certainly would have compromised creative vision and forced such changes on all versions of the game to have parity across all platforms. Whether Apple's revised stance on the game was truly something that had to be clarified due to an error, or a change brought about by pressure, it is the mix of identity, politics, and gameplay focusing on the plight of immigrants that makes the lessons conveyed by *Papers, Please* so meaningful.

Thou Shalt Not Pass

Papers, Please was released in 2013. If you have ever played a game in a magazine in which you have to look at two almost identical pictures side-by-side and find the ten differences between them, that is not too far removed from what players do in this game. If such gameplay was all this game offered, asking people to get skilled at processing paperwork might have gone down as one of the worst video game ideas ever. That idea for a game in the abstract is simply not very exciting. However, the hook to this game is that the people whose papers players must inspect speak back to the player. Many emotionally and ethically charged scenarios result from such interactions.

Players control an immigration officer on the border of a fictional Cold War–era Eastern Bloc country, Arstotzka. The country has just ended a six-year war with its neighboring country. The player's job as an immigration officer is to control the flow of people entering the country by inspecting their documents. The information matching gameplay consists of making sure people have the required entry tickets, passports, and other documents. Sometimes players need to compare the current date with the expiration date on documents. Other times a name or number may not be consistent from one document to another. Because a war just ended, required documents also change over time. Citizens of Arstotzka need only show their identification to enter the country, but foreigners are required to produce entry tickets, passports, work passes, and even certifications of vaccination. The requirements become more cumbersome as government worries about the dangers posed by foreigners increase. If players note missing information in the documents provided by someone, or discrepancies in the information provided, they can question the person standing in front of them at their inspection desk. People entering for work sometimes try to stay longer than their work passes allow, and if players do not catch the difference between their allowed duration in the country and how long they claim they will be working, players can be docked pay.

Gameplay proceeds in a cycle of days. After each day is over, players will be paid based on how many people they correctly admitted or turned away. They will be docked pay for mistakes made. Making as much money as possible is important because the player's character has a family and needs money for daily necessities like food and heat, in addition to buying medicine for sick family members. If players do not make enough money, family members may have to go without heat or food. All of this should seem straightforward so far. All players need to do is correctly inspect and match documents so they get paid and are able to take care of their family. However, this game is not that simple. The most interesting aspect of *Papers, Please* is that the people crossing the border and handing documents to players tell stories and explain their reasons for crossing the border while players inspect their documents. Those stories can potentially make players stop following the rules of the game, as these narratives place real emotional pressure on those who continue to play exactly according to the rules.

Some people are trying to cross the border because they are hoping to visit dying relatives, smuggle in medicine for sick loved ones, or escape sex trafficking and almost certain death. One woman comes to the player's desk claiming the man behind her is selling her into sexual slavery, begging that he not be let through. If players take the woman at her word (and they have no reason not to in terms of gameplay, since her paperwork is in order), the man next in line is a criminal. However, as far as immigration is concerned, he is also free to pass. One man comes through the line without trouble and lets you know his wife is right behind him in line. Her paperwork is incomplete. Another person has invalid paperwork but claims to be smuggling in medicine that relatives need for survival, medicine unavailable in Arstotzka. Sometimes a character will sound sympathetic with a moving story but end up being a suicide bomber who detonates not far from the player's immigration booth. In these situations, doing the right thing morally that goes against the rules of the game can have consequences for the player's family. People approach the border with devastating stories, but players still need to pay for food, heat, rent, and medicine.

Some of these immigrants are attempting to enter the country illegally, but with morally justified reasons, such as the people trying to smuggle in needed, otherwise unavailable medicine. Others' situations are just unfortunate, such as when a husband and wife are moving to start a new life together but only one of them has proper documentation. Players can do whatever they want in these situations. They can play by the rules or draw their own lines regarding what cases of human suffering or attempts at helping others permit bending the rules. However, bending rules to do the right thing becomes increasingly difficult as players have their pay docked when they improperly process immigrants and their papers. If players want to make sure they have enough money to provide for their family, doing the right thing may not always be easy. If players do not process immigrants by the book, some family members could eventually die. Alternatively, players can do the right thing, have their pay docked, and skip paying rent to pay for medicine to ensure sick family members survive, but that can result in a game-over scenario in which the entire family is kicked out of government housing for failure to pay. All these tensions are escalated as the game progresses due to a series of violent attacks in Arstotzka that are blamed on foreigners. On some days the player is ordered to let nobody from certain countries past the checkpoint, even if they claim to be fleeing certain death in their home countries.

As briefly noted in the introduction to this chapter, *Papers, Please* is also a remarkable achievement in terms of representation in games. It depicts legitimate reasons immigrants flee to other countries despite not having the necessary credentials. It also does a wonderful job of representing transgender individuals without tokenizing them. Early in the game, it is possible to be penalized for incorrectly processing someone because their identification does not list their gender correctly. This penalty could be interpreted as a glitch in the game, because all the documentation seems correct. However, later in the game, when Arstotzka greatly heightens security after more violence inside its borders, the situation becomes clear. At that point in the game, full body scanners appear at the player's inspection point, with instructions from the government that all foreigners are required to submit to full body scans that reveal their naked bodies if they wish to enter the country. Sometimes people will have female listed on their identification card, but a scan will reveal the person has a penis. It is not directly stated anywhere in the game, but at that point players should realize that they are working in a country that does not support transgender rights, or even acknowledge the existence of transgender individuals. The times I was docked pay earlier in the game suddenly made sense, even though I disagreed with them.

The game also has numerous endings, and in one of the most poignant, the player's family ends up relying on the kindness of a government employee inspecting their papers, just like the player's character has been inspecting others' documents. Depending on how the game has been played, that ending may involve the player's character attempting to flee with their family to another country using forged documents. Just as the faces of others have been calling out to the player to help them cross the border of Arstotzka, the game ends with the player's own face calling out for a response.

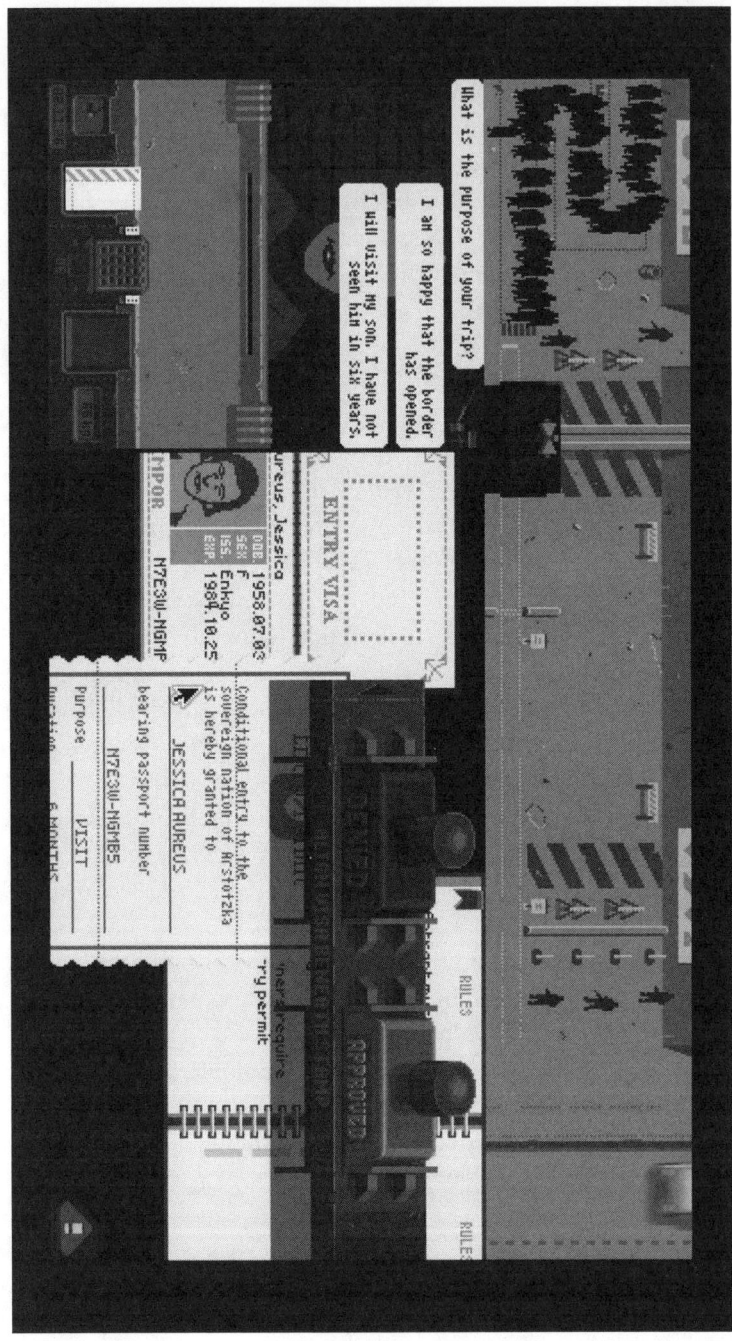

FIG. 5-1. A woman explaining her reason for trying to enter Arstotzka in *Papers, Please* (2013).

Others have also noticed the excellence of *Papers, Please*. Though he did not win awards for theological excellence, Pope did well during the 2014 video game award season. *Papers, Please* won the "Innovation Award" and "Best Downloadable Game" at the Game Developers Choice Awards.[5] At the Games for Change Awards, Pope's game won in the categories of "Most Innovative" and "Best Gameplay."[6] I find that latter award significant, because as already noted, the document-inspecting gameplay of *Papers, Please* does not come across as the best of anything, at least when considered in isolation. What makes the gameplay so commendable is how it works in concert with and places pressure on the ethical scenarios within the game. Fortunately, *Papers, Please* does not stand alone within the game industry as a game highlighting the experiences of immigrants and the ethical issues surrounding those experiences.

For Those Left Behind

Bury Me, My Love is another moving game focused on migration and immigration. Players control Majd, the husband of Nour, a woman fleeing from Syria to France. The studio that made the game, Playdius, claims the game is based on the real experiences of immigrants. The game takes place within a chat app on a smartphone as players communicate with Nour on her journey. Players offer Nour advice, support, and sometimes information to help her decide where to travel. For example, in one situation Nour is unsure whether to head to the Hungarian or Croatian border on her way to France, and the player, as Majd, can help her assess her options. However, because the situation in Syria is constantly changing and reception on smartphones is not always reliable, Nour is not always available when Majd tries to reach her. This effect is achieved by the game playing out in real time. If Nour is out of range to use her phone for a day or two, the player will not receive messages from her during that time and will be left to wonder whether she is alright or if a game-over screen announcing her death is coming. This was a great decision by the developers, as it makes playing *Bury Me, My Love* feel like a real interaction between two people via their phones, the sort of interaction that does not always result in immediate responses.

Nour is also her own person and does not always follow Majd's advice, improvising out of necessity when chaos erupts. It is impressive how gripping and engaging this game is, despite the fact that it often takes control away from the player. Things do not always turn out for the best, and players cannot force others to make the right decision, even if they know what that is. Just as *Gone Home* can control the player's emotions to some extent, *Bury Me, My Love* takes control away from players to convey the helplessness of being caught within profound geopolitical turmoil. That sense of helplessness is intensified in many of the game's nineteen endings. Sometimes, near the end, the time between messages from Nour grows longer, and the messages sent are brief and discouraging. The indication is that the only help Majd may be able to provide in a helpless situation is burying Nour once everything is over. The game has since been followed up by a prequel to the game's story, *Nour's Choice*. It is a brief experience of thirty minutes or so that reveals more of the backstory between Nour and her husband, as well as the reasons she chose to flee Syria. As Nour's story shows, not all attempts to flee countries are successful, but some people do not even have the opportunity to flee danger in their home country in search of safety elsewhere.

This War of Mine focuses on the experiences of those who cannot flee wartorn countries. Players control civilians, not trained military personnel, who are stuck in an Eastern European civil war. The gameplay occurs in cycles of day and night. During the day, the player needs to take care of chores inside a crumbling structure that their small group of civilians calls home. Structural repairs are required and sources of heat need to be found before night arrives. During the night, it is possible to explore other locations in the town. Players can look for supplies like food and medicine, as well as other survivors, some of whom can join the player's group. However, it is also possible to come across armed and dangerous survivors while scavenging. Any survivor the player controls can die, be it from sickness, starvation, or a bullet. Any death makes continued survival all the more difficult with fewer people cooperating to help one another. Running into other armed scavengers at night is a truly harrowing experience, because some of them attack on sight, while others are armed but friendly. To add more emotion to such a potentially anxiety-inducing game, the developers added an expansion to the game, *This War of Mine: The Little Ones*. That expansion added children to the game, creating more mouths to feed in a time when resources are already hard to find. The developers have stated they made the expansion to increase the difficulty, because wars are not easy and people in real life do not simply abandon their children in difficult situations.[7]

There is ludonarrative dissonance in these games, meaning a discrepancy between what players need to do to play "correctly" according to the rules of a game and how the game allows them to play for a variety of reasons. It can also refer to a discrepancy between gameplay and a game's narrative.[8] In short, ludonarrative dissonance refers to the difference between player-created moments and the official framed narrative created by the developers. Such discrepancy only heightens the relevance of such games for theological reflection. Playing *Papers, Please* correctly would entail accurately inspecting all documents and admitting or turning away all people at the border strictly according to the rules of Arstotzka's government, no matter what sorts of pleas from virtual others face the player. However, players can also play incorrectly and have their pay docked. The game allows players to embrace such incorrect play, and arguably encourages it by having immigrants tell such moving stories to the player while their documents are being inspected. That is ludonarrative dissonance in action. Such a discrepancy between the technical rules of a game and what it allows, at least in this case, heightens its importance for theological reflection. It places the responsibility we all have toward others directly in the hands of players.

When these ideas were first tested out with Curry College students in the course Philosophy in Pop Culture, everyone played games together as a group in class. *Gone Home* and *Papers, Please* were the focus of the video game portion of the course. Some Tillich was covered in that course, but the reason for using *Gone Home* and *Papers, Please* was to try and help students gain an introductory understanding of what Levinas means by ethics starting with the face of the other. Some of the more engaged students were helped by *Gone Home*, but Levinas really started to connect with students upon their finishing *Papers, Please*. The fact that faces of others are literally staring at the player and telling stories is likely a large reason why, combined with the fact that the wide gap between following the rules and what the game allows players to do in order to help others only intensifies the moral choices present in the game. To paraphrase an "aha!" moment one student had in class, *Papers, Please* puts players face to face with the face of the other, literally and figuratively.

In the context of games about immigration, safety, and those who do not always make it to the other side of the border, at least one more game is worth mentioning. *A Mortician's Tale* was released in 2017, takes one hour at most to play, and has nothing to do with war or immigration. It involves players controlling a mortician running a funeral home and preparing the bodies of the deceased for funerals, providing others with care even in death, care that they possibly never received while living. What happens on screen while playing *A Mortician's Tale* is reminiscent of the old board game *Operation*. Players click on the bodies of deceased individuals while handling various instruments to prepare them for a burial or cremation. What is striking is the tone and care with which this game addresses such work. Daily industry emails that the player can read provide accurate information about cultural differences regarding customs surrounding death, as well as different needs of different people. Transgender people are often intentionally misgendered by their families at funerals by having their hair cut and name changed.

After learning this information, players must handle a similar case within the game. At one point, a massive corporation purchases the small family-owned funeral home in which the game starts. Later, that corporation accepts a lucrative contract from the city to handle unclaimed bodies. At that point, the tone of care and respect the game has conditioned the player to approach the mortician's job with leads to paying the same respect to deceased homeless people, even though there is nobody present to witness such acts, and no family members to congratulate the player and thank them for caring.

The difference between the mechanics of preparing bodies and the attitude taken to such work, as well as the emotional space occupied during it, results in this game's own sort of ludonarrative dissonance. It is hard not to think about people mistreated in life, who had their lives cut short, while playing this game. The entire game is honest about death in a refreshing way that is also quite beautiful. That alone should be a theological lesson about the importance of being honest about the finality of death rather than referencing Heaven as a supposed means of explaining away death's real sting. While having such thoughts, it is also hard not to think that this game is not really about death, but is calling upon its players to show others this same amount of respect in life so that death is not the only time others experience it. Even if no one else in the universe will ever know, whenever the other calls out for respect, they will know how their call was met.

Video Games and the Courage to Be

In the introduction to *The Courage to Be*, Peter Gomes notes a great paradox about the time at which Tillich was writing. Two wars had just happened, and yet recovery was going well and people were optimistic. "Material prosperity was an ambition and a fact of life."[9] None of this impressed Tillich much. Externally majestic church structures that were spiritually empty inside is what caught his eye. People were losing their unconditioned depths as they tried to satisfy themselves with conditioned goods. The assessment Gomes gives of Tillich's continued relevance could have been written not in the year 2000 as it was, but right now.

> At the end of the twentieth century, despite all of the superficial signs of religious vitality in American life and culture, where presidential candidates are obliged to boast of their intimacy with Jesus Christ, the nagging clouds of doubt and meaning continue to rain on our religious parade. In an era of unprecedented economic growth and material prosperity, where more people have more faith in the chairman of the Federal Reserve Bank than in the president of the United States, their remains at the heart of the culture a grave and disquieting anxiety.[10]

Gamergate produced the anxiety of emptiness in a very direct way by trying to prevent Quinn and Wu from participating in their chosen industry through the games they created. In that regard, it is interesting that Tillich notes periods of anxiety in history correlate with the end of an era: "Conflicts between the old, which tries to maintain itself, often with new means, and the new, which derives the old of its intrinsic power, produce anxiety in all directions."[11] This can be seen as the political establishment derides and dismisses legitimate critiques of neoliberal capitalism that draw support from so many young people. It happened in Gamergate, the end of an era of innocence in which games were "just" games and, like toys, nothing to be taken too seriously. It would also be the end of the time that developers and critics could get away with ignoring inaccurate or even harmful representations of anyone not white, male, straight, and cis in video games. As *Papers, Please*; *Bury Me, My Love*; and *This War of Mine* show, the era of making immigration illegal in favor of an overly conservative fear-based nationalism may also be coming to an end in favor of something new.

Courageous action in the face of such fearful yet powerful political forces is inherently risky for immigrants as well as their supporters. However, because such courage depends upon the power of being-itself, which transcends the threat of nonbeing and annihilation, each person can accept the risks they face with that courage and boldly step into an unknown future through acts of self-affirmation. "Courage is the self-affirmation of being in spite of the fact of nonbeing. It is the act of the individual self in taking the anxiety of nonbeing upon itself by affirming itself either as part of an embracing whole or in its individual selfhood."[12] In the case of the games mentioned in this chapter, their theological significance is not so much that the player is impacted by the encounter with the other, as was the case with *Gone Home*, though that element is certainly present. Rather, players experience characters in these games who face problematic situations with real-world counterparts, and they get to see those marginalized digital immigrants and refugees facing those situations with courage. What makes *Papers, Please* so full of depth is the nuance that comes from showing the same care and sympathy for people who work in jobs related to immigration. While it is easy to vilify Border Patrol officers if one is in favor of immigrant rights, those officers also have families and need to perform certain duties in order to keep their jobs and be paid. *Papers, Please* does not provide easy answers about the moral problems involved with immigration. Rather, it makes sure the complexity of the situation is clear to those playing it. In *Papers, Please*, both the player's character and the others they interact with in the game are facing problematic situations with courage.

The courage coming from the depths of these digital characters is God made manifest in their overcoming of doubts about the future. These digital others are heroic in acting to make a better future real, despite uncertainty about that future, as is especially the case for Nour in *Bury Me, My Love*. As Tillich noted, when doubts and fears subside, at least enough to enable action, that is when God is present: "The courage to be is rooted in the God who appears when God has disappeared in the anxiety of doubt."[13] Or, as Gomes summarizes Tillich's theological thoughts on courage, it is an affirmation of "hope that appears when the situation is beyond hope itself, or hopeless."[14] The immigration situation for many people around the world today is hopeless, as is the plight of so many trying to flee genocide and tyranny, or just shelter in place and survive. However, the very lives of the characters in these games, just like so many people in the real world, are evidence of God's reality as they act to be more and demand more of others.

Both Tillich and Levinas developed philosophical theologies in which polar opposites need each other and are brought together, but only through something beyond either component of that pair. If only more people could realize that safety through separation or pluralistic participation are not exclusive options, that a society encouraging the greatest participation possible is also a safer society, Tillich's point would be realized. Levinas argued we need other persons, to look otherwise than being, to find true infinite lasting goodness in responsibility toward those others. If only leaders would turn their gaze and hear the call of the other instead of creating laws and upholding principles that twist and pervert that ethical call into a dangerous call that can easily be dismissed, the world would be a better place. The games covered in this chapter are all somewhat anxiety-inducing because they reflect real issues that countries around the world are not adequately addressing, and players experience only a fraction of the anxiety the characters in the games are going through while trying to escape or survive war. Nonetheless, all the characters are facing such fraught situations with courage. Out of their very depths, they are finding the courage to be in the world and assert their right to live free from war, tyranny, and the regular threat of nonexistence. Furthermore, out of that courage comes the ability to respond to and help others, even if larger forces at work are not similarly cooperative.

Someone emboldened by the ground-of-being should respond to every other, should make sure everyone realizes who they are in the divine depths. Once someone courageously affirms who they are due to their grounding in God, they should turn otherwise and help others to make sure they can do the same. Even though soldiers are preventing people from fleeing, and armed survivors pose a threat, the group of allies that players control in *This*

War of Mine can live up to their ethical responsibilities to one another in a way that would make Levinas proud. Such seemingly futile acts of care amid more powerful immoral political forces also serve as reminders from Levinas that we have a special moral obligation to respond to the marginalized. Or, as Tillich would put the same point, heteronomous forces must be resisted in hopes that a new theonomous situation can be brought about, one in which in which they too, no longer being heteronomous, can participate. However, without the initial resistance, the theonomous situation will never be achieved. The same is true for Levinas. Even though we have an ultimate moral duty to respond to the call of others, the reality of concrete situations is not so neutral. Sometimes it is necessary to privilege some calls and suppress others; otherwise, no ethical responsibility will be possible. Tillich and Levinas allow for a nuanced appreciation of the tensions and plights explored in these games. Divine potential is within both oppressor and oppressed, the soldiers at the border and the immigrants fleeing for their lives. However, in such polarized *and imbalanced* situations, special responsibilities are due to the marginalized and oppressed, as Tillich clearly emphasized.

> Nobody can say where the final limits of human power lie. In his encounter with the universe, man is able to transcend any imaginable limit. But there is a limit for man which is definite and which he always encounters, the other man. The other one, the "thou", is like a wall which cannot be removed or penetrated or used. He who tries to do so, destroys himself. The "thou" demands by his very existence to be acknowledged as a "thou" for an "ego" and as an "ego" for himself. This is the claim which is implied in his being. Man can refuse to listen to the intrinsic claim of the other one. He can disregard his demand for justice. He can remove or use him. He can try to transform him into a manageable object, a thing, a tool. But in doing so he meets the resistance of him who has the claim to be acknowledged as an ego. And this resistance forces him either to meet the other one as an ego or to give up his own ego-quality.[15]

While this passage might seem to violate Tillich's hope for theonomy, that would be a mistaken impression. It is not that one pole is chosen over the other, that of the immigrant over the immigration officer, but that special ethical responsibilities exist toward one group in this situation, while the other must be resisted, so that restitutions can be made and conditions restored in which everyone can have their lives realized.

As Tillich would assert in one of his more famous sermons, "You Are Accepted," we should accept what God does for us even though we cannot know what that will mean for the future with certainty: "*You are accepted*, accepted by that which is greater than you, and the name of which you do not know. Do not ask for the name now; perhaps you will find it later. Do not try to do anything now; perhaps later you will do much. Do not seek for anything; do not perform anything; do not intend anything. *Simply accept the fact that you are accepted!*"[16] It is not naïve to hold onto hope and assert one's true identity in the face of Gamergate supporters trying to suppress that identity and crush hope. It is not pointless to personally resist authoritarian structures even though no single person can tear them down. These are manifestations of courage, something which lives, dwells, and thrives in paradox and is supported despite that paradox because it is grounded in God: "The courage to be is the ethical act in which man affirms his own being in spite of those elements of his existence which conflict with his essential self-affirmation."[17] Living between one age and another, or one movement and a countermovement, is where Tillich found himself, and where the present argument about theology, video games, and Gamergate can be located. Countering everything destructive and living toward the new is risky, but Tillich provides resources for taking that risk up within ourselves and acting with courage to do what is necessary nonetheless. Police states may also be on the verge of something new, as protests across the United States and the entire earth in 2020 cried out for an end to the militarization of police and the atrocities they commit against people of color. Those protesters are manifestations of God in their courageous insistence that they have the right to exist directly to the forces who so often snatch that right from them. It is to the God found in and supporting such courageous protests that the argument now turns, first in Iran, before examining how the video game industry has protested police brutality.

Level Six
Other Races and Religions in Protest

Just as the Me Too movement has called out sexism and sexual assault across industries, emboldening more voices to come forward with their stories, a chorus of voices within the video game industry has refused to remain silent after Gamergate. The video game industry is also in the midst of dealing with long-overlooked allegations of sexism and abuse, and that situation will be briefly surveyed near the closing of this book. On other fronts, the industry has done an astounding job of living up to its responsibility when faced with the call of the other, at least in the case of another worldwide movement, Black Lives Matter, especially in light of a recent string of murders of unarmed Black people by police officers and armed civilians across the United States. Games that have dealt with race and protest will be the topic of this chapter, in addition to evidence regarding how shifts in the video game industry since Gamergate have galvanized video game communities to actively realize some of the moral potential that exists within video games and the communities around them.

The person who has most visibly spearheaded protests over depictions of nonwhite and non-Christian people in video games is Rami Ismail. He is a game developer who formerly made up half of the small Dutch game development studio Vlambeer. Ismail is also a Muslim who has been vocal about the importance of pluralism in both video games and theology.[1] As proof of how rare it is for Muslims, and people from the Middle East in general, to be able to tell their own stories in their own way in video games, Ismail felt compelled to give a scathing critique of one of the video game industry's biggest franchises at the 2015 Game Developers Conference (GDC). The yearly event is the largest gathering of professionals working in the video game industry held in the United States. That year, Ismail gave several talks, and devoted one to emphasizing how far the industry still has to go if it wants to be inclusive and diverse. The main point of that talk is impossible to deny.

Ismail represents a growing segment of the video game industry that, in the spirit of Tillich, does not want the existing video game culture to continue unchallenged. While working within the video game industry and fitting within Tillich's theology of culture in which theological import can appear in the seemingly nonreligious, Ismail also delivers an explicitly religious critique to the video game status quo. His 2015 GDC talk was titled "We Suck at Inclusivity: How Language Creates the Largest Invisible Minority for Games." In it, he criticized one of the biggest video games from 2011, *Battlefield 3*, published by one of the largest companies in the industry, Electronic Arts. Its $100 million budget resulted in a game in which all enemies are brown, heroes white, and Muslims terrorists. Ismail pointed out the problematic nature of this game at the end of his thirty-minute talk, after he spent about twenty-five minutes giving his audience a very basic introduction to reading Arabic. Despite such brevity, the audience was able to notice a major blunder by the developers of *Battlefield 3*.

One of the game's major scenes takes place as players are in a shootout near a crumbling hotel in the region of the border of Iran and Iraq. The hotel's sign is constantly on screen, but there is one problem. When Ismail showed a picture of the scene and asked the audience if they could spot the problem, someone immediately noticed it with only Ismail's twenty-five minutes of training to help. "Hotel" was spelled backward in Arabic. Ismail took the fact that the developers of *Battlefield 3* could not be bothered to spell an Arabic word correctly in one of their game's major scenes as a personal insult. "One hundred million dollars to make sure you can kill my people, and nobody took the time to make sure the text on this enormous set-piece was right. . . . This isn't just a translation error, it's a gross disrespect towards an entire culture, to spend tens of millions of dollars on rag-dolls, but not have courtesy to have someone review the writing."[2] *Battlefield 3* was a distortion of deeper meaning that can be manifest in cultural creations. For example, national pride has meaning that can be positive, but it can also be distorted just like everything relating to culture. When national pride directly harms millions of lives, its meaning has ceased to be positive and has become demonic. As if to show how little the industry cares about Muslims by displaying how little time it takes to do a better job, Ismail has since whittled a version of his talk down to just over eighteen minutes.³ He has also not restricted his activism to video games and criticized HBO for making the same mistake with a different word in their series *Westworld*.⁴ Ismail represents a prophetic voice concerning what it means to be truly human, and how that truth can burst forth in pieces of pop culture like video games. Those who would deny such expression, who prefer the status quo even though it actively harms others, are not simply expressing personal preference for one type of video game over another. They are demonically distorting human life.

Ismail did not end his GDC presentation on such a stinging note. He closed his talk by announcing gamedev.world, an initiative providing language support to developers in non-English speaking countries in an effort to help them break into the industry. Ismail and his team use that website to make some of the best presentations and tech support, previously only in English, available in other languages. As would happen in a theonomous culture, Ismail noticed how heteronomous forces of the video game industry's existing structure were preventing the majority of the world from fully participating in the industry and realizing their dreams of making games, merely due to a language barrier. How inclusive is an industry when the majority of game developers in the world are excluded because they do not speak English? By creating gamedev.world, Ismail disrupted those given structures, and in that violent disruption destroyed a barrier and allowed a new reality to shine through. From June 21–23, 2019 gamedev.world livestreamed a global game developer conference featuring dozens of speakers from across the world, with closed captioning in addition to translations of all videos into Arabic, Simplified Chinese, English, French, Japanese, Brazilian Portuguese, Russian, and Spanish.⁵ Their efforts have not ended with such virtual global conferences. Given the global pandemic caused by the COVID-19 virus, GDC was cancelled in 2020. Many game developers were unable to get refunds for visas, travel costs, and lodgings. Others were stuck abroad away from their homes due to lockdown orders and flight cancellations. To help, gamedev.world raised $81,636.13 that went to help marginalized video game developers in such situations.⁶ In light of Ismail's rightful protests within the video game industry and his efforts to make it better, a video game that contains a protagonist saying "Allāhu akbar!" during prayer instead of while committing acts of terror notably stands out.

People, Not Ragdolls

1979 Revolution: Black Friday was created by Iranian-born game developer Navid Khonsari and released in 2016. Coincidentally, like Lucas Pope, Khonsari once worked for one of the juggernauts of the industry, Rockstar Games, developers of the controversial and massively successful *Grand Theft Auto* series. He left to follow his own interests, starting his development studio iNK Stories for the explicit purpose of telling underrepresented cultural histories. In the case of *1979 Revolution: Black Friday*, he is telling the story of the Iranian Revolution.

Players take control of Reza Shirazi, a young photographer living in Tehran during the penultimate days of the Iranian Revolution, as indicated by "Black Friday" in the game's title. Reza wants to document the revolution as an impartial photojournalist but not actually get involved. He is split on whether he supports peaceful protesters or those who want to fight back against the military. He is also unsure whether Muslim rule under Ayatollah Khomeini is better than a secular alternative. The game goes further than presenting such an introductory version of the revolution and even includes comparatively progressive figures like Ayatollah Shariatmadari in the game. Players can hear audio clips from real speeches delivered by all these figures, depending on which characters they speak to within the game. As the story of the game unfolds, despite Reza Shirazi's wishes, remaining neutral does not remain an option for him for very long. However, as the bloody events of September 8, 1978, occur, there is beauty in the simplicity and very grounded approach the game takes to depicting such a situation.

There are no superheroes in this game. Everyone is a typical Iranian citizen motivated by some combination of social change, justice, and national pride. Reza draws motivation for change from the death of his own cousin, while others are engaged in motivational speaking at rallies or seeking violent justice and payback against the military. Reza eventually finds himself with hundreds of thousands of other people protesting on the streets of Tehran. On those streets he encounters the walking wall of martyrs, a man wearing graphic pictures of murdered protesters and revolutionaries all over his body. The man later invites Reza to pray with him as he thinks it might help Reza center and find himself during trying times. However, the choice is in the player's hands, and turning to or away from Islam as a means of coping with the situation becomes an option in the game. Regardless of their choice, players can read copies of real-world prayer cards recreated in game that outline the steps of a call to prayer. Those cards are also placed in front of an accurate washing station within the game. Players can properly go through all the steps during a call to prayer, praying out loud with others taking part in the prayer.

Recall that theonomy does not reject the free choices of individuals or cultures, but indicates how ultimate meaning is either revealed or hidden by those choices. Players can come to their own conclusions regarding whether protests should be violent or peaceful, and can actively choose whether or not to pray. But the characters in this game, as well as the video game industry as a whole, are responding to destructive situations with a vision for creating something new, as would happen in a theonomous society. Whether a player turns to God in prayer or dismisses the idea as nonsense, the events that unfold in the game's plot are a reminder that superheroes are not necessary. Everyday people listening to one another and working together can bring about great change. However, because choices about embracing or rejecting Islam and the government are present in the game, as opposed to unqualified support of Iran, Khonsari has since been labeled a US spy by Iranian tabloids. As a result, he fears returning to visit family still living in Iran.[7]

Khonsari was a child still living in Iran during the revolution and aimed to represent what his people went through as thoroughly as possible using the medium of video games. He adopted several unique strategies to achieve this goal. He went through his family's home videos of himself as a child and selected some to use in the game, in which they are presented as videos of Reza when he was younger. This decision by Khonsari helps convey the sense that Reza is a living, breathing, fully formed character. During development Khonsari also interviewed over forty people who lived through the Iranian Revolution. He used their stories to create some of the in-game dialogue spoken by other characters and to craft notes found in the world and screens about historical background that pop up to give players accurate information about some of the people and places in the game. From the main menu players can access all this information and read it at their leisure, as well as learn which fictional characters in the game were based on the life experiences of real people described in Khonsari's interviews. In stark contrast to the mistakes of *Battlefield 3*, Muslims are depicted as fully formed people, complex characters, and a collective working together to protest for the future of their country.

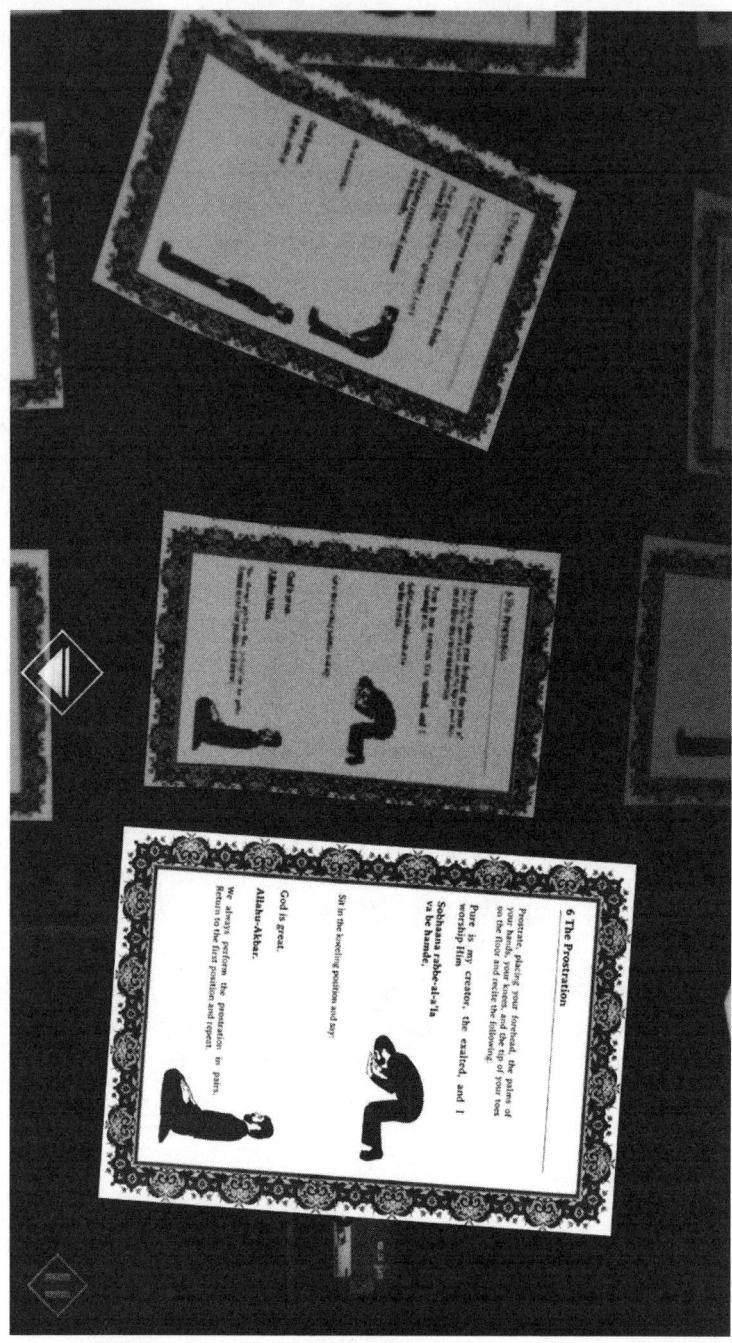

FIG. 6-1. Instructions for prayer found in *1979 Revolution: Black Friday* (2016).

FIG. 6-2. Reza Shirazi participating in a prayer in *1979 Revolution: Black Friday* (2016).

An Unfortunately Rare Success Story

1979 Revolution is notable because its story is unfortunately rare within the video game industry. The game was well received, with overwhelmingly positive review scores from most outlets. Other attempts at telling the stories of Muslims have not been so successful.

The Sun Also Rises was a failed video game project attempted by developer Horse Volume. The two-person team presented their mission within the industry as follows: "to expand games as an art form and create new kinds of experiences. We believe in inclusivity and advocacy as core motivators for our projects."[8] The game was ambitious, perhaps too ambitious. *The Sun Also Rises* was meant to be a war game without bullets, explosions, or violence. Rather, the goal was to use the game to increase empathy for those too often forgotten as casualties of war. In this case, that was going to mean stories of vulnerability and uncertainty from US soldiers, as opposed to merely glamorizing war and the soldiers fighting. The developers also planned to gather and use stories from the families of US soldiers left alone at home, as well as Afghan citizens, to craft the game's story. The gameplay was going to consist of exploring environments across the globe amid the War on Terror and something the developers called passive multiplayer. The idea behind such multiplayer gameplay was that the choices of one player would impact the sort of game world experienced by another player. The two players would not directly interact or play with one another. Rather, their choices would impact what the other experienced in game, with the result being that players might realize how everyday citizens are impacted by war and develop greater empathy for them in the process. Unfortunately, the project never came to fruition.

The Sun Also Rises was successfully funded on Kickstarter, a crowdfunding platform most prominently, though not exclusively, featuring video game projects. However, the ambitions of Horse Volume may have outstripped their resources. The last update from the development team on the game's progress was given on June 27, 2016. The developer's website no longer exists,[9] and the same is true of another website devoted solely to *The Sun Also Rises*.[10] If only the industry had heeded the words of Rami Ismail, perhaps some funding would have been made available for a project that was trying to get representation right, as opposed to the majority of money going toward games that still misrepresent and abuse Muslims within their digital worlds. There is a positive lesson in this failed project, however.

The founding figure of American pragmatism, Charles S. Peirce, placed significant value in ideas and projects that end up going nowhere. When it comes to inquiry into any subject, he wrote about the important roles of abduction and retroduction, the creation of novel hypotheses that would, if true, explain vexing problems at hand. There are competing interpretations of quantum mechanics in existence right now, including the possibility that in parallel worlds all unrealized possibilities, all the choices each of us did not make, have been made manifest. Novel and incredibly creative hypotheses might be needed to explain novel and incredibly bizarre phenomena. *The Sun Also Rises* was a sort of abductive hypothesis about how to positively represent both soldiers and the people who innocently suffer from their actions in a way that has not currently been realized within the video game industry. Peirce referred to abduction as "a method of forming a general prediction without any positive assurance that it will succeed" and retroduction as "reasoning from consequent to antecedent" when creating hypotheses.[11]

In either case, whether developing a new hypothesis from scratch or creatively revising an existing idea, a core component to Peirce's way of thinking is that seemingly absurd ideas might be the most useful. Sometimes the correct solution to an incredibly confusing problem, or the explanation for an unknown phenomenon, is completely improbable according to current ways of thinking. In a way, the failure of *The Sun Also Rises* was a demonic distortion of meaning, as not enough people saw the ultimate potential of the game to bring it to fruition. It was also a bold abduction in Peirce's sense, as it tried something daring, new, and needed within the video game industry. Rather than be scared away by its unfortunate ending, developers should be inspired to follow its lead and tilt the direction toward which new ideas in the industry are leaning. That direction, though improbable now, might be exactly what is needed. If others are empowered by such a failure to support future projects better representing Muslims, that will be a case of theological ethics informed by Tillich and Levinas in action.

Just as Tillich's theological lens helped him identify deeper possible meaning within cultural distortions, *Battlefield 3* and the failure of *The Sun Also Rises* contain distortions of national pride and the cautious nature of power structures. However, it should be possible to identify the religious aspect of culture, even while that aspect is being distorted by the very culture in which it is identified. The possibility of making such an identification is what makes this approach to culture theological—placing culture in the context of that which is beyond it, both judging it and saving it in that very judgment. James Luther Adams compared this vision of Tillich's to that of Jackson Pollock.

> Pollock saw in paint not a passive substance to be manipulated but a storehouse of pent-up forces for the painter to release; and he intended to release them by pouring and spattering his colors on a large canvas instead of transmitting the paint from the tip of the brush. The consequence is that the billowing and surging shapes and lines on the immense canvas reveal the internal dynamics of his material and of the process releasing energy, so to speak, in a field of combat.[12]

Ending on the combat analogy was a good choice by Adams. The power of being is in distortions as well as clear revelations, contradictions as well as essential realizations. Sometimes the tensions and polarizations experienced in life are clues that we should stop, think otherwise, and in doing so be opened up to the depths of our being. This makes perfect sense according to Tillich's way of thinking, because religion is not a realm apart from the rest of culture and God is not a being independent of the world. Rather, God is the depth of reality which, by breaking through the surface in disruptive, destructive moments, brings new possibilities into being.

Hope, anticipation, and failure followed by learning from failure and doing better are important parts of the process of uniting what a polarized culture has torn asunder. Ismail's critique is a paradigmatic example of how there is positivity in failure when failure becomes an opportunity for realizing something better. Likewise, the developers of *The Sun Also Rises* should not give up on making video games. Even if further attempts fail, they will have imaginatively opened up a route out of the problematic present to something better. That is how the story of *The Sun Also Rises'* incompletion should be told. The industry needs developers to attempt such games, even if they fail, because such visions have power over the present. Even if those attempts fail, they will empower other developers to make similar attempts until more games like *1979 Revolution: Black Friday* are successful. At that time, both the world and the video game industry will be better for the failures that precede such success. Tillich reminds us that we need the courage to risk all in order to find the courage to be.

> Every living thing drives beyond itself, transcends itself. The moment in which it no longer does this, in which it remains bound within itself for the sake of internal or external securities, the moment in which it no longer seeks to take upon itself the experiment of living, in that moment it loses life. Only where life risks itself, stakes itself, and imperils itself in going as far as possible beyond itself, only there can it be won.[13]

It is inspiring that some video game developers are willing to take such risks, which makes the lack of such bold vision and willingness to attempt change in so many institutions molding the shape of the world all the more glaring.

Theonomy, Protest, and Special Responsibilities

Beyond the video games discussed so far, and many more that could be listed, it is also the communities that have developed around such games that matter. The communities developing around these nontraditional styles of video games have been perhaps an even better example of Tillich's theology of culture at work. Seeing the potential in video games, these communities have pushed developers to bring forth their meaningful depths rather than block the way to meaning by falling back on outdated and incorrect tropes. Just as there is a paradoxical affirmation of transcendence in immanence in video games, God's universal presence as the ground-of-being is also realized by particular historical communities when objections like the one offered by Ismail become more commonplace.

I have personally witnessed such community support in action when speaking at various professional video game conferences in the Boston area. Boston Gameloop is an un-conference, a one-day event where people discuss what topics they want to cover first thing in the morning, gather as one large group to pitch those topics as sessions, and then vote on which sessions will actually happen in the afternoon. At Boston Gameloop 2015 and 2016, I pitched sessions on the importance of diversity in the industry, as well as religion and video games. Both sessions received many votes and were well attended. Just like my reception at Women in Games Boston, the reason had nothing directly to do with me. Nobody except for one person knew who I was, and only one person who was present both years had any interest in religion (they actually earned a Master of Divinity degree before pivoting to the video game industry). Rather, those who have felt marginalized within the industry have been clear that they will take validation wherever they can get it. When gay rights were thought to have been achieved but are being opened up again for debate in some places, and conversations about transgender rights are largely nonexistent in the culture at large, interacting with a transgender character or playing a gay character can be genuine sources of relief and validation. When Muslims are demonized by political leaders, voices like that of Ismail and games like *1979 Revolution: Black Friday* ultimately matter. Just as important as the games themselves is the fact that communities develop around real-world issues represented in video games, and events like Gameloop allow for discussions of their importance. When all this happens, people in marginalized communities will engage. It does not matter that each person's situation is not the same. Oppressed people can recognize the plights of other oppressed people. As would happen in a theonomous culture, people are thirsting for deep meaning in video games, rather than just taking them at face value as nothing more than a fun hobby. When that thirst is met in video games and people are validated, they in turn organize and act to make the same possibility available for others, despite societal structures and political forces that can hinder such efforts.

THEONOMY AND PROTEST

Tillich did not just think big thoughts and develop an intricate theological system. He was actively politically engaged. The video game industry after Gamergate is not in a dissimilar place to his hope for Christian socialism after the failures of the culture he grew up in during the wars. Both the video game industry and the theological world after their respective tragedies represent people in need of redemption who are also the means for that redemption. The very disruption of someone's beloved culture, rather than mere disruption, can be exactly what is necessary to realize what is ultimately true and worthwhile in life. In light of such theological judgment that places culture in the context of that which is beyond it, both judging it and saving it in that very judgment, protestation can be both righteously angry and lovingly peaceful, pointing to and working to realize something better in its very disruption of the given.

The video game industry is not just making and supporting new kinds of games that fully affirm the humanity of the marginalized. The industry has applied such support to real-world issues. It rallied to support protests rising up across the United States in an effort to raise money for causes supporting social justice and bail funds for those detained by overly aggressive police forces. In the summer of 2020, in the wake of the murders of George Floyd by Minneapolis police officer Derek Chauvin, Breonna Taylor by Louisville Metro Police Department officers Jonathan Mattingly, Detective Brett Hankison, and Myles Cosgrovethe, Ahmaud Arbery by Georgia citizens Gregory and Travis McMichael, and the thousands of other people of color murdered by police who went before them, the video game industry responded along with the rest of the world. At the end of May 2020, a few large video game websites shifted their coverage from just video games to responding to others in need.

E3, or the Electronic Entertainment Expo, is the largest video game event in the United States, perhaps only dwarfed worldwide by the much larger Gamescom held in Germany. Both events occur yearly and are open to both fans and industry professionals. However, in light of the worldwide COVID-19 pandemic, E3 had to be canceled. Like practically every other industry trying to operate in light of stay-at-home orders meant to slow the spread of the virus, outlets that cover video games and normally make in-person coverage of E3 their most important content of the year shifted to online coverage. GameSpot is one of the longer running video game websites in existence, with a following to match their longevity.[14] GameSpot had plans to stream interviews with developers and previews of games to try to make up for the cancellation of the physical E3 convention, but those plans rapidly changed in light of peaceful protests demanding racial justice across the United States.

GameSpot's online replacement for E3, Play For All, was set to start on June 1, kicking off a month of coverage meant to more than make up for the loss of a physical E3. The entire schedule was changed in light of the new wave of Black people being murdered in the United States. The scheduled interview meant to be a sort of opening ceremony was still held. The CEO of Epic Games, Tim Sweeney, was interviewed, but the change in the interview's tone signaled further changes to come. Epic creates the Unreal Engine, a piece of software that many game developers use to create the amazing graphics in their games. However, instead of focusing on technological breakthroughs involving the next video game consoles planned for release within a year of the interview, Sweeney spoke about how Epic would be supporting charities devoted to social justice.[15] GameSpot changed their entire schedule of programming for the month, directing all traffic to their new E3 schedule through their article "Black Lives Matter, Black Voices Are Important."[16] This article stated that all scheduled live video streams would include a donation component to raise money for charity. Just as important is the fact that GameSpot updated the article over the summer with lists featuring Black creators in the video game industry, one list highlighting Black creators working on projects about the Black experience and the other listing Black creators, regardless of the subject matter of their projects. This swift change in strategy as a reaction to police brutality against people of color was only the first in what became a tidal wave.

At around 8:37 p.m. on June 5, 2020, itch.io launched the "Bundle for Racial Justice and Equality."[17] itch.io is an online platform that helps the nontraditional sorts of games described in previous chapters to reach a wider audience. It is not a publisher taking a cut of profits but a depository of creative, often experimental, independent games that has crafted an identity for itself as one of the first places to go for those seeking alternatives to AAA games. It is like an online farmer's market for smaller video game development teams, and it does not charge a fee for a developer to list their game on the website. Most games on the site are made by small development teams, some by students. Almost none of the games on the platform reap the huge profits of the industry compared to their larger big-budget alternatives. In this bundle of games for charity, 564 developers originally agreed to make 742 video games available for a minimum of $5, with no maximum on how much people could choose to pay. The normal retail price of those games would have been $3,468. The special offer was set to run for ten days, with all proceeds going to the NAACP Legal Defense and Educational Fund and Community Bail Fund. The fundraising goal for ten days was set at $100,000.

To say that the video game community responded would be an understatement; it raised $80,000 in under two hours. After four hours, the total reached $160,000, and two hours after that, just over $230,000. By 7:30 the next morning, the new total was $370,000, and a new goal of $500,000 set. By noon the total amount of money raised to support racial justice in the wake of police brutality stood at $540,000, and the goal was raised to $1 million. Later that day, just twenty-four hours after announcing a ten-day fundraising campaign with an initial goal of $100,000, $1.3 million dollars had been raised. Just before midnight on June 8, the total reached $2.7 million. Along the way, more developers joined the cause so that the bundle included over a thousand games, and organizers set a new fundraising goal of $5 million. By 9:00 a.m. on June 12, the bundle reached $5.4 million and included 1,637 games valued at over $8,500. When sales finished on June 16, the bundle had raised $8,158,561.31 from 814,659 people who purchased the bundle of 1,741 games normally valued at $9,519. However, the industry was not finished.

On June 6, 2020, Lucas Pope, the creator of *Papers, Please*, put that game on sale for $3 for twenty-four hours, down from its standard price of $10. He committed to doubling all proceeds from sales during that time up to $50,000 and donating all the money to the NAACP, ACLU, and Equal Justice Initiative.[18] When all sales were tallied, he raised $100,000, plus his own contribution of $50,000, for a total of $150,000 raised for charities fighting for racial justice.[19] Independent game studio Klei Entertainment donated $1 million to the ACLU and NAACP Legal Defense Fund.[20] Contigo Games, a small publisher that specializes in working with independent developers, came to an agreement with their developer partners to make twenty games available as part of their "Black Lives Matter Support Bundle," which was also made available on itch.io.[21] The money raised was split between Black Lives Matter and the National Bail Fund Network, with all of the money going to Black Lives Matter beyond an initial $5,000 being directed to local chapters. Contigo Games set their goal at $99,999.99 and raised $113,941.36. This bundle also linked to a website dedicated to resources for educating oneself on related topics, such as volunteering, voting, protesting, and petitioning elected officials. The description of their fundraising bundle concluded with "Rest in Power George Floyd, Breonna Taylor, Ahmaud Arbery, David McAtee, Tony McDade, and all Black people who have lost their lives at the hands of police."[22]

Beyond itch.io, the Humble Bundle organization created its own initiative for charities. Humble Bundle is a website that sells collections of digital books and video games, with prices beyond a certain level freely determined by consumers and proceeds split between charities and developers. They created the "Fight for Racial Justice Bundle," composed of $1,234 worth of both video games and books that could be purchased for a minimum of $30, though people were free to pay more.[23] The Bundle was on sale for one week and was purchased 134,087 times, raising $4,385,310.63. All proceeds went to charity via the PayPal Giving Fund. This bundle supported the NAACP Legal Defense Fund, Race Forward, and the Bail Project.

The McElroy brothers, who run a veritable podcast empire on the Maximum Fun Podcast Network, donated advertising proceeds from a week's worth of their shows, which range from general entertainment and audio playthroughs of Dungeons & Dragons to broader video game talk. In response to the killing of trans women Dominique Fells and Riah Milton, they gave all advertising proceeds from their tabletop roleplaying podcast, *The Adventure Zone*, to the Okra Project Mental Health Funds, named in honor of Tony McDade and Nina Pop. Those funds support Black trans people emotionally struggling at the intersection of racial and gender violence, with one fund focused on supporting Black trans women and the other Black trans men.[24] In addition to such mental health support, the Okra Project is a grassroots initiative that seeks to address food security in the Black trans and gender nonconforming community.²⁵ Donating this advertising money was not merely a symbolic, insubstantial gesture by the McElroys—*The Adventure Zone* podcast is so popular that the graphic novel based on it debuted at number one on the *New York Times* bestseller list.²⁶ Donations from the McElroy brothers were also in addition to the initial $15,000 that the Okra Project fronted to get each mental health fund started.²⁷ The entire partnership is not a coincidence, as there are popular trans characters in *The Adventure Zone*.

While these examples should have sufficiently demonstrated how the video game industry can be an example of theological ethics in action, here is one more example. Tanya DePass, founder of I Need Diverse Games, a nonprofit based in Chicago, hosts a video-game streaming channel on the website Twitch.tv (a popular video live-streaming platform) under the username cypheroftyr. They started a live stream playing *Animal Crossing: New Horizons* on the evening of June 6 with the humble goal of raising $500 for The Bail Project. Six hours later, over $150,000 had been raised.²⁸

Just like Ismail tries to hold the industry in which he works accountable for its mistakes, many segments of that industry are holding the United States and its police departments accountable in the wake of excessive violence toward communities of color. Hundreds of thousands of people (close to a million combined for only the fundraising efforts mentioned) have shown they understand the importance of video games through their actions. Not only do they seem to grasp the personal importance of video games but also the importance of video games to the society in which they live. Most importantly, those hundreds of thousands of people have turned such recognition into impactful action. Critiques are being extended beyond the industry and turned into protest in the wider world. People are starting to hold institutions accountable rather than proceeding with business as usual. When immigrants and Muslims are represented in games, resulting support can be seen flowing out from such respect in the digital world to the real one. When communities develop around such issues represented in video games, people in marginalized communities will engage. As would happen in a theonomous culture, people are thirsting for deep meaning in video games, and they are taking that meaning with them to act courageously and make sure those same values are enacted in society.

Such sustained efforts on the part of video game communities are also further evidence supporting the claim that video games can help lift Levinas' argument about ethical responsibility off the page, or out of the screen, and into everyday behavior. I have frequently used the following example at video game conventions to indicate what video games can do better than other forms of activism: What are you likely to do if someone with a clipboard walks up to you on the sidewalk asking for your thoughts on LGBTQ+ rights? People by and large give similar responses. Someone against gay rights would tell the person to get lost, and supporters of gay rights would likely note their support before similarly ignoring the street activist. Games like *Gone Home* and *If Found . . .* can be much more effective at making people face an issue like LGBTQ+ equality, and the same is true of issues like police violence and racism. Furthermore, players can encounter such people unencumbered in video games. In many parts of the world, the same players may have met many gay people, for example, but never realized it because many people repress who they are daily out of self-preservation in prejudiced societies. It is not necessary to know the other to respond to their call, because the ethical call is prior to knowing anything about the one to whom a response must be given.

However, if the other occupies a marginalized place in society and their call is more likely to be ignored, games that directly confront players with the reality of such marginalized lives can help players realize the greater responsibilities they have toward those others. The theological significance of video games is not just that they can help marginalized people affirm their essence, but that people who are not marginalized can learn to be more accepting and loving by playing video games. Video games can help players become exemplars of Levinasian responsibility. Video game communities are not ignoring the person with the clipboard. Rather, when the digital equivalent appeared in the form of several fundraising efforts, they put over $12 million into action. Tillich believed theology could provide the courage to be to those experiencing existential meaninglessness during his lifetime. Such fundraising efforts just described show the video game industry is bringing Tillich's vision to fruition today.

Empowering someone to be themselves and cultivating ethical behavior go hand in hand. When you are face to face with someone, their call cannot be ignored. Granted, it is possible to fail to live up to one's responsibility when faced with the call of the other, but even ignoring such a call is acknowledging it was made. Video games make such ethical failures more difficult to comfortably get away with, as they confront players with the face of the other and its ethical call in a much more direct manner than books and lectures. The necessity of responding, and the fact that ignoring the needs of the other is also a response which acknowledges their call, is brought to the forefront because video games are interactive. Players literally cannot avoid responding to the other, unless they turn off the game they are playing. When marginalized people are empowered by representations of themselves in video games, and they in turn are more bravely themselves in society, the same confrontation between the face of other and those who might ignore its call is more forcefully brought out of the digital realm and into daily life. Just as Tillich viewed problematic world events as signs that divine truth is ready to break into the world and destroy existing forms in favor of something new, true, and beautiful, the reckoning now being faced by Gamergate and right-wing movements hostile to the other can be taken as a similar sign. The end of their days is preparing the way for ultimate truth to break through, to be revealed as it shatters such distortions and makes the call of marginalized others impossible to ignore.

Level Seven

Economic and Social Polarities

If you recall the financial numbers briefly mentioned in the introduction, you might have the impression that everyone making video games is financially comfortable. After all, it is true that the video game industry as a whole earns more money than the movie and music industries combined.[1] However, a snapshot of an entire industry necessarily glosses over some details. Not everyone in the industry is thriving, and those struggling to make ends meet are more likely to be the developers making nontraditional games. While such inequity is a problem that needs to be resolved within the industry, the gap between video game haves and have-nots also supports the argument of this book. Some smaller developers are making, and losing money on, smaller games because they find them important to make, be it as learning projects, for the sake of artistic expression, or a sense of personal meaning. Compare the enthusiasm with which video game communities jumped at the opportunity to support Black people across America, evidenced by the amount of money they contributed in such a short period of time, with the responses of some of the richest people in the world.

While billionaire Robert Kraft, owner of the New England Patriots NFL team, only pledged $1 million to racial equality,[2] several different initiatives from nontraditional game developers and publishers raised well over $12 million in support of the same cause. The independent development community and the people who love it also raised more than the

$10 million donated by Amazon, a company owned by the richest person in the world.[3] Klei Entertainment, an independent development studio of about thirty-five people working out of Vancouver, Canada, matched Kraft's efforts by giving $1 million out of its own pockets.[4] Numerous people who allowed their games to be part of such fundraising efforts, or even went out of their way to volunteer their work, could have used some of that large sum of money, as they currently make no money from their games. Many contributors to the itch.io bundles lose money or barely break even on the games they make, even those whose games were critically well received. Nonetheless, they did what they knew was right by doing what was within their ability to help those in need. Despite being in a position of financial need themselves, they heard the call of the other and responded.

According to reporting from Kotaku, in 2010 there was a gap of $58,953 between what people in the video game industry working for larger developers and publishers made that year compared to their smaller independent counterparts. The average employee in the industry that year made $85,733, much more than the $26,780 earned by developers who identified as independent.[5] In 2013 things went from bad to abysmal for one-person game development projects, which earned merely $11,812 on average. However, the situation was better for small development teams, whose members earned $50,833 on average.[6] Shockingly, entry-level positions in the industry were seeing an increase in wages in 2010 (from $37,905 to $49,009), an increase that still dwarfed the earnings of established independent developers, despite being earned by novices. Even the previous year's "bad" earnings number for entry-level employees would make many people working on nontraditional games envious. Perhaps even more shocking is the fact that individuals working within the business and legal portion of the industry, people who have absolutely nothing to do with creating the video games making so much money, surpassed everyone with average earnings of $106,452. Eighty-five percent of those high earners even reported additional income by way of bonuses and other nonmonetary incentives. Compare such comfortable earning figures with the fact that merely paying publishing costs to have an independent game released on various platforms could cut into someone's already meager earnings to the tune of thousands of dollars.[7] Most of the games in this book are exceptions. *Papers, Please* made much more than a few thousand dollars for Lucas Pope. As of August 2016, it had sold 1.8 million units,[8] which gave Pope the financial security to not rush development of his next game, which was not released until 2018, five years after *Papers, Please*.[9] For other small, independent developers of nontraditional games, when already making so little per year, and with other bills to pay, is paying to publish another game worth the risks? What if that game is not a success and one's yearly income drops significantly the following year?

These business realities make the previously mentioned charity work all the more impressive. None of the large sums of money raised was the result of one or two rich donors. One contributor to the Humble Bundle gave $20,000, but the next highest contribution was $3,000, and only eleven contributions were at or above $1,000. The average purchase price was just over $32. The average contribution of $40.12 to the "Black Lives Matter Support Bundle" was just over the minimum of $40 required to purchase the entire bundle, and the average contribution to the itch.io bundle that raised over $8 million and exceeded all expectations was $10.01, with the largest contribution being only $5,000. To put these numbers in a context that makes them even more impressive, remember that these fundraising efforts were occurring during the COVID-19 pandemic, which caused widespread unemployment and spread many budgets thin. Just as impressive as supporting others financially while money is tight is the fact that such support came from so many people rather than a few wealthy donors. The impressiveness of such a feat should not be minimized, because it can be difficult to do the right thing when times are tough.

Economics and Responsibility in Tension

In *Cart Life* players control either an immigrant struggling to make ends meet and take care of his beloved cat while operating a food cart, or a mother trying to start a business in order to earn custody of her child in an upcoming court hearing. There is also Vinny, a bagel merchant who will work slowly if not properly caffeinated, as he is addicted to caffeine. He has never been able to hold a stable job and is trying to change that fact. Whichever character players choose to control, they need to work at a business to make money, but they can also seek social relationships and pursue leisure activities, tasks made difficult by economic realities. However, if the player's character does not find fulfillment outside work, there are devastating psychological consequences. If they find such fulfillment outside of work but do not work enough and run low on funds, starvation or eviction could result.

Melanie Emberly is a single mother in the game. She is recently divorced, and she is not particularly fond of work. She is very fond of her daughter Laura, however, whom she cares for above all else in the world. Melanie needs to work, in spite of her distaste, because she has an upcoming custody hearing. She wants to be able to present herself as stable enough to take care of her daughter. However, if she works too much and does not spend enough time with her daughter, her mental health will deteriorate. Andrus Poder is an immigrant who had a tumultuous time getting to the United States. Now that he has arrived, he is ready to get over past traumas and start his life over with his cat, Mr. Glembovski. Adrus and Mr. Glembovski do not own an apartment or a house. They are staying at a hotel that does not allow pets, but Andrus sneaked in his cat, whom he could not live without. While Andrus needs to make money to start his new life on the right foot, he also does not know what he would do without the comfort of Mr. Glembovski in his life. However, that cat has a proclivity for going on adventures by himself. At one point, one of Andrus' hotel neighbors even catches Andrus looking for Mr. Glembovski after the cat gets out one night. She promises to keep his secret, but her following through on that promise may depend on the quality of the relationship the two maintain.

The genius design decision that went into *Cart Life* is that all these concerns need to be balanced, but the game does not force any schedule on players. Players can choose to never go to work at their cart, spending all day with their daughter or cat instead, but the results will be predictable when they make a poor showing in court or are unable to pay for the hotel. Conversely, players could spend all their time working, to the point that their character collapses from exhaustion and needs to be taken home by someone else. Spending all one's time in the game working, to the neglect of Laura and Mr. Glembovski, would also spell the end of those relationships. Given how important each is to Melanie and Andrus, such consequences would also be devastating for their mental health. If the game sounds like a panic attack in waiting and in some sense miserable to play, that is because in many ways it is.

The person who developed *Cart Life*, Richard Hofmeier, calls the game a "retail simulator," but it is really a simulation of the struggle to survive poverty in the United States. It is an excellent representation of how living in such a situation provides few good options. Unlike *Gone Home, If Found. . .*, and other games already discussed, some of the most meaningful exposition in this game is not delivered through written text or spoken words. While working at their cart, players will mash keys on the keyboard to make food and drinks for people, and type phrases on their keyboard to complete other jobs. It can be both monotonous and frantic, just like a real minimum wage job. Despite being sad and tired, these characters are also courageous in the way they persist. Melanie finds respite in walking her daughter to school and chatting about what is happening in their lives along the way. Andrus finds comfort in spending time with his cat. These characters also remind those not in dire economic straits that achieving what might appear like simple goals can be anything but simple because of the way capitalism works.

Every moment of work chips away at mental health, which is a measured meter in the game, because long hours in low-paying jobs take so much time away from other needs. Every moment spent with loved ones brings pangs of guilt when that time could be spent working: money is needed for basic necessities, and there is currently no disposable income. When unexpected challenges arise—and this game throws more than a few at players—a middle-class person with some extra money might be able to withstand them with relative ease. But for the characters in this game, such unwelcome events turn life into an outright nightmare. Choices in *Cart Life* are about time and money, because both are limited. Hunger is also a meter in the game which needs to be filled, or the player's character will collapse. Such a balancing act becomes a complete juggling routine as each character has to fill meters representing the most basic needs of survival while also meeting their other goals of either winning custody of a child or moving on from a harsh life overseas while keeping a beloved pet alive.

For those who are not struggling financially, playing this game, in all its unpleasantness, really gives a *feeling* of what living in poverty is like, because players get to try that balancing act out for themselves. They also get to experience how little society helps or cares about the difficulty of accomplishing that act. Hofmeier has since made the game free and even made the source code for it available to the public. He did so explicitly to help in education. He is a one-person indie development team, and the game became a success story for him, both in terms of reviews from critics and financial success. He released the source code for the game so students in game designs programs could tinker with it and learn from a small project that will probably be closer to the projects they will initially be working on after graduating in contrast to big-budget AAA titles.[10] Since *Cart Life* was released, other video games have also depicted the anxieties and difficulties of handling life's responsibilities while poor.

FIG. 7-1. Andrus must hide Mr. Glembovski from others, or he risks losing the cat in Cart Life (2010).

In *Diaries of a Spaceport Janitor*, players experience exactly what the title indicates, the life of an alien janitor in a world that looks like a science-fiction Saturday morning cartoon. While the style makes the game appear much more frivolous than *Cart Life*, this game is also a meditation upon the mix of monotony and anxiety that comes from needing to perform repetitive tasks to make money instead of spending time pursuing one's dreams. In the case of *Diaries of a Spaceport Janitor*, the janitor wants to one day leave the planet and explore space. The job in the game is to collect trash and destroy it in an incinerator, which happens to be part of the main character's alien physiology. Players are paid for every piece of garbage eliminated. Like *Cart Life*, players have no schedule forced upon them. However, the basic routine is to work, find food, eat, sleep, pray, and then do it all again. There is a fictional religious aspect to the game in which players can choose a god out of a pantheon and pray to them daily. The gods in the game bestow what seem to be entirely random degrees of luck upon players which will impact how much trash players find and money they make as well as the odds when playing a lottery in the game. The randomness to this religious component serves as a reminder that nobody chooses to be born into poverty or great wealth.

Life starts in a way that nobody chooses, and each of us is left to deal with the reality of the situation in which we find ourselves. A message on the game's tutorial screen tells players, "Don't stress too much about being poor or unlucky. You'll get off this planet someday!" Luck factors heavily into how and when the game will end. Players can try to work as much as possible, but just as in *Cart Life* there are basic constraints on trying to earn one's way out of poverty as quickly as possible. Players need to make money in this game, but the character they control also runs on batteries, which charge the incinerator. This fact means that every time the player makes money as a janitor, they are also reducing the number of times they can make money before having to sleep, recharge, and wait until the next day. These features of the game cause players to think about misconceptions behind questions about why people just do not work harder or take control of their lives to escape poverty. *Diaries of a Spaceport Janitor* conveys a feeling of little to no control. From gods impacting luck to batteries running down, players do not control how the game unfolds as much as they have events happen to them. The player may be motivated to work their way out of poverty as the goal of the game, but the game's systems are literally rigged against them.

As already noted, the themes of various video games in this book are interrelated, and the feeling of being a pawn moved around by capitalist forces is also present in *A Mortician's Tale*. The life of a mortician does not occur the way players might expect upon starting the game, which begins with players controlling a character working in a family-owned business. However, that business is struggling, and its owner soon sells to a massive national organization to at least preserve the company name and make sure employees, like the one players control, can keep their jobs. The original funeral home offered affordable funeral services presented without judgement, whether surviving family members wanted the most basic or most complex funeral services. Once the business is taken over, only bronze, silver, and gold packages are offered, with very partial wording in the description of each package pressuring families into providing their deceased loved ones with the most expensive services. The packages are also tied to expected attendance numbers for funeral services and imply someone being given a bronze funeral service must not have been very important or loved. At one point, when the player's character learns that a family wants to have an at-home funeral because their mother and grandmother would have never accepted anything less intimate, the CEO rejects the player's petition to respect the family's request and steps in to pressure the family into buying one of the more expensive packages. However, amid such an unfortunate turn of events, the touching main theme of this game remains the same. While capitalism and the CEO enthusiastically abuse people in the name of profit, the player's character is able to provide what care to others they can during their final moments.

Digital and Theological Disruptions

LGBTQ+ individuals, immigrants, Muslims, racial minorities, and the economically disadvantaged are marginalized across the world. Tillich, Levinas, and video games have resources to empower and respond to the marginalized. Video games are deeply theological even when focused more on social and political concerns than on overtly theological topics. However, according to Tillich, such a focus is perfectly theological. In *The Religious Situation* he was not really interested in speaking to religious people or addressing churches. In its pages he tried to assess the entire situation in which he was living and discover forgotten or ignored religious values. In such assessment, sociopolitical forces are of the utmost importance because something more than the future of the church is at stake. If something was lacking in all the circumstances that led up to a problematic moment, then finding creative forces that will transform institutions and policies is crucial.

Tillich wrote about the decline of capitalist society after global war, and this book has been dealing with Gamergate and its associated ethical and political issues. Both problems should be viewed as opportunities to usher in something new. Almost all the video games described previously do not contain overtly religious language, and yet the ultimate, eternal source of meaning bursts forth within them. H. Richard Niebuhr referred to Tillich's position that the real divine ground-of-being is present everywhere rather than in some supernatural realm as "belief-ful" realism because this God cannot transgress our experienceable reality.[11] That is, God must be present here and now, not elsewhere, and yet still be God, not reducible to any piece of our reality. Faith embraces the risk of claiming God is present in changing circumstances rather than somewhere settled and secure. God is in the lesbian teenager Sam, not in her as a lesbian, but that which empowers her to live that life. God is in Muslim immigrants, not because God is identical to Muslims, but because God is that giving them courage to be themselves in the midst of racist and xenophobic sentiment. God is in the poor and struggling, not because God likes poverty, but as the reality that reminds anyone who will listen about the importance of lives capitalism trampled.

Tillich was a realist regarding history. God is not a divine being ensuring unending progress. God also does not provide a syllabus outlining ethical behaviors that will stand forever. Tillich rejected the notion of an absolute struggle between good and evil that would eventually be overcome in some final victory. While he positively regarded revolutionary impulses, he did not think they would result in an absolute victory either. He was even more critical of conservative impulses that thought absolute truth had already been located in the past and that nothing new and worthwhile could be anticipated in the future. Tillich had no time for idealistic utopians or conservative defenders of the faith.[12] He focused on *kairos* moments in the present, moments that shatter what conservative impulses may hold dear and cannot guarantee the direction of the future, but in which the role of singular individuals grounded in God may be decisive. Resting content with what is the case and defending it as ultimately meaningful is a stance that will resist necessary revivals, resulting in a denial of divine transcendence that breaks through in disruptive moments. Merely waiting for God to enact a better future amounts to denying that God's presence has any meaning for the world now. Rather, God's immanence is that which is intimately present within actions in the present moment, even in the face of uncertainty about the future because such action is empowered by that divine presence. When theologically assessing historical upheavals while trying to decide upon a plan of action, the answer is never to let things be as they are or instinctively work to roll back whatever changes have been wrought. The answer is not to hope for an ideal future essentially different than the uncertain present moment. The theological answer is always to act now because the meaning of God is found in the present in our actions.[13]

A fulfilled *kairos* moment is invaded by God, but that unconditional eternal reality will not be present to act with predetermined ends in mind. Each *kairos* moment is different due to different cultural and historical circumstances, but different historical moments can be connected to God amid those differences. Concrete actions can be taken when a culture has drifted away from theonomy through exercises of autonomous and heteronomous power: "What happens in the kairos should be absolute, and yet not absolute, but under judgment of the absolute. This demand is fulfilled when the conditioned surrenders itself to become a vehicle for the unconditional."[14] The divine ground-of-being does not bring about justice for Black transgender people who were murdered, and then stop. God is always present to propel those who experience that presence into action when necessary. God disrupted the video game industry in the United States when Gamergate and police brutality brought problems to light, and God propelled video game developers and communities to swiftly and decisively respond. Historical upheavals are a sort of divine judgment against what the present is lacking, be it equal treatment of women in the video game industry or nonwhite people in society. Acting to bring such societal disruptions to completion through protest and resistance is not actually disruptive in the end but productive. Understanding the presence of God as the ground-of-being is almost like a challenge to proclaim meaningfulness in a seemingly meaningless situation without explaining away aspects of tragedy and loss within that situation by referencing Heaven, but by instead digging deeper in the now.

Tillich was not envisioning an end to history, its perfect culmination in an ideal set of cultural or religious institutions. Rather than bringing a dialectical method to a halt, he would keep tension alive in history while nonetheless locating the ultimate ground-of-being across history with all its tensions. No historical fact or movement will have the final say, but neither is any event devoid of meaning, even a failure like Gamergate. Recall Tillich's definition of *kairos* as "a moment in which the eternal breaks into the temporal, shaking and transforming it and creating a crisis in the depth of human existence."[15] There will be different right times, many *kairos* moments with differing characteristics, because history and culture shift and change. However, all *kairos* moments are connected to ultimate meaning amid their differences.[16] God has a negative power in such moments in that even destructive energy and forces are filled with meaning and greater productive possibilities. In *kairos* moments God brings to judgment those who brought about the crisis and lifts up those who have been damaged and hurt, filling violent disruptions with meaning insofar as they are opportunities to address imbalances of love, power, and justice in favor of something new. The next phase of history, the next culture, the next form of religion, all these will be judged in a similar way when they are found wanting and need to pass away in order for something else to take their place.[17] As Tillich warned, in defending genuine truth it is easy to be shaped into the form of those attacking it.[18] He would remind us that the possibility of crisis should always remain present in our personal and collective consciousness, lest the correct positive assessment of what is happening in history turn dogmatic and into something else that must be firmly rejected.[19]

God embraces culture, embraces everything conditional rather than forcing conditioned cultural forms to adhere to some alternative religious structure. This is Tillich's point, but it is also intimately tied to the concerns of Levinas because Tillich did not have totalizing dogmatic adherence in his ontological scheme. Tillich would not reduce the meaning of individuals to their role in cultural or historical movements. Such is what would happen under the control of heteronomous forces. Tillich sought theonomy, in which all others are affirmed not because they are like me, or because their depths of meaning have already been made clear, but because ultimate potential undergirds and supports everything, even personal and historical failures. While phrased differently, Levinas affirmed these same points. As Purcell notes, "the unique individual is its own signification, signifying with a signification irreducible to any cultural, historical, religious, or economic totality. Quite simply put, even idiots demand a hearing, despite the meaningless of what they say (*le dit*), because more to be respected than what is said is the one who is doing the saying (*le dire*)."[20] There is something essentially particular and historical about responsibility toward others. We find ourselves where we happen to find ourselves when the other provokes a response in us. But while this encounter is concrete, particular, and historical, the *face* of the other is rather unhistorical.

Each face will phenomenologically differ, but the notion of encountering the demand of the face of the other is a general basic feature of personal experience. Both Tillich and Levinas have important nonhistorical concepts in their work that are crucial for that work to matter in different and unique historical situations. In a sense, both are existentialists. Understanding a person fully, in their depth, is to understand them as already open to more, something beyond them that makes them who they are most fully, but without tacking on something supernatural. Rather, the human phenomenon already points beyond itself. Without referencing Tillich, Purcell wonderfully summarizes how Tillich and Levinas share sensibilities on this point: "In short, if the human person is constituted or created in such a way that he or she is open to a revelation, capable of receiving a word from another who is excessive or infinite, then one might say that the human person is to be understood as response to an initiative which is not of his or her own devising."[21] Or, as Tillich claims, the reality of God is evidenced by responsibility toward the other. "Where one is grasped by a human face as human, although one has to overcome personal distaste, or racial strangeness, or national conflicts, or the differences of sex, of age, of beauty, of strength, of knowledge, and all the other innumerable causes of separation—*there* New Creation happens!"[22] Whether through the notion of responsibility or the presence of the unconditional God in the conditional, Tillich and Levinas agree that we are not slaves to the past but also that we should not defer to an ideal future. Levinas also criticized mythical elements of religion, idolatrous concepts that do nothing to change the world and nothing to access God. Ethically responding to the other is the means to achieving both. We do not receive orders from God, but a calling, an ethical role, should we accept it.[23]

We should not understand ethics in terms of a specific list of demands. The answers will differ by situation, and we can never be sure without ambiguity that we have responded correctly. People and their institutions can recover their true identities and become something new, ethical, and responsible. For Levinas this implies a transcendence of each human being to one another, just as Tillich's infinite unconditioned God is the source of realizing our new being. In a sense, both Tillich and Levinas agree the source of genuine human freedom is outside any person but only realized in the activity of those persons.

Tillich calls such a person reacting with courage a centered person, one who does not pick one pole in life over another but correlates with both. For example, rather than self or world, both are affirmed, and the same is true for individual identity versus participating with others.[24] Another way of stating this point is that the same is always also permeated by the not-same, self by the world, isolated individuation with participation, or even wealthy and poor. A truly centered person needs to be open to having their sense of identity decentered by those other influences in order to develop a truly holistic and healthy, and ultimately meaningful, identity. It is more important to be always ready to properly relate to others than it is to supposedly discover one's essence and then erect walls and shy away from all external influences. James DiCenso summarizes Tillich's centered person as "permeated by otherness and by negativity (in the sense of nonbeing as the not-yet and the other-than-what-is), and hence remains open to possibility and transformation."[25] As Tillich puts the point, "the self-affirmation of being without nonbeing would not even be a self-affirmation but an immovable self-identity."[26] Just as for theology and religious institutions, so for individuals—openness to future possibilities, even if unknown and risky, rather than closure. Or, as Levinas would remind, the other remains other rather than known and nameable. The opposite of this open approach tends toward idolatry and the demonic, turning God into a being among beings or morality into a settled list of commands. The courage to be, as opposed to being closed off and withdrawing from others, relates to seeing things otherwise.

If someone chooses to help another financially by supporting raised taxes in service of universal healthcare or even embracing a form of socialism as Tillich did, these are actions that take nothing away from the one giving but only make their life more rich and complete. Such sharing of resources achieves such a feat despite superficial appearances of only taking because it helps lead to a theonomous situation, rather than one in which some may have autonomy, but others are suffering and having their choices and desires crushed by unjust systems. "The courage to be is the ethical act in which man affirms his own being in spite of those elements of his existence which conflict with his essential self-affirmation."[27] The anxiety of economic realities does not go away immediately given God's presence, but courage to continue on behalf of the one so oppressed is real. More importantly, the courage to acknowledge such a genuine divine encounter by helping that other through easing their burden and doing what is possible to lessen the anxiety is an act emerging out of the very same courage.

Real-World Takeaways from Video Games

It is not difficult to find pie-in-the-sky arguments that view technology in ultimate terms, basically as a replacement for the promises of religion, one that is more capable of delivering on those promises. *TechGnosis* by Erik Davis, *The Religion of Technology* by David Noble, and *The Pearly Gates of Cyberspace* by Margaret Wertheim will provide a representative sample for those interested in such perspectives. However, while religious in tone and optimistic outlook, the arguments in such books are not theological. Rather, they present technology as a replacement for religious traditions and theological thinking, and a better replacement at that. The Pied Piper for such technological utopianism was Marshall McLuhan, who was so optimistic regarding virtual communities that he referred to the possibility of a worldwide community enabled by technology as "the ultimate harmony of all being."[28] However, as Gamergate has taught, interactions fostered by virtual communities are not free from all the bigotries and prejudices found in face-to-face interactions.[29] If you want further proof, just browse Twitter or Facebook for five minutes.

The situation created by Gamergate revealed that video games cannot be ignored because they are full of genuine power and potential. Such power and potential can be leveraged for both good and for bad, just as every cultural form participating in the ground-of-being is ambiguous. Gamergate's defenders created a heteronomous situation in which they defined video games in such a way as to be wielded as a possession of only certain sorts of video game fans, who were emboldened and encouraged by that definition to criticize and harass all others. Gamergate revealed the potential demonic distortion of video games. The result was a culture war in which one group was pitted against another, which could have been avoided in favor of a theonomous situation if everyone embraced the fact that video games are for all and nontraditional games do not take away from those who like to play other more action-packed games. Such a failure within the industry represents the pitfalls and promises of the demonic. However, even such failures participate in God as the ground-of-being. Demonic distortions like Gamergate would not tempt people if they were not distorting some greater potential.[30] They too draw their power from God, the ground-of-being. But just as Levinas and Tillich looked at the historical failures of wars they lived through with hope for new theological meaning and ethical behavior, the reactions to Gamergate by game developers and gaming communities can be viewed as a sign that there is still a thirst for transcendent meaning that transforms the present. Playing video games, at least the nontraditional ones that have been described, can be deemed a religious experience in that God cannot be separated from culture, and must necessarily appear in cultural forms.

The following list is not exhaustive, but represents key points repeated over and over in conversations about theological ethics with video game developers and fans at various conventions and conferences that have been exemplified throughout these pages. There are important ethical themes that arise simply from playing video games, which also impact the way people view themselves and behave in the world when not playing a game.

WITHIN-GAME POINTS

1. Validation. Interacting with representations of people other than straight white males in video games is a validation of those other identities. The video game industry has been dominated by games featuring straight white men for most of its existence. Those who have felt marginalized within the industry will take validation wherever they can get it. When gay and transgender rights are being openly debated, interacting with a transgender character or playing a gay character can be a genuine source of relief and validation. The *Dragon Age* and *Mass Effect* series are perhaps the most popular examples of this phenomenon. Both games were early examples of players being able to romance characters in game through flirtatious conversations that can eventually lead to virtual sexual relations. As noted in chapter 4, between the two franchises, gay, lesbian, bi, and transgender characters are represented. The same is true for non-Christians. When Muslims are still demonized as terrorists in many countries across the world, controlling an Iranian main character who can turn to Islam within the game is a protest against such real-world propaganda, and a source of validation that Muslims ultimately matter. This point extends beyond historically marginalized communities and even applies simply to nontoxic forms of masculinity that can be found in a game like *Dream Daddy*.

2. Autonomy. Strong female lead characters are more prevalent than ever in video games. As *Gone Home* shows, video games are actively overturning the trope that saving a fragile young woman, often an object of sexual desire, must be the driving force of adventures. *Papers, Please* more radically and fundamentally subverts this trope, since at the end of that game the player's character and their family need saving by the other computer-controlled characters in the game. As the industry morphs into a more inclusive one in the wake of Gamergate, cis male players who consider themselves allies and who have sometimes tried to play the role of the white knight and publicly support the marginalized can start taking a back seat. Those historically marginalized in the industry are gaining more power than ever, and it is time to move beyond conversations about the importance of diversity and why such marginalized groups need time in the industry's spotlight to actually letting them have it by featuring games they create and enjoy.

OUT-OF-GAME POINTS

3. Political pressure. The communities growing up around games like the ones mentioned, in online message boards and in the real world at fan conventions, are also sources of validation and spaces to explore alternative identities. These communities have also kept pressure on companies to keep improving when it comes to representation. Rami Ismail has used his place as a developer working within the industry to point out its failures, and now more members of the press and fans are also refusing to be silent when egregious mistakes are made. There is already some excellent scholarship on how women are designing identities for themselves in games as a deliberate form of political protest against societal structures that often prevent such identities from being openly expressed and valued.[31] When it comes to whether or not games will continue to positively represent others, the persistence of these communities will factor heavily. Representation is more than escapism. While video games may provide digital spaces to which marginalized players can escape from daily oppression, representation is also the acknowledgment that the people represented exist and cannot be ignored.

4. Who sets policy. This point is related to the previous one, yet distinct. Pressure placed on people in positions of power does not necessarily result in change if those people are able to resist the pressure. Some people from marginalized communities do not find representation of people *like them* to be especially important in video games. Their reasoning is not that representation does not matter, but simply that even they would like the chance to encounter a more diverse spectrum of people and cultures in video games.[32] Even though marginalized and underrepresented in video games, they would still rather see characters unlike themselves in video games. They want to turn otherwise, not inward, to echo Levinas. Such representation is tied to active political change and impacts who gets to set policy—not just political policy, but policies within development studios or church institutions.

Representation matters and representation in games is not simply a fantasy divorced from reality. There are parallels to the 2018 US midterm elections in that people who define themselves in explicit contrast to toxic white masculinity are taking on leadership roles to combat its effects. In chapter 3 it was noted that pluralistic communities are important for realizing ethical responsibility to the other, because exposure to a diversity of people will help overcome natural in-group biases and help people live up to their responsibilities toward others. If those who are able continue to encourage such diversity among leadership of the communities in which they are involved, such work will also be part of living up to one's responsibility before the face of the other.

Remaining Missions

Here near the end, you may still be thinking, "So what? Stories exist in other mediums, and those mediums have matured over a much greater time. What is really so special about video games?" It is true that many video game stories are laughable compared to the plots of decent novels. However, the industry is comparatively young and has matured a great deal. It is now the largest grossing entertainment industry in the world, and that money is being put back into the products to improve their quality. Besides such evidence of maturation, it is possible to interact with stories in video games in ways unlike any other medium. It may be trite to claim the medium is the message, but it is also true. One could create a simple binary and state that books are not interactive, but that would be disingenuous. One's imagination and personal history are greatly involved in interpreting the meaning of words on a page. However, there is a definitive, qualitative difference when interacting with a video game story. It is like the emergence of mind from matter; something new is happening.

Tom Bissell has referred to the "evolutionary long jump" to which commentary on video games is susceptible. Advances in technology change the industry so drastically that any given argument about video games may be woefully out of date in a few years.[1] While that may be the case, the points made in this book are desperately needed and worth making, even if they come packaged with out-of-date technology from the perspective of future readers. Furthermore, the argument that has been made is not likely to be made technologically irrelevant for several reasons. The experience of the other in the games mentioned will not be eliminated if everyone is playing photorealistic virtual reality games in several decades. If anything, such games would likely enhance the claims made about virtual others and ethical responsibility. Beyond a dependence on technology, there is something about the interactivity of games, no matter their chosen graphical styles, that does something theological that books and lectures cannot achieve.

Video games possess great potential to transform individual lives and problematic political structures, though there is still further work to be done. The good news is that there is evidence these sorts of changes can happen. Recall that when it comes to changing people's opinions and the way they behave toward others, *Gone Home* is directly responsible for changing the minds of at least some players who reported being against gay rights prior to playing the game, but now support rights like gay marriage due to questions the act of playing the game made them think about.[2] A Pew survey linked playing video games with others to being more civic-minded, with a greater percentage of teenage players raising money for charity than their peers who do not play games. A greater percentage of teens who play games also committed to political participation and protesting.[3] Despite such positive features of video games, there is still much more work to be done.

Dealing with the Dark Underside of Video Games

While Gamergate was the setup for this book, and positive reactions to it have been dealt with throughout, there continues to be a dark side to the video game industry. Games like *Battlefield 3* are still being made, and the nontraditional games that have been described are still far from being the most important games in the industry in terms of monetary success. The way the Arabic-speaking world has been depicted in video games has been overwhelmingly embarrassing, and that arguably limits the ability of players to comprehend the reality of conflicts within the Middle East as well as the reality of the daily lives of people living there.[4] The version of *Call of Duty* released in 2019 literally turned real US war crimes from the Gulf War into acts committed by Russians as a means of justifying violence against the foreign power by American troops, who are presented as heroes due to in-game twisting of facts.[5] When the reality of an entire people is distilled into being terrorists in video games, real-world support for those very people who have had their lives distorted is less likely to follow. The sort of attitude that drove Gamergate is less prevalent but still present, as evidenced by the review bombing that *The Last of Us Part II* experienced for including a trans character and telling LGBTQ+ stories.[6] Some people still defend something like a Platonic notion of a "gamer" that is defined by only playing certain sorts of games that are telling certain sorts of stories. While everything I have written about the video game industry responding to Gamergate is true, that industry is still far from a perfect place.

There are also problematic business aspects to the video game industry. Women are still frequently mistreated, and it is much harder for them to succeed as developers or members of the press compared to their male counterparts.[7] While in the midst of writing this book, a wave of sexual assault allegations spread across the industry.[8] Famed video game writer Chris Avellone was accused of gross sexual harassment and rape.[9] Apparently management at various development and publishing studios knew about his conduct but covered it up because of his status as an industry icon. Similar accusations from over fifty people who broadcast themselves playing video games on Twitch, a popular video live-streaming platform focused on games, resulted in over twenty popular streamers and the head of one streaming management firm leaving the platform.[10] While it does not minimize the tragedy of any of this behavior, such problems put the video game industry on par with the rest of society as issues of sexism and assault continue to arise. However, what stands out as something this industry handles comparatively well is the swiftness with which the accusations are brought to light, often through social media, and dealt with in the form of firings, leaves of absence, or actually learning and making positive changes.[11] Compare that to the relative slowness with which religious institutions have dealt with related problems such as the sexual abuse of children.

There are also links between video games and real-world violence in the form of the military. The US Army uses video games in recruiting, a potentially benign strategy that could also prey on the marginalized by associating a deadly job with an entertainment.[12] They have used games from *Doom* to the *ARMA* franchise in actively recruiting young people, and video game technology, including some of the exact same games available for consumers to purchase now, has become a regular component of training soldiers for battle.[13] The Chinese government has even used the competitive first-person shooter *Counter-Strike* to test antiterrorist strategies for its police.[14] While the following practice has since largely ended, developers of war-based first-person shooter games like the *Call of Duty*, *Battlefield*, and *Medal of Honor* franchises have subsidized the real-world firearms industry by paying for the use of three-dimensional models of real guns within the games.[15] However, none of this is especially unique to modern times.

Tennis for Two, a 1958 video game that was likely the first ever made, was created by the same person who developed timers for the atomic bombs dropped on Japan.[16] Military research and development funds have helped develop games since that time, and after *Battlezone* was released in 1980, games have been modified by military programmers for use in training simulations.[17] Even though video games have been used for military purposes—purposes benign at best, and insidious at worst—such efforts suggest the military has noticed the naturalness with which people who grew up with games find meaning in them. That is also good news for theologians, even if they find the military connection to video games troublesome. When Tom Bissell was embedded with Marines in 2005, he found video game consoles everywhere and a fan of shooters in every uniform: "Was this all spiritually akin to World War I–era soldiers keeping a copy of Homer or Tennyson at the ready? Did the shooter allow these Marines some small, orchestrated sanity within the chaos of war? When I asked a non-shooter-playing lieutenant about this, he reminded me that chess, too, is a war simulator."[18] Beyond connections with the military, if the video game industry truly wants to continue its support of the Black Lives Matter movement, it will need to reconsider how the police are unequivocally presented as forces of good in video games.[19]

There is also another connection to violence that the video game industry will need to think about moving forward. Even though claims that violent video games cause violent behavior have been debunked, moral lines regarding violence will need to be rethought as technology keeps improving. When is shooting someone in game with a real-world weapon, modeled realistically, with realistic viscera resulting, just too much, not something anyone wants to make or play? What if all of that occurs in virtual reality? Beyond photorealism, the interactivity of games should make developers think about how putting people in control of such situations will impact them, as Bissell notes: "For designers who want to change and startle gamers, they as authors must relinquish the impulse not only to declare meaning but also to suggest meaning. They have to think of themselves as shopkeepers of many possible meanings—some of which may be sick, nihilistic, and disturbing."[20] These problematic aspects of video games as well as the industry as a whole deserve serious theological consideration in the future.

Real Teaching Resources

Gone Home costs fifteen dollars and can be completed between one minute (a hidden secret in the game) and two or three hours. It also contains nuance in its stories that can be explored for many hours more. It is likely more affordable and accessible than your favorite text on theology and sexuality. If *Papers, Please* sounds like a valuable resource as the world faces worldwide refugee crises, compare its cost of ten dollars and completion time of four hours with your preferred books on the plights of immigrants. *1979 Revolution: Black Friday* can provide a crash-course in Iranian politics and the plight of Iranian Muslims in two or three hours for only six dollars. *Cart Life*, as already noted, is now free and can be completed in about five hours. Sales regularly reduce the price of all these games to around the cost of a cup of coffee, and they are sometimes even given away for free. Since the style of these games is nontraditional, these titles are widely accessible regardless of someone's skill level or familiarity with playing video games. And for people with disabilities, control devices provided by the AbleGamers Charity designed to enhance accessibility for people without use of certain parts of their body are a means of overcoming remaining obstacles. Every game featured in this book is also capable of running on very modest, inexpensive computers. The cost, length, and overall accessibility of these games should lead to them being deemed as real teaching resources that are one means of addressing the digital divide.

The digital divide is a situation in which there is not equal access to information through technology across racial and economic lines. The once-celebrated idea was that computers would provide access to information in a way not hindered by socioeconomic constraints. The term is most often referenced as coming from *Falling Through the Net*, a report from The US Department of Commerce's National Telecommunications and Information Administration (NTIA), but they admit they borrowed the term from a source they cannot remember.[21] The ambiguity of origins extends to ambiguity as to how the term can be used. It could refer to those optimistic or pessimistic about the possibilities of new technology, as already mentioned. It could reference Al Gore's distinction between those who do or do not have adequate access to such technology in K–12 education. It could reference changing over from analog to digital technology.[22] It could refer to unfair discrimination regarding compensation found in tech industries.[23] Access, as in the NTIA report, could also reference either ownership of technology or effective use of owned technology, very different things.[24] The idea goes back to the early days of the internet and is sometimes viewed as irrelevant to today, but the divide continues to be very real. Some rural communities have little to no internet access, and many communities still rely on libraries and other public resources for computer usage. In light of the divide's continued relevance, assigning any of the games highlighted in this book to undergraduate or graduate students would be cheaper than one typical college textbook. Of course, if video games are important yet expensive, that would seemingly increase the equity problem. Such would be the case with AAA games that cost sixty dollars when newly released, but that is not a problem with nontraditional games. Beyond the issue of access, these video games should be part of educating people because they lead to real change. The entire argument of this book should have already demonstrated this point, but one more example will be given.

Andrew Shapiro, in *The Control Revolution*, demonstrates how advances in computer technology democratize power, create more autonomy, and extend power to virtual communities while taking some power away from hegemonic institutions. Of course, those traditional systems of power will resist by trying to control access to such technologies in return. When players started organizing around real-world events such as elections within video games like *World of Warcraft*, reports from media outlets were largely derisive, their headlines dismissing such organizing as nothing more than a bunch of nerds trying to elect their favorite politician as the president of a fantasy land. However, some people saw the potential within video games to get younger people engaged in real-world causes. One study on the ability of players to organize in game and discuss political issues, as well as continue those discussions online outside of the game, now comes across as particularly prophetic about how games can lead to civic engagement.[25] Now Democrats like Joe Biden and Alexandria Ocasio-Cortez are rightly praised for their wise, strategic decisions to engage with video game communities.[26] Unfortunately, there are positive and negative aspects of civic engagement, as Gamergate was extremely well organized too. Video games and the communities around them are also places where legitimate learning is stored, as if in the cloud.[27] The video game communities that are greatly concerned about racial justice are more reliable and more in-depth storehouses of knowledge on the subject than many news stories on race-related matters from major news outlets, because people in those communities are intimately involved in enacting social change. Video games like *Minecraft* also started a revolution not touched upon in this book, one in which players create their own content in games and regard that creation as a large part of the fun. These games could be called participatory cultures in which barriers to participate are low and support from others is readily available.[28] Already in 2005, half of all teens created their own digital content of some sort, and a third shared their creations online.[29] Such creative and technical knowledge driven by interest in video games will be relevant beyond the games themselves.

An underlying, if unspoken, theme weaving through this book is that teaching content, such as 2+2=4, or a list of the properties of the Trinity as outlined by Thomas Aquinas, hinders, or at least does not help, innovation and creative problem solving. Video games can help here. Some games have content that many people would readily embrace as part of learning, but that content would be straightforward and fact-based. Sid Meier's *Civilization* series contains some accurate text descriptions of world history, but there is nothing about *that* presentation of information that does anything more than the same facts listed in a history book. However, if viewed with an open mind, the sorts of games that have been described can help when it comes to learning and applying ethics. Content is cheap and now readily available online. What we need is not plain facts but to cultivate better creative thinking, and people who can learn from meaningful experiences to better act and react in the future.

There are great organizations dedicated to using video games to think creatively about and improve things like human health and political institutions, such as Gamesforhealth.org, Gamesforchange.org, and Seriousgamessource.com. Technical and fact-based knowledge now needs to be integrated with emotional intelligence.[30] Barbara Ehrenreich's *Nickle and Dimed* is about the inability of poor people to get by due to the way society complicates their lives. The author tried to live in poverty, and the book is about her struggles to live in the situation that so many do daily. Video games, like that book, can touch upon emotional intelligence. If that book provided a window into the lives of people living in poverty, how much more could *Cart Life* and *Diaries of a Spaceport Janitor* achieve in that regard? Individuals who can step back and gain perspective on themselves and others rather than immediately reacting are the sorts of people who can learn from nontraditional video games. Doing so will help them better collaborate with others instead of immediately coming to snap judgments about whether others are enemies or allies. Video games can help cultivate such social intelligence and empathy,[31] especially if those who play games representing marginalized groups also interact with the communities that have developed around those games.

Theology of Trauma and Video Games

The subject of theology and trauma, or theology and suffering, is one with a well-established body of literature.[32] This area of theological research is ripe for cooperation with the video game industry. *That Dragon Cancer* is an independent video game that shares the experience of a real family dealing with childhood cancer and death. The design team was led by Ryan and Amy Green, whose son Joel died from pediatric cancer at age four. The game conveys their experience of living through the ordeal, from learning of the cancer to Joel's death, in a fictionalized setting that is nonetheless based on their reality. The game has since been used in courses on pastoral counseling at Trinity Western University, with the course's professor, John W. Auxier, drawing the conclusion that the game is indeed a useful tool in developing skills for pastoral care.[33] Such practical pastoral training in seminaries could be supplemented by a number of games, such as *What Remains of Edith Finch*. That game is a walking simulator like *Gone Home* and takes advantage of what can be achieved in video games by wrapping the experience of death and losing children within science fiction and fantasy scenarios that players get to explore. There are many games that deal with subject matter related to trauma, but two more will be briefly mentioned.

Papo y Yo is a game about a boy with an imaginary friend who becomes a monster that tries to hurt the boy once it has consumed too many poisonous frogs. The game was designed by Vander Caballero and conveys his experience of living with his father who abused alcohol and drugs, as well as how video games were his escape from that world into a place that made him feel happy.[34] *Bound* is a game about a child living through her parents' divorce. That child loves to dance, which is how her character moves through the game world, transforming things that cause her pain into things of beauty. Not only are these games strongly connected to work on theology and trauma in theme, but they could also be therapeutic for those who have experienced the traumas they depict. If games that deal with trauma can also be a source of relief from trauma, the immersion in virtual reality should only amplify that effect, though the feasibility of that possibility will only be determined through such collaborative work in the future. However, research already indicates games can be used to fight ADHD and detect early onset Alzheimer's, and the companies behind that work are seeking FDA approval for some games as medical devices.[35] Early evidence is that one game made to detect Alzheimer's, *Sea Hero Quest*, is working.[36] Furthermore, Wesley Wildman has convincingly argued that while theologians tend to focus on the importance of positive aspects of life such as community, joy, and love, from a ground-of-being perspective, darker undersides to life such as loneliness and intense experiences of pain are also revelatory of the manner in which God's presence is always with us.[37] God is present in tragedies, social disruptions, and whatever follows in their wake, not solely in happy endings. Future interactions between those working on theology of trauma, theologians who focus on suffering, and video games depicting such themes should be very fruitful.

Conclusion: Video Games in Aid of Theology

One definition of technology is that it is largely about exerting control.[38] Consider the nontraditional games that are emerging after Gamergate. With often unspoken, prejudiced cultural assumptions working against marginalized people, what better way to control one's narrative than to make a game about one's experiences, something that is also a means of opening up those experiences to others? Considering how our species has told meaningful stories with the technologies available—from the Stone and Bronze Ages to the age of print—why not a video game age? However, also consider how Thomas Hughes describes the experience of Silicon Valley tech startups as moving from vision for the future to business as usual: "eureka moment, simultaneity of invention, formation of a development team, acquisition of funding, acquisition of momentum, and transfer of management from inventor-entrepreneurs to management entrepreneurs."[39] Something novel becomes controlled and eventually calcifies. The outsider spirit is lost as inventive entrepreneurs become the new insiders dictating what is supposedly possible. This is as true for theology as it is for tech monopolies.

Indie developers of nontraditional games stand outside, or even against, this narrative. That is why it is important for prophetic voices such as Rami Ismail's to speak up to prevent Gamergate evangelists from turning games into dangerous idols. What nontraditional games point to is the importance of thinking differently for new truths to emerge. Technologies allow us to *control*, and successful technology companies want to control both their tech and their successful image. Ismail is one of the voices revealing the rough edges of the video game industry rather than pretending they do not exist, and standing in the darkness of disruption is revelatory. Now that more voices have joined his, refusing to pretend the industry has no problems with its depictions of Muslims, women, LGBTQ+ individuals, and other marginalized people, it will become possible to disrupt controlling forces that would prevent the ground-of-being from being made manifest in video games with better representation. Furthermore, getting to play gay, Muslim, and disenfranchised characters in a game is in some cases more liberating and real than living in such bodies in the real world, at least when that world actively hinders their full expression.

Technology has greatly extended our creative powers. We can travel and communicate over distances and at speeds unimaginable a hundred years ago. The same is true for the essence of human lives. In video games, they can be set free as people fully realize themselves. Prophet of technology Marshall McLuhan knew this even before video games were the pop culture heavyweight they are today: "Technological environments are not merely passive containers of people but are active processes that reshape people and other technologies alike."[40] As a cultural form, video games are just waiting to be creatively used and transformed into something that bears the ultimate. This theological potential of games is also where Tillich and Levinas align with one another. God is brought forth in meeting the other and realizing one's ethical responsibility to them in the cultural form of video games. As the ground of all, and therefore of all culture, God is simultaneously supporting the video game industry and breaking it as something new and better emerges. The results can be revolutionary. We can be different, and better, in the way we deal with both ourselves and others in the world based on an encounter with God in the other within video games.

Mark C. Taylor interpreted the internet and speed of modern communication as hastening the rise of irreligion as far back as 1993. People no longer need to search for meaning in some transcendent realm because seemingly anything can now be delivered in the present moment at lightning speed. An "eternal now" has supposedly replaced the need to find the eternal somewhere else.[41] If Taylor is correct, this fact is not necessarily bad for religion. The video games and associated communities described in this book are not examples of shallow forms of fulfillment being sought for right here and right now. People are actively working toward, rather than waiting for, the right moment, a *kairos* which includes reconfiguring the way we relate to others responsibly and ethically. While painfully dated in some ways thanks to the rapid pace of technological change since its writing, a particular remark from Tom Beaudoin regarding the relation of culture to Generation X in the late 1990s is still on point regarding why nonreligious games should matter to those interested in religion: "GenX pop culture also reminds institutions of Xer's awareness that we are on our own, seeking the religious outside their framework. Whereas boomer self-reliance partly results from the economic and social advantages they had in their upbringing, Xer self-reliance is a form of 'making do.' Xers challenge institutions to prove that they will not let us down."[42]

I have found the millennials and even younger people I speak to at gaming conventions and conferences to be more religious than many older, supposed sages defending the institutions that younger generations have left behind. People who love video games, and the people who make the games they love, are actively responding to others in need of help, rather than holding debates over many years about what institutional stance toward others will be adopted. The speed with which the industry raised so much money to support racial justice proves that point. People are not simply seeking entertainment in video games, or validation of themselves but not others. In video games people are finding deep meaning that speaks to everyone, as well as the ability to face current issues with courage and a ferocious confidence. Beaudoin already knew this was true in the 90s: "Xers challenge religious institutions to recognize the prophethood of all believers, not just those in control of religious institutions. Institutions can search out and heed these prophetic GenX voices."[43] The same is true of the relationship between people who make and play video games and religious institutions.

It is possible to make an analogy between more conservative theologies and AAA games. The approach in each is very hierarchical, top-down, and determined from on high. Things are settled upon release (creation), and God (the developer) has to break in through a miracle to change anything. Meanwhile, nontraditional indie games are closer to the process and relational models of God more frequently found in liberal theologies. They take fan feedback into account more often, especially regarding representation of those historically marginalized. Rather than highly scripted gameplay experiences, there is growing interest in emergent gameplay, encouraging the players to make their own fun as they explore and behave in the virtual world as they wish. Not only does this impact gameplay, it also affects how the story unfolds and what it means to the player. *Papers, Please* allows players to create what the game means for them as they choose how to respond to the face of the other at a border crossing. It is the difference between fulfilling predefined roles and exploring our roles, finding ourselves in that very process of exploration.

The problem waiting for a theological answer today is not so much meaninglessness and a lack of depth per se but inattentiveness to others. Young people in the video game industry and video game communities are incredibly sensitive to the way people they know and love who belong to minority groups are marginalized and blatantly mistreated. They empathically extend that concern to others they do not directly know and love. If reconnecting with our divine depth is going to happen today, those depths also need to be understood in the *encounters with others*.

In relation to Tillich's ontology, in finding ourselves through encountering the other, the other becomes a source of salvation, a way of overcoming estrangement and realizing our essence. Both Tillich and Levinas are aware of the great discomfort that often accompanies experiences of existential anxiety and calls from others, and both are trying to emphasize the importance of engaging those experiences with courage and responsibility instead. The ethical demand of the other cannot be predicted beforehand, but the ethical risk can be embraced. Both anxiety over personal meaning and the ethical responsibility toward the other lack specific referents, being instead general features of the human condition. For both Tillich and Levinas, these basic troubling features of our lives are not removed just because we responded to them well once or twice. Living courageously does not eliminate estrangement and anxiety; it does let us realize who we truly are amid the pushes and pulls of life. The other will be no less different if we perform our duty in responding to their call, as they will continue to call for responsible self-formation through ethical response.

Meanwhile, polarized groups deny the validity of any people who do not conform to their movement's defining characteristics. An ideal form of democratic group conformity would limit extreme and dangerous forms of self-expression without limiting expression to a mere collective in which everyone must agree and act or look the same. Those who proclaim that "All lives matter!" do not see the irony in their statement. They do not see that special attention to Black lives is to pay attention to all lives, while claiming all lives matter in response to such special pleading is to deny meaning to all, despite what the slogan claims. Levinas was aware of imbalances of power that impact face-to-face encounters. Sometimes a pressing existential need to defend oneself or one's family can, and should, take precedence over the ethical ideal of responding responsibly to all others.[44] This point is not new. It can be found in Deuteronomy 10: "For the LORD your God is God of gods and Lord of lords, the great God, mighty and awesome, who is not partial and takes no bribe, who executes justice for the orphan and the widow, and who loves the strangers, providing them food and clothing."[45] In order for God to be for everyone, sometimes God needs to be especially for certain people and groups. Evidence that old insider versus outsider ways of thinking about video games, race, and policing are fading away is often found in proportion to how viscerally those forces push back against their much-needed protestation.

Tillich describes the combination of meaninglessness and courage as resulting in the ability of meaning to break through in new forms that dismantle the old. This happens when "categories which constitute ordinary experience have lost their power."[46] He also correctly notes how the old structures, especially ones that exercise near total control on the production of cultural forms, resist such novel meaning. Such systems are fearful of facing reality as it is, as opposed to the way their systematic control has tried to skew reality. But art, of all things, can help theologians open the eyes of those clinging onto control. "Modern art is not propaganda but revolution. It shows that the reality of our existence is as it is. It does not cover up the reality in which we are living."[47] As a representative of contemporary creative reinterpretations of Tillich, Wildman seems to agree with this point. A ground-of-being approach to theology makes it possible to affirm God's genuine ultimacy while directing our gaze to the world around us rather than some other realm. It allows us to see and engage the world as it is and see God in both the good and the bad, rather than engaging what we see through wishful theological lenses that distort the reality in which we are participating.[48] There is something ultimately true right here right now, already realized yet waiting for us to come to the same realization and accept that truth.

Tillich opens volume one of his *Systematic Theology* by rejecting fundamentalism in religion for speaking beyond all current situations, particularly by being stuck in the past.[49] Not only is such theology, by its own definition, incapable of speaking to the present, but it excludes everyone not similarly stuck in the past for not being identical with their fundamentalist identity. Tillich, conversely, has turned his theological gaze to the present and immediate future. He thought risk was a theological virtue. Once realized in the present, the reality of God's presence cannot be clutched to our chests out of fear, for that manifestation will pass and something new will take its place. Anxiety of the unknown is understandable, but with assurance that it too will be grounded in the ground-of-being, that unknown future can be eagerly embraced. Genuine historical achievements can succumb to polarization that reveals their limits; this does not diminish these achievements, but does help us accept their necessary passing for something new.

In terms of how the promises and perils of technology have been leveraged theologically, it is hard to argue that liberal theologians have been more successful than their conservative counterparts. Gamergate, Donald Trump, Brexit, and other right-wing movements have manipulated digital mediums to achieve political victory. Such examples make it hard to argue technological idealists were correct, at least if judged in terms of what has happened thus far.[50] Progressive religious groups have fared no better than progressive politicians. Conservative Christians put their money and strength in numbers to work to ensure their supernatural God who dominates and punishes nonbelievers is also the more powerful and dominating presence of Christianity on the internet.[51] The reciprocal relationship between conservative Republican politicians and conservative Christians who often make grand shows of their public support for one another is an example of such money and power in action. However, an alternative possibility for progressive liberal theology is conceivable.

When detached from real-world factors such as membership and finances that make it difficult for liberal theologies and their counterpart churches to become more widespread, heterodox trajectories of liberal religion should be able to better flourish. Video games could be a place where such growth occurs. In contrast to those pessimistic about technology, Michael Heim, in *The Metaphysics of Virtual Reality*, argued such virtual worlds are actually the most real and true—they free us from Plato's cave of matter and let us enter the world of pure form.[52] This is understandably an attractive possibility for the mathematically minded. The equations driving technology seem less invented than discovered, but that is not how the internet or video games work. People create them and fill them with human experiences. Players enter an impersonal realm that becomes personal as they explore it with others. This is clear in the case of multiplayer games but also true of narrative-based games in which personal experiences pulse through the gameplay and story. Those interactive experiences, from a supposedly impersonal medium, in turn reflect back and shed new light on the experiences, beliefs, and actions of players. Outside of the larger, more powerful conservative institutions that resist progressive liberal causes, video games can help foster alternative narratives.

This book encourages all theologians to consider what steps they could take to do more, and what they could be doing differently. Video games are not important only because they are relatively cheap compared to most theology books. Many churches host game nights during which youth groups can gather and play video games together. Courses on theology and film are rather easy to find in the curriculums of many schools of theology and divinity schools. The takeaway from this book should not simply be that more video games should be added to youth group gatherings and film courses should be supplemented with video games. The experiences and opportunities for learning that have been shown to be present in video games are at least as important as sermons and theological curriculum. How could theology, both its creation and its teaching, look different if video games and the communities supporting them were taken more seriously? Tripp Fuller's *Homebrewed Christianity* platform provides one possible example.

Fuller produces a series of podcasts featuring conversations with top-tier theologians, and in doing so spreads awareness of their work to thousands of listeners. The *Homebrewed Christianity* book series features excellent theologians like Donna Bowman and Jeffrey Pugh extending their reach to Fuller's large audience. During the COVID-19 pandemic, Fuller hosted TheoCon with Sarah Lane Ritchie and the University of Edinburgh School of Divinity, a free theology conference held through Zoom and featuring many theologians from Edinburgh and the Claremont School of Theology, among others. Related to what traditional academic activities can be performed online, perhaps even extending their reach, a collaboration between Northwind Theological Seminary and the Center for Open and Relational Theology started a new online Doctor in Theology and Ministry program in 2019 led by Thomas Jay Oord.[53] Not only does this program give students the chance to learn from an expert in Wesleyan and process theology, but it is more affordable and can be completed in less time than traditional Ph.D. programs in the United States.

These alternative forms of theological education and dissemination are especially important in light of the rising costs of higher education, declining college enrollment numbers, and the widespread attack on the humanities in light of those financial realities. *Homebrewed Christianity* has a crowdfunding component in which financial backers gain access to special podcast episodes, discounts on tickets to public talks, and the opportunity to attend online courses.[54] As was shown by the response video game communities gave to the Black Lives Matter movement, people will seek meaning where it is to be found and support such efforts. Other than because it is how it has always been done, there is no reason theological education and dissemination needs to occur exclusively through universities tied to physical locations. If theologians believe their work really matters, why not make the extra effort to leverage the internet and reach more people? Beyond the internet, what would theology look like if video games were incorporated into theological work and the way it is taught? Why are books almost always the only medium ever assigned to students? Some of the first podcasts ever were created by websites focused on video games, and now the format is so respected that National Public Radio produces numerous podcasts. If all culture is full of religious truth, and religion potentially embodied in any culture, then theologians would be wise to follow Fuller and Oord in leveraging the possibilities. Just like nontraditional video games after Gamergate, there are many people hungering for good theology if it is made available to them. Many of those people are not in seminary classrooms or churches on Sunday, but they might be online and in video game communities. Anxiety over trying something new is understandable, but the situation in the video game industry has revealed that people are ready to find God in new ways.

Gamergate produced anxiety in a very direct way, by trying to prevent Quinn and Wu from participating in their chosen industry through the games they created. It is interesting that Tillich notes major periods of anxiety in history correlate with the end of an era: "Conflicts between the old, which tries to maintain itself, often with new means, and the new, which deprives the old of its intrinsic power, produce anxiety in all directions."[55] This point can be seen in action currently as the political establishment derides and criticizes legitimate critiques of neoliberal capitalism that draw support from so many young people. A clear majority of younger liberals supported and voted for Bernie Sanders in the 2020 Democratic Party presidential primaries. He and Alexandria Ocasio-Cortez are not fringe leftists. They represent the future of liberal politics in the United States. Gamergate also represented the end of an era, one of innocence in which games were "just" games and, like toys, nothing to be taken too seriously. It was also the end of the time that developers and critics could get away with ignoring inaccurate or even harmful representations of anyone not white, male, straight, and cisgender in video games. Gamergate signaled the end of an era in which marginalized people could easily be ignored and mistreated, even if the new era is not yet fully formed and still has its problems. Theologians need to boldly step into that *kairos* moment Gamergate has revealed. There is much theologians can learn from video games about finding personal meaning through responding ethically to the other.

Video games should influence the forms inhabited by religious practice and theological ideas, just as art forms like literature and cinema have left an impact. Allow video games to challenge accepted doctrines and beliefs. It is time to admit the sorts of lives depicted in video game stories convey ultimate meaning about the human condition, rather than restricting that revelatory capacity to grand poetry found in Milton and Byron or only the popular works of overtly religious (and usually Christian) figures such as C. S. Lewis. Furthermore, the influence of video games is not strictly confined to the games. As has been shown, understanding what has been happening in the video game industry reveals a way forward out of culture wars and polarized conflicts. Nontraditional games and their communities show a path to something more collective, collaborative, and inclusive. There is something powerful about being who you are and collaborating with others amid difference to help others who are different similarly be themselves and join the movement. This possibility is real, emerging, and growing, as exemplified by the video game communities that rallied around Black lives.

Theologians would do well to learn from video games and join the movement. Such a possibility is eternally true, was always possible, but there is a *kairotic* drive to realize it now. Out of Gamergate the video game industry was elevated to something new, a higher calling, which was also an indication that the threats and harassment of Gamergate were in their death throes. That process of dying can take a while and is still unfolding, but so is the new reality taking its place. Video games and supportive communities surrounding those games provide real reasons to believe in and push for justice, cooperation, and care for others. The lesson is stronger than simply not getting in anyone's way, or mere tolerance. Tillich argued socialist movements fail by trying to force politically what can only be achieved organically by grassroots bottom-up movements.[56] Without such organic support, traditional powers will take back their supposedly rightful place in the world. Video games have shown that situation is not inevitable. The industry is rebelling in protest against powers of the past that want their distortions of culture tolerated but which do not see that same desire for respect in others.

Criticisms of big-budget video games for continuing to put outdated and offensive tropes in their games are destroying the sense of self-sufficiency in the industry—that making a best-selling game is all that matters. Sometimes the most important religious movements are happening outside traditionally recognized organized religion.

There are clear theological messages from the sphere of video games, if only theologians are willing to listen. They are saying "no" to heteronomous forces that deny the pleas of the other. They are saying "no" to self-sufficient autonomy, to an erasure or covering up of the eternal. They are crying out that the eternal is in the autonomous, that God is in everyday life, in video games and the other in those games. A theological eye, or perhaps a theonomous one, turned to video games should accept them on their own terms while also understanding them as expressions of eternal meaning. The critical aspect of that vision is important, for it accepts the present cultural situation while protesting its distortions and taking one additional step. The protest is followed by an elevation in which culture moves beyond freedom from controlling forces to that through which ultimate meaning shines. The "no!" to Gamergate needs to be followed by a "yes!" enthusiastically affirming the importance of the responses to Gamergate. Theologians interested in theology that engages and learns from the world, and transforms the world into a more inclusive, pluralistic place, should embrace video games and the others depicted in them as an essential part of their work.

Source Code

Loading...

1. Scott Tilghman and Daniel Ernst, "Plugging into the Video Game Market: Trends, Challenges and Opportunities in the Interactive Entertainment Market," *Hudson Square Research Report*, October 2009, accessed November 1, 2019, https://nanopdf.com/download/presentation-5afdbf8055284_pdf.
2. "Global Games Market Report Free Version 2019," Newzoo, accessed June 24, 2020, https://newzoo.com/insights/trend-reports/newzoo-global-games-market-report-2019-light-version/.
3. Anna Brown, "Younger Men Play Video Games, but So Do a Diverse Group of Other Americans," Pew Research Center, September 11, 2017, https://www.pewresearch.org/fact-tank/2017/09/11/younger-men-play-video-games-but-so-do-a-diverse-group-of-other-americans/.
4. Paul Tillich, *The Religious Situation*, trans. H. Richard Niebuhr (Cleveland: Meridian Books, 1956), 25–27. I am not just a lifelong fan of video games. I have devoted over six years to engaging fans and creators with my work at events ranging from massive fan conventions to professional game developer conferences. Perhaps more importantly, I have been able to consider their responses to my philosophical and theological interpretations of video games, which gives me a unique ability to speak to the importance of video games for philosophical theology.
5. In defining his philosophical theological project, Neville systematically lays out the connections between such a theology and world religions, the sciences, arts, and practical normative disciplines like ethics, law, and politics. As such, philosophical theology is not so much one discipline that one individual can master entirely, but a form of multidisciplinary inquiry to which many individuals contribute. This is a pragmatic strategy, with many different individual strands

contributing to the strength of a rope, and it exists in contrast to foundational approaches in which missing any link in the chain means the end of inquiry. See Robert Cummings Neville, *On the Scope and Truth of Theology: Theology as Symbolic Engagement* (New York: T&T Clark, 2006), ix–xviii, 101–26.
6 For a representative sample, see the work of theologians like Karl Barth, Rowan Williams, George Lindbeck, and Hans Frei.
7 Neville, *On the Scope and Truth of Theology*, 114–23.

Tutorial

1 Levinas scholars debate whether to capitalize or refrain from capitalizing "other" when translating his work into English. Some suggest capitalizing "other" when it refers to a personal other and making it lowercase when it refers to another form of difference, such as the otherness of the natural world. However, that strategy is not consistent with the original French texts, in which Levinas switches back and forth in violation of this proposed rule. When the other is mentioned in relation to ontology, it could also arguably be capitalized. Given that this book is not an exegetical work exclusively for Levinas scholars, "other" will be kept in lowercase throughout the text for the sake of simplicity, consistency, and clarity for readers. Quotations from authors who have chosen to use capitalization are included unaltered.
2 Given that ethics is first philosophy for Levinas, who also upheld the typical phenomenological suspicion regarding the scientific attitude, some readers may be surprised by this chapter that critiques Levinas by using science. However, the fallible revival of large-scale metaphysical thinking outlined in the preface allows for dialogue between the natural and social sciences without older naïve, imperialistic attitudes about such a conversation. Rather than another case of scientific totalization, fallibility and openness to correction mean the product of such inquiry cannot be a totalizing scheme. Bringing as many relevant perspectives into the fold as possible means more chances for correction and better results. Critical theory, Continental philosophy, and phenomenology are helpful in pointing out when and where science becomes blind to things like the socially constructed nature of its practices or overgeneralization from hyperspecialized domains of inquiry. However, such cautionary reminders do not undermine the cross-cultural success of science in unveiling various, nearly universal features of human life or eliminate the viability of drawing general conclusions. For philosophical theology, as I have described it, overcoming epistemic foundationalism and finding natural science philosophically and theologically useful can go together, rather than the former resulting in the rejection of the latter.
3 Eric A. Weed, *The Religion of White Supremacy in the United States* (Lanham, Md.: Lexington Books, 2017).
4 Zaid Jilani, "Gamergate's Fickle Hero: The Dark Opportunism of Breitbart's Milo Yiannopoulos," Salon, October 29, 2014, https://www.salon.com/2014/10/28/gamergates_fickle_hero_the_dark_opportunism_of_breitbarts_milo_yiannopoulos/.

5   Kyle Wagner, "The Future of the Culture Wars Is Here, and It's Gamergate," Deadspin, October 14, 2014, https://deadspin.com/the-future-of-the-culture-wars-is-here-and-its-gamerga-1646145844. Wagner's article contains the one of the best summaries of events that led up to and followed Gamergate, including their ramifications to this day.

6   Nathan Grayson, "The Indie Game Reality TV Show That Went to Hell," Kotaku, March 31, 2014, https://kotaku.com/the-indie-game-reality-tv-show-that-went-to-hell-1555599284.

7   Phil Owen, "4 Video Games That Help You Understand and Deal with Your Depression," Kotaku, April 19, 2013, https://kotaku.com/4-video-games-that-help-you-understand-and-deal-with-yo-473476131.

8   Callum Borchers and Dennis Keohane, "Citing Threats, Game Maker Pulls Her Company from PAX East Fest," *Boston Globe*, February 24, 2015, https://www.bostonglobe.com/business/2015/02/24/pax-east-withdrawal-reveals-sexist-side-video-game-culture/SiRAzMnuI6iea0woo9ob6I/story.html.

9   Anita Sarkeesian, "Damsel in Distress (Part 1) Tropes vs Women," Feminist Frequency, March 7, 2013, video, 23:34, https://feministfrequency.com/video/damsel-in-distress-part-1/.

10 Anita Sarkeesian, "Lingerie Is Not Armor," Feminist Frequency, June 6, 2016, video, 16:41, https://feministfrequency.com/video/lingerie-is-not-armor/.

11 Jennifer Allaway, "#Gamergate Trolls Aren't Ethics Crusaders; They're a Hate Group," Jezebel, October 13, 2014, https://jezebel.com/gamergate-trolls-arent-ethics-crusaders-theyre-a-hate-1644984010.

12 Kari Paul, "GamerGaters Are Targeting People Who Were Victims of the Patreon Hack," Vice, October 14, 2015, https://www.vice.com/en_us/article/4x3k8n/gamergaters-are-targeting-people-who-were-victims-of-the-patreon-hack; Phil Owen, "WTF Is Wrong with Video Games?" Polygon, September 28, 2015, https://www.polygon.com/2015/9/28/9370821/wtf-is-wrong-with-video-games-excerpt.

13 Monica Anderson, "A Majority of Teens Have Experienced Some Form of Cyberbullying," Pew Research Center, September 27, 2018, https://www.pewresearch.org/internet/2018/09/27/a-majority-of-teens-have-experienced-some-form-of-cyberbullying/.

14 Brown, "Younger Men Play Video Games."

15 Maeve Duggan, "Gaming and Gamers," Pew Research Center, December 15, 2015, https://www.pewresearch.org/internet/2015/12/15/gaming-and-gamers/.

16 David Jenkins, "PAX East Attendance Figures Up by 17,000," gamesindustry.biz, March 15, 2011, https://www.gamesindustry.biz/articles/2011-03-15-pax-east-attendance-figures-up-by-17-000.

17 Nathan Grayson, "Was PAX East's Diversity Lounge a Success? I Asked People Who Went," Kotaku, April 21, 2014, https://kotaku.com/was-pax-easts-diversity-lounge-a-success-i-asked-peopl-1564499083.

18 Leigh Alexander, "'Diversity Lounge'? PAX Has a Lot of Work to Do," Gamasutra, December 19, 2013, https://www.gamasutra.com/view/news/207402/Diversity_Lounge_PAX_has_a_lot_of_work_to_do.php.

19 Jessica Conditt, "Fighting Depression in the Video Game World, One AFK at a Time," Engadget, March 25, 2016, https://www.engadget.com/2016-03-25-mental-illness-video-games-take-this-please-knock.html.

20 Benjamin J. Chicka and Andrew Tripp, "The Science of Online Bullying: A Lesson in Diversity," filmed March 8, 2015, at PAX East, Boston, Mass., video, 1:15:09, https://www.youtube.com/watch?v=Dh9z_A5Td2k.

21 *TheoNerd Podcast*, accessed April 13, 2021, https://www.breaker.audio/theonerd-podcast.

22 "About us," Women in Games, accessed April 13, 2021, http://www.womeningames.org/about-us/.

23 "About Arisia," Arisia Inc., accessed June 25, 2020, https://www.arisia.org/AboutArisia.

24 "Code of Conduct," Arisia Inc., accessed June 25, 2020, https://www.arisia.org/Code-of-Conduct.

25 Crystal Huff, "Why I'm Not at Arisia Anymore: My Rapist is President. Again." October 25, 2018, http://www.jimchines.com/2018/10/arisia-rapist/.

26 "Arisia Settles Cancellation Fees with Westin and Aloft Hotels," Arisia Inc., last modified December 30, 2019, http://corp.arisia.org/Arisia-settles-cancellation-fees.

27 Fran C. Blumberg, *Learning by Playing: Video Gaming in Education* (New York: Oxford University Press, 2014); Constance Steinkuehler, Kurt Squire, and Sasha Barab, eds., *Games, Learning, and Society: Learning and Meaning in the Digital Age* (Cambridge: Cambridge University Press, 2012); Harry J. Brown, *Videogames and Education* (London: Routledge, 2015).

28 Andrew Fishman, "Blame Game: Violent Video Games Do Not Cause Violence," *Psychology Today*, July 16, 2019, https://www.psychologytoday.com/us/blog/video-game-health/201907/blame-game-violent-video-games-do-not-cause-violence. Fishman's article contains a summary of relevant research, including a well-vetted list of studies providing more in-depth explanations of the research; also see Jason Schreier, "Why Most Video Game 'Aggression' Studies Are Nonsense," Kotaku, August 14, 2015, https://kotaku.com/why-most-video-game-aggression-studies-are-nonsense-1724116744. Schreier's article links to many of the same scientific studies as Fishman's, but Schreier summarizes their findings in a way that is accessible to a wider audience.

29 "Technical Report on the Review of the Violent Video Game Literature," American Psychological Association Task Force on Violent Media, accessed March 20, 2020, https://www.apa.org/pi/families/review-video-games.pdf; American Psychological Association's Society for Media Psychology and Technology, "News Media, Public Education and Public Policy Committee," *The Amplifier Magazine*, June 12, 2017, https://div46amplifier.com/2017/06/12/news-media-public-education-and-public-policy-committee.

30 Lawrence Kutner and Cheryl K. Olson, *Grand Theft Childhood: The Surprising Truth about Violent Video Games and What Parents Can Do* (New York: Simon & Schuster, 2009).

31 Seymour Feshbach, "The Catharsis Hypothesis of Interaction with Aggressive and Neutral Play Objects," *Journal of Personality* 24 (1956): 449–62. Feshbach's idea was applied to video games by Barrie Gunter, "Psychological Effects of Video Games," in *Handbook of Computer Games Studies*, ed. Joost Raessens and Jeffrey Goldstein (Cambridge, Mass.: MIT Press, 2005), 145–60.
32 Blay Whitby, "The Virtual Sky Is Not the Limit: Ethics in Virtual Reality," *Intelligent Tutoring Media* 4, no. 1 (1993): 23–28.
33 Nancy E. Dowd, Dorothy G. Singer, and Robin Fretwell Wilson, eds., *Handbook of Children, Culture, and Violence* (Thousand Oaks, Calif.: Sage Publications, 2006).
34 Michael Heim, *Virtual Realism* (Oxford: Oxford University Press, 1998), 42.
35 Derek Stanovsky, "Virtual Reality," in *The Blackwell Guide to the Philosophy of Computing and Information*, ed. Luciano Floridi (Malden, Mass.: Blackwell, 2004), 167–77.
36 Andrew Calcutt, *White Noise: An A-Z of the Contradictions of Cyberculture* (New York: Saint Martin's Press, 1999).
37 Michael Benedikt, "Introduction," in *Cyberspace: First Steps*, ed. Michael Benedikt (Cambridge, Mass.: MIT Press, 1991), 16.
38 Plato, *Phaedrus*, trans. James H. Nichols Jr. (Ithaca, N.Y.: Cornell University Press, 1998).
39 Neil Postman, *Technopoly: The Surrender of Culture to Technology* (New York: Alfred A. Knopf, 1992), 3–39.
40 Mark Slouka, *War of the Worlds: Cyberspace and the High-Tech Assault on Reality* (New York: Basic Books, 1995), 1.
41 The point is not to equate the Holocaust or the horrors of two world wars with Gamergate, but to highlight agreement between Tillich and Levinas that major human failures indicate the need for our intellectual and practical work to be rethought and reconfigured. Such agreement is illuminating when considering how the video game industry has changed since Gamergate.
42 Stephen Butler Murray and Aimee Upjohn Light, eds., *God and Popular Culture: A Behind-the-Scenes Look at the Entertainment Industry's Most Influential Figure*, 2 vols. (Santa Barbara, Calif.: Praeger, 2015). This two-volume set is a paradigmatic example of the nearly complete neglect of video games. Its thirty-six essays touch upon film, television, music, and other cultural forms. However, video games are never mentioned once.
43 S. Brent Plate, "Religion is Playing Games: Playing Video Gods, Playing to Play," *Religious Studies and Theology* 29, no. 2 (2010): 215–30.
44 Robert M. Geraci, *Virtually Sacred: Myth and Meaning in "World of Warcraft" and "Second Life"* (New York: Oxford University Press, 2014).
45 Scott R. Paeth, "The Moral Complexity of Video Games: Virtual Good and Evil," *Christian Century* 192, no. 6 (2012): 22–25.
46 Rachel Wagner, *Godwired: Religion, Ritual and Virtual Reality* (Abingdon, UK: Routledge, 2012).
47 Vít Šisler, Kerstin Radde-Antweiler, and Xenia Zeiler, eds., *Methods for Studying Video Games and Religion* (New York: Routledge, 2018); Heidi A. Campbell and

Gregory Price Grieve, *Playing with Religion in Video Games* (Bloomington: Indiana University Press, 2014).
48 Kevin Schut, *Of Games and God: A Christian Exploration of Video Games* (Grand Rapids: Brazos, 2013).
49 J. Sage Elwell, *Crisis of Transcendence: A Theology of Digital Art and Culture* (Lanham, Md.: Lexington Books, 2011).
50 Jaco J. Hamman, *Growing Down: Theology and Human Nature in the Virtual Age* (Waco, Tex.: Baylor University Press, 2017); George Pattison, *Thinking about God in an Age of Technology* (New York: Oxford University Press, 2005).
51 Frank G. Bosman, *Gaming and the Divine: A New Systematic Theology of Video Games* (London: Routledge, 2019).
52 Bosman focuses on five ways religion is present in video games: (1) Explicit content in game related to religion and references to real religious traditions that exist outside the game; (2) Reflection on existential themes associated with religion; (3) Ritual behavior typically associated with religion; (4) Story or environmental elements referencing religion or goals connected to religion; (5) Identifying the experience of playing a game as religious. The difference between such an approach that sets limits on what can be deemed religiously relevant in video games and the current approach informed by philosophical theology that rejects all doctrinal limits on theology should be clear.

1 Tillich and a Theology of Pop Culture

1 Paul Tillich, *The Irrelevance and Relevance of the Christian Message* (Cleveland: Pilgrim Press, 1996), 62.
2 Paul Tillich, *Theology of Culture*, ed. Robert C. Kimball (New York: Oxford University Press, 1959), 163–64.
3 Paul Tillich, *The Protestant Era* (Chicago: University of Chicago Press, 1948), 60–65, 266–67; *Systematic Theology*, vol. 3, *Life and the Spirit; History and the Kingdom of God* (Chicago: University of Chicago Press, 1963), 369–72.
4 Paul Tillich, *The Shaking of the Foundations* (New York: Charles Scribner's Sons, 1948), 9.
5 Paul Tillich, *My Search for Absolutes* (New York: Simon and Schuster, 1967), 23–54.
6 Paul Tillich, *Main Works/Hauptwerke*, vol. 4, *Writings in the Philosophy of Religion*, ed. Carl Heinz Ratschow (Berlin: Walter de Gruyter, 1987), 190 (my translation).
7 Paul Tillich, "Relation of Metaphysics and Theology," *The Review of Metaphysics* 10, no. 1 (1956): 58.
8 Paul Tillich, *The System of the Sciences according to Objects and Methods*, trans. Paul Wiebe (Lewisburg, Penn.: Bucknell University Press, 1981), 203.
9 Paul Tillich, "The Two Types of Philosophy of Religion," in *Main Works*, 4:292–94.
10 Paul Tillich, "The Philosophical Background of My Theology," in *Main Works*, vol. 1, *Philosophical Writings*, ed. Carl Heinz Ratschow (Berlin: Walter de Gruyter, 1989), 418.

11 Paul Tillich, *Systematic Theology*, vol. 2, *Existence and the Christ* (Chicago: University of Chicago Press, 1957), 10–13.
12 Tillich, *Theology of Culture*, 61.
13 James Luther Adams, *Paul Tillich's Philosophy of Culture, Science, and Religion* (Washington, D.C.: University Press of America, 1982), 187–98.
14 Tillich, *Theology of Culture*, 24–25.
15 Tillich, *Theology of Culture*, 23; and Paul Tillich, *Love, Power, and Justice: Ontological Analyses and Ethical Applications* (New York: Oxford University Press, 1954), 39.
16 Adams, *Paul Tillich's Philosophy of Culture, Science, and Religion*, 207.
17 Tillich, *Theology of Culture*, 61.
18 Adams, *Paul Tillich's Philosophy of Culture, Science, and Religion*, 207.
19 Raymond F. Bulman, *A Blueprint for Humanity: Paul Tillich's Theology of Culture* (Lewisburg, Penn.: Bucknell University Press, 1981), 73.
20 Paul Tillich, *Political Expectation* (New York: Harper & Row, 1971), 25.
21 Tillich, *Theology of Culture*, 27.
22 Adams, *Paul Tillich's Philosophy of Culture, Science, and Religion*, 33.
23 Paul Tillich, *The Interpretation of History*, trans. N. A. Resetzki and Elsa L. Talmey (New York: Charles Scribner's Sons, 1936), 8.
24 Paul Tillich, *Systematic Theology*, vol. 1, *Reason and Revelation; Being and God* (Chicago: University of Chicago Press, 1951), 85.
25 Tillich, *Theology of Culture*, 7 (emphasis original).
26 Tillich, *Political Expectation*, 63.
27 Bulman, *Blueprint for Humanity*, 95 (emphasis original).
28 Tillich, *Theology of Culture*, 61.
29 Tillich, "Philosophical Background of My Theology," 418.
30 Paul Tillich, *Biblical Religion and the Search for Ultimate Reality* (Chicago: University of Chicago Press, 1955), 22.
31 Tillich, *Systematic Theology*, 1:242.
32 Adams, *Paul Tillich's Philosophy of Culture, Science, and Religion*, 32.
33 Tillich, *Political Expectation*, 155.
34 Jaron Lanier makes a similar observation regarding problems that arise when social media boils people down to information on a profile aggregated as data to be sold to advertisers. "Emphasizing the crowd means deemphasizing individual humans in the design of society, and when you ask people to not be people, they revert to moblike behaviors. This leads not only to empowered trolls, but to a generally unfriendly and unconstructive online world." Jaron Lanier, *You Are Not a Gadget: A Manifesto* (New York: Vintage Books, 2011), 19.
35 Tillich, *Theology of Culture*, 50–51.
36 Tillich, *Protestant Era*, 57.
37 Tillich, *Biblical Religion and the Search for Ultimate Reality*, 4.
38 Tillich, *Biblical Religion and the Search for Ultimate Reality*, 22.
39 Exod 3.
40 Tillich, *Biblical Religion and the Search for Ultimate Reality*, 24.
41 Tillich, *Systematic Theology*, 1:59–66.

42 Adams, *Paul Tillich's Philosophy of Culture, Science, and Religion*; Bulman, *Blueprint for Humanity*.

43 Russell Re Manning, "Tillich's Theology of Art," in *The Cambridge Companion to Paul Tillich*, ed. Russell Re Manning (Cambridge: Cambridge University Press, 2009), 152–72.

44 In some ways, this argument is a more forceful follow-up to Jonathan Brant, *Paul Tillich and the Possibility of Revelation through Film* (New York: Oxford University Press, 2012). Brant is correct that Tillich's theology should be applied more systematically to popular culture than it has been so far. For an example of this need, consider Clive Marsh and Gaye Ortiz, introduction to *Explorations in Theology and Film: An Introduction*, ed. Clive Marsh and Gaye Ortiz (Malden, Mass.: Blackwell, 1997), 1–6. Marsh and Ortiz credit Tillich for displaying the importance of theological engagement with the arts, but deem his system as lacking the resources to engage the state of arts today. In what follows, their reservations will be shown to be misplaced. In *The Blackwell Guide to Theology and Popular Culture*, Tillich receives due treatment, but the bibliography does not even list video games as a "zone" of popular culture among categories such as film, television, the internet, and music to which theology can relate. Video games are entirely missing from the index. For more resources on Tillich and film, see Carl Skrade, "Theology and Films," in *Celluloid and Symbols*, ed. John C. Cooper and Carl Skrade (Philadelphia: Fortress, 1970); Michael Bird, "Film as Hierophany," in *Religion in Film*, ed. John R. May and Michael Bird (Knoxville: University of Tennessee Press, 1982); and David John Graham, "Uses of Film in Theology," in *Explorations in Theology and Film: Movies and Meaning*, ed. Clive Marsh and Gaye Ortiz (Oxford: Blackwell, 1997).

45 Tillich, *Religious Situation*, 57.

46 Paul Tillich, *The Boundaries of Our Being* (London: Collins, 1973), 331.

47 Re Manning, "Tillich's Theology of Art," 157–61; Victor Nuovo, "Tillich's Theory of Art and the Possibility of a Theology of Culture," in *Religion et Culture: Actes du Colloque International du Centenaire Paul Tillich, Université Laval, Québec 18–22 août 1986*, ed. Michel Despland, Jean-Claude Petit, and Jean Richard (Laval, Quebec: Presses de l'Université Laval/Éditions du Cerf, 1987), 394.

48 Paul Tillich, "On the Idea of a Theology of Culture," in *Visionary Science: A Translation of Tillich's "On the Idea of a Theology of Culture" with an Interpretative Essay*, trans. Victor Nuovo (Detroit: Wayne State University Press, 1987), 26 (emphasis original).

49 Jesper Juul, *Half-Real: Video Games between Real Rules and Fictional Worlds* (Cambridge, Mass.: MIT Press, 2005); Noah Wardrip-Fruin and Pat Harrigan, eds., *First Person: New Media as Story, Performance, and Game* (Cambridge, Mass.: MIT Press, 2004).

50 James Paul Gee and Elisabeth R. Hayes, *Women and Gaming: "The Sims" and 21st Century Learning* (New York: Palgrave Macmillan, 2010), 43.

51 Gee and Hayes, *Women and Gaming*, 50.

52 Paul Tillich, *My Travel Diary: 1936: Between Two Worlds*, ed. Jerald C. Brauer, trans. Maria Pelikan (New York: Harper & Row, 1970), 104.

53 Paul Tillich, *On Art and Architecture*, ed. John Dillenberger and Joan Dillenberger, trans. Robert P. Scharlemann (New York: Crossroad, 1987), 95.
54 Tillich, *Religious Situation*, 86.
55 Paul Tillich, *Gesammelte Werke*, vol. 2, *Christentum und Soziale Gestaltung: Frühe Schriften zum Religiöse Sozialismus*, ed. Renate Albrecht (Stuttgart: Evangelisches Verlagswerk, 1962), 29.
56 Tillich, *Religious Situation*, 54–55.
57 Tillich, *Religious Situation*, 55.
58 Kelton Cobb, "Reconsidering the Status of Popular Culture in Tillich's Theology of Culture," *Journal of the American Academy of Religion* 63, no. 1 (1995): 78.
59 Re Manning, "Tillich's Theology of Art," 167–68.
60 Tillich, "On the Idea of a Theology of Culture," 26.
61 Re Manning, "Tillich's Theology of Art," 168.
62 Tillich, *Religious Situation*, 41–53.
63 Tillich, *Systematic Theology*, 3:67.
64 Tillich, *Theology of Culture*, 43.
65 Francis Fukuyama, *Our Posthuman Future: Consequences of the Biotechnology Revolution* (New York: Farrar, Straus and Giroux, 2002); N. Katherine Hayles, *How We Became Posthuman: Virtual Bodies in Cybernetics, Literature, and Informatics* (Chicago: Chicago University Press, 1999); Jeanine Thweatt-Bates, *Cyborg Selves: A Theological Anthropology of the Posthuman* (Burlington, Vt.: Ashgate, 2012).
66 Pattison, *Thinking about God in an Age of Technology*, 45.
67 Mirror neurons respond primarily to the expressions on someone's face as they react to something that harmed them or gave them pleasure. While absent on the internet, apart from video-based content, it is conceivable that advances in graphical technology and animation techniques have made animated movies and some video games capable of triggering mirror neurons.
68 Paul Tillich, *The New Being* (New York: Charles Scribner's Sons, 1955), 20.
69 James Luther Adams, foreword to Bulman, *Blueprint for Humanity*, 19.
70 Tillich, *Religious Situation*, 176.
71 Tillich, *Political Expectation*, 8.
72 Tillich, *Political Expectation*, 130 (emphasis original).
73 Tillich, *My Search for Absolutes*, 38.
74 Tillich, *My Search for Absolutes*, 31, 39, 50.
75 Tillich, *Love, Power, and Justice*, 39.
76 Tillich, *My Search for Absolutes*, 46.
77 Tillich, *Political Expectation*, 61.

2 Turning to the Other in Video Games

1 Jacques Derrida, *The Work of Mourning*, ed. Pascale-Anne Brault and Michael Naas (Chicago: University of Chicago Press, 2001), 202. Derrida is recalling Levinas responding to him in a conversation the two had in Paris.

2   As already noted, it is conventional for Levinas scholars to capitalize "other" when Levinas is referring to the human other and use lowercase when the word refers to nonhuman otherness. Besides problems with this method that have already been noted, this convention glosses over places where, in the French, Levinas writes about God as the "Other" encountered. For more on this debate, see Adriaan T. Peperzak, preface to *Emmanuel Levinas: Basic Philosophical Writings*, ed. Adriaan T. Peperzak, Simon Critchley, and Robert Bernasconi (Bloomington: Indiana University Press, 1996), xiv–xv. For the sake of simplicity and clarity, "other" will not be capitalized here, unless quoting an author who chose that strategy.

3   Jeffrey L. Kosky, *Levinas and the Philosophy of Religion* (Bloomington: Indiana University Press, 2001), vi.

4   Emmanuel Levinas, "Signature," in *Difficult Freedom: Essays on Judaism*, trans. Seán Hand (Baltimore: Johns Hopkins University Press, 1990), 291–95.

5   Michael L. Morgan, *Discovering Levinas* (Cambridge: Cambridge University Press, 2007), 9.

6   Thomas Merton, *The Seven Storey Mountain* (San Diego: Harcourt Brace, 1999).

7   "Thomas Merton," PBS Religion and Ethics Newsweekly, June 4, 2009, video, 10:54, https://www.pbs.org/video/religion-and-ethics-newsweekly-thomas-merton/.

8   While Levinas rarely mentions the Holocaust in his writing, numerous commentators have noted it is always lurking in the background informing his thought. In particular, see Robert Plant, "Levinas, Philosophy, and Biography," and Robert Eaglestone, "Levinas and the Holocaust," in *The Oxford Handbook of Levinas*, ed. Michael L. Morgan (New York: Oxford University Press, 2019). Plant and Eaglestone contend that understanding Levinas as reacting to the tragedy of the Holocaust is important to understanding his development of an ethically responsible philosophy. Biography for Levinas, Tillich, and those impacted by Gamergate is significant and cannot be brushed aside to look at the quality of an ethical argument in abstract.

9   Emmanuel Levinas, *Otherwise Than Being or Beyond Essence* (Boston: Martinus Nijhoff, 1981), vii.

10 Michael Purcell, *Levinas and Theology* (Cambridge: Cambridge University Press, 2006), 4.

11 Morgan, *Discovering Levinas*, 13.

12 Morgan, *Discovering Levinas*, 367–68.

13 Emmanuel Levinas, "Is Ontology Fundamental?" in *Emmanuel Levinas: Basic Philosophical Writings*, ed. Adriaan T. Peperzak, Simon Critchley, and Robert Bernasconi (Bloomington: Indiana University Press, 1996), 1–10.

14 Levinas, "Is Ontology Fundamental?" 4.

15 Levinas, *Otherwise Than Being*, 47.

16 Levinas, *Otherwise Than Being*, 47.

17 Levinas, *Otherwise Than Being*, 55.

18 Kosky, *Levinas and the Philosophy of Religion*, 87.

19 Kosky, *Levinas and the Philosophy of Religion*, 88.

20 Levinas, *Otherwise Than Being*, 139.

21 Kosky, *Levinas and the Philosophy of Religion*, 89.

22 Purcell, *Levinas and Theology*, 82.
23 Purcell, *Levinas and Theology*, 88.
24 William James, *Sciousness*, ed. Jonathan Bricklin (Guilford, Conn.: Eirini Press, 2006).
25 Purcell, *Levinas and Theology*, 94.
26 Emmanuel Levinas, *Time and the Other*, trans. Richard A. Cohen (Pittsburgh: Duquesne University Press, 1987), 67.
27 Levinas, *Otherwise Than Being*, 123.
28 Morgan, *Discovering Levinas*, 89.
29 Emmanuel Levinas, "Philosophy and the Idea of Infinity," in *Collected Philosophical Papers*, trans. Alphonso Lingis (Pittsburgh: Duquesne University Press, 1998), 47–48.
30 Levinas, *Time and the Other*, 83.
31 Morgan, *Discovering Levinas*, 68 (emphasis original).
32 Morgan, *Discovering Levinas*, 79.
33 Emmanuel Levinas, *Totality and Infinity: An Essay on Exteriority* (Pittsburgh: Duquesne University Press, 1969), 215.
34 Levinas, *Otherwise Than Being*, 87, 192–95.
35 Roger Burggraeve, "'Fraternity, Equality, Freedom': On the Soul and the Extent of Our Responsibility," in *Responsibility, God and Society: Theological Ethics in Dialogue*, ed. Johan de Tavernier, Joseph Selling, Johan Verstraeten, and Paul Schotsmans (Leuven: Uitgeverij Peeters, 2008), 5.
36 Levinas, *Otherwise Than Being*, 82–87.
37 Levinas, *Otherwise Than Being*, 138.
38 Burggraeve, "Fraternity, Equality, Freedom," 13.
39 Vasily Grossman, *Life and Fate*, trans. Robert Chandler (London: Harvill Press, 1995), 805–6.
40 Tillich, *Love, Power, and Justice*, 42.
41 Tillich, *Love, Power, and Justice*, 48.
42 Tillich, *Love, Power, and Justice*, 49.
43 Tillich, *Love, Power, and Justice*, 49–50.
44 Emmanuel Levinas, *Entre Nous: Thinking-of-the-Other*, trans. Michael B. Smith and Barbara Harshav (New York: Columbia University Press, 1998), 105.
45 Emmanuel Levinas, "Ethics and Politics," in *The Levinas Reader*, ed. Seán Hand (Oxford: Basil Blackwell, 1989), 291–92.
46 Emmanuel Levinas, *Nine Talmudic Readings*, trans. Annette Aronowicz (Bloomington: Indiana University Press, 1990), 25 (emphasis original).
47 Morgan, *Discovering Levinas*, 36.
48 Levinas, "A Man-God?" in *Entre Nous*, 60.
49 Levinas describes God as a "third" that emerges in encounters between the face of the other and the one having to respond to that other: "I and you and the Third who is in our midst. And only as a Third does He reveal Himself." Levinas, *Levinas Reader*, 247.
50 Levinas, *Collected Philosophical Papers*, 165–66 (emphasis original).

51. Kosky, *Levinas and the Philosophy of Religion*, xix.
52. Morgan, *Discovering Levinas*, 174–207.
53. Kosky, *Levinas and the Philosophy of Religion*, 170.
54. Emmanuel Levinas, *Beyond the Verse: Talmudic Readings and Lectures* (Bloomington: Indiana University Press, 1994), 126–27.
55. Kosky, *Levinas and the Philosophy of Religion*, 175.
56. Purcell, *Levinas and Theology*, 99.
57. Levinas, *Totality and Infinity*, 151.
58. Levinas, *Collected Philosophical Papers*, 21.
59. Michael L. Morgan, *The Cambridge Introduction to Emmanuel Levinas* (Cambridge: Cambridge University Press, 2011), 143 (emphasis original).
60. Levinas, *Totality and Infinity*, 78–79.
61. Levinas plainly states that his view is "diametrically opposed to the traditional idea of God" in *God, Death, and Time*, trans. Bettina Bergo (Stanford, Calif.: Stanford University Press, 2000), 207.
62. Morgan, *Discovering Levinas*, 181.
63. For a detailed elaboration on the meaning of height in relation to the other and God, see Richard Cohen, *Elevations: The Height of the Good in Rosenzweig and Levinas* (Chicago: University of Chicago Press, 1994).
64. Levinas, *Otherwise Than Being*, 93–94.
65. Morgan, *Discovering Levinas*, 193.
66. The following is how Morgan argues such a point on behalf of Levinas.

    > [A] key term in Levinas's account, perhaps *the* key term, is "*illeity.*" There is a tendency for commentators to treat it as any other name or designation and to look for its referent. But this is a mistake; the term does not denote. It does signify something by helping us to appreciate that the face does not supplicate and command in virtue of its own features, shape, skin color, expression, and so forth; the face calls me into question insofar as it is a trace of a distant thing that is no thing, of an absolute absence. That absence, as present in the face, so to speak, is *illeity*. It is not a thing or entity or object nor literally a manifestation of one. It is not a you or Thou. In a sense, it *is not*. But without *illeity*, the face cannot mean what it does to me. It is what accounts for the particularity and transcendence of the face and for the infinity of my responsibility, for *illeity* is why the face carries weight with me and demands of me—why it matters to me.

    Morgan, *Discovering Levinas*, 203.
67. Morgan, *Discovering Levinas*, 180 (emphasis original).
68. Levinas, *Difficult Freedom*, 17.
69. Emmanuel Levinas, *Of God Who Comes to Mind* (Stanford, Calif.: Stanford University Press, 1998), 69.
70. As Purcell summarizes this point, "God withdraws in order in order to create a space wherein the individual can achieve the stature of humanity which is 'responsibility for-the-other.'" Purcell, *Levinas and Theology*, 71.

71 Levinas, *Totality and Infinity*, 58–59.
72 David J. Gunkel, *Thinking Otherwise: Philosophy, Communication, Technology* (West Lafayette, Ind.: Purdue University Press, 2007).
73 Morgan, *Discovering Levinas*, 47–48.
74 Kosky, *Levinas and the Philosophy of Religion*, 189.
75 Marshall McLuhan, *Understanding Media: The Extensions of Man* (Cambridge, Mass.: MIT Press, 1994), 18.
76 Levinas, *Totality and Infinity*, 181–82.
77 Kosky, *Levinas and the Philosophy of Religion*, 21.
78 Joeri Schrijvers, *Ontotheological Turnings? The Decentering of the Modern Subject in Recent French Phenomenology* (Albany: SUNY Press, 2011), 167–68.
79 Kosky, *Levinas and the Philosophy of Religion*, 22.

3 Boss Fight: Philosophical Theology and Science

1 Paul J. Zak, *The Moral Molecule: The Source of Love and Prosperity* (New York: Dutton, 2012), 97.
2 Mark Lewis Taylor notes that the suspicion of ontology in modern philosophy, especially in relation to ethics, is unnecessary. While modern theology and ethics tend to emphasize the particular, and Tillich wrote about universal essences, works like *The Socialist Decision* contain critiques of abstract ontology. Tillich's promotion of democratic socialism and proclamation of *kairos* moments amounted to the affirmation that distinct features of the present must break apart abstract, unchanging metaphysical theories. Even though God is technically universally present, individual experiences and choices decide how that presence is manifest, without which God's universality means practically nothing. Rather than a case of ontology hiding and needing disruption by the other, Tillich's ontology actually helps him affirm the other. See Tillich, *Love, Power, and Justice*, 87–88 and *The Socialist Decision*, trans. Franklin Sherman (New York: Harper & Row, 1977), 155–66; Mark Lewis Taylor, "Tillich's Ethics: Between Politics and Ontology," in *The Cambridge Companion to Paul Tillich*, ed. Russell Re Manning (Cambridge: Cambridge University Press, 2009), 189–207.
3 Calvin O. Schrag, "The Problem of Being and the Question about God," *International Journal for Philosophy of Religion* 45, no. 1 (1999): 73.
4 James J. DiCenso has argued Tillich turns infinity, the ground-of-being, into that which allows people to open themselves up beyond a potentially damaging self-enclosure. Through this lens DiCenso links Tillich to Levinas' argument that relating to the infinite in human relations amounts to relating to God. "As with Tillich, the Levinasian sense of the divine becomes manifest in existential situations and relations. . . . For both thinkers, the term 'God' designates a quality inherent in reality itself, especially the sphere of human relations." In this context, DiCenso approvingly casts Levinas as crafting a project similar to Tillich's when Levinas states that God "comes to me in the concreteness of my relation to the other man, in the sociality which is my responsibility for the neighbor." See James J. DiCenso, "Anxiety, Risk and

Transformation: Re-Visiting Tillich with Lacan," in *Secular Theology: American Radical Theological Thought*, ed. Clayton Crockett (London: Routledge, 2001), 52–53.

5   Nathan Eric Dickman, "Anxiety and the Face of the Other: Tillich and Levinas on the Origin of Questioning," *Sophia* 48, no. 3 (2009): 267–79.
6   Dickman, "Anxiety and the Face of the Other," 268.
7   Dickman, "Anxiety and the Face of the Other," 268, n.3.
8   Tillich, *Systematic Theology*, 1:163.
9   Tillich, *Systematic Theology*, 1:164.
10 In *Biblical Religion and the Search for Ultimate Reality*, Tillich regularly comments that subject and object are not really separated but always occur at once in the same place.
11 Dickman, "Anxiety and the Face of the Other," 273.
12 Robert P. Scharlemann, *Reflection and Doubt in the Thought of Paul Tillich* (New Haven, Conn.: Yale University Press, 1969), 201.
13 Robert Neville, *Metaphysics of Goodness: Harmony and Form, Beauty and Art, Obligation and Personhood, Flourishing and Civilization* (Albany: SUNY Press, 2019), xv.
14 Neville, *Metaphysics of Goodness*, 3.
15 Robert Smid has delivered a similar criticism of Neville's argument about goodness, though developed from within Neville's system using Neville's own argument against his conclusion that *all things* are good. Part of what it means to have form, on Neville's account, is to be determinate with essential and conditional features. Conditional features are how anything relates to everything else, and essential features make each thing unique rather than reducible to those relations. Smid locates the following problem with arguing everything is good within such a framework. When something has determinate form, it is a harmony of essential and conditional features. When it becomes a component in something else through the interrelation of their conditional features, those conditional features, which are part of the determinate form of anything, should be deemed bad or evil when they are destructive of others to which they relate. Thus, rather than all things simply being good due to having determinate form, it seems the correct conclusion to draw is that some things are evil because damaging conditional relations are part of their determinate form. See Robert Smid, "The Metaphysics of Relative Goodness: Or, Recovery of the Axiological Measure," *The Pluralist* 15, no. 3 (2020): 27–37.
16 Tillich, *My Search for Absolutes*, 73.
17 Tillich, *My Search for Absolutes*, 106–7.
18 Merold Westphal, "Thinking about God and God-Talk with Levinas," in *The Exorbitant: Emmanuel Levinas Between Jews and Christians*, ed. Kevin Hart and Michael A. Signer (New York: Fordham University Press, 2010), 224.
19 Kevin Hart has lent some credence to my claim that Levinas and Tillich are not so incompatible as it might seem with his argument that negative or apophatic forms of theology are not unlike deconstructive movements in philosophy. See Kevin Hart, *The Trespass of the Sign: Deconstruction, Theology, and Philosophy* (New York: Fordham University Press, 2000), 43.

20 For an example of the typical assumption that Levinas is incompatible with any ontological theological project, because ontology necessarily excludes, see Purcell, *Levinas and Theology*, 126.

21 For a nuanced discussion as to why shared sensibilities about the sort of work in which philosophical theologians should be engaged matters, at least as much as very specific disagreements and incompatibilities, see Wesley Wildman, *Religious Philosophy as Multidisciplinary Comparative Inquiry: Envisioning a Future for the Philosophy of Religion* (Albany: SUNY Press, 2010), 72–83.

22 Wildman, *Religious Philosophy*, 81.

23 Wildman, *Religious Philosophy*, 83.

24 Tillich, *Protestant Era*, 57.

25 Levinas scholars and postmodern readers may be suspicious of this turn to science, if they do not immediately reject it as irrelevant. It is true that identifying unreflective yet accepted ideas is key to making corrections and progress in inquiry. Popular glosses on scientific achievements that reach mass markets might be guilty of such errors. However, rather than amounting to a rejection of systematic thinking, antifoundational and fallible forms of philosophical theology as defended in the preface align nicely with critical theory and the phenomenological suspicion of the scientific attitude as naive such as was carried on by Levinas. Rejecting nominalism and positivism is why philosophical theology is interested in all relevant hypotheses that can shed light on subject matter, including scientific ones. No discipline has a monopoly, not even science, but all are to be valued for their contributions. Furthermore, there are still standards of knowledge and of plausible truth claims, even if foundationalism is bunk. Pragmatist philosophers enthusiastically embrace the genuine results of science while noting its social and political entanglement. Science is an important narrative that is ignored to the detriment of philosophy and theology, but it is not the only narrative, and certainly not the master narrative. However, the alternative of cutting science out of any explanatory picture creates greater problems than not criticizing science in the first place. Reasons as to why this is the case could not be put better than they have been by Wildman: "Cutting biology out of the explanatory picture makes unintelligible both the structurally universal features of human cultures and the universality of ideological processes and interestedness in interpretation. This in turn leads to overestimating the degree of arbitrariness and irrationality in ideologically loaded social and interpersonal transactions, underestimating the degree to which power transactions penetrate every kind and level of discourse, and missing relevant strategies for management—strategies that become easier to identify in the presence of a biological framework of interpretation." Wildman, *Religious Philosophy as Multidisciplinary Comparative Inquiry*, 69. For his extended remarks on why it is dangerous and intellectually dishonest to ignore science, see pages 63–72 in that same book.

26 Beyond reasons already outlined as to why phenomenological and postmodern thinkers should not reject science, the scientific data regarding the effects of oxytocin covered in the next section overwhelmingly supports Levinas. While the data necessitates a minor adjustment to his philosophy, the science aids in understanding

how tendencies to be hostile toward the other can be criticized and transformed into instances of responsibility. Suspicion of science is the last thing someone interested in Levinas and otherness should affirm.

27 Paul J. Zak, "The Neurobiology of Trust," *Scientific American* 298, no. 6 (2008): 88–92, 95; Paul J. Zak, Robert Kurzban, and William T. Matzner, "Oxytocin Is Associated with Human Trustworthiness," *Hormones and Behavior* 48, no. 5 (2005): 522–27.

28 Paul J. Zak, Karla Borja, William Matzner, and Robert Kurzban, "The Neuroeconomics of Distrust: Sex Differences in Behavior and Physiology," *American Economic Review Papers and Proceedings* 95, no. 2 (2005): 360–63.

29 Zak, *Moral Molecule*, 80–82; Paul J. Zak et al., "Testosterone Administration Decreases Generosity in the Ultimatum Game," *PLoS ONE* 4, no. 12 (2009): 1–7; Terence C. Burnham, "High-Testosterone Men Reject Low Ultimatum Game Offers," *Proceedings of the Royal Society: Biological Sciences* 274, no. 1623 (2007): 2327–30.

30 Participants can also be infused with oxytocin through the nose, and those participants demonstrate considerably more generosity than those given a placebo. In exit interviews they also report being perfectly content leaving the lab with less money, because they are leaving with more than when they entered and they were also able to help another person leave with more money.

31 Morgan, *Cambridge Introduction to Emmanuel Levinas*, 10.

32 Levinas, *Otherwise Than Being*, 11.

33 Levinas, *Nine Talmudic Readings*, 171.

34 Burggraeve, "Fraternity, Equality, Freedom," 19–20.

35 Andrew Shepherd has leveled a similar critique against Levinas, noting that discernment is a crucial component of making sure others are receiving appropriate care. When others are in conflict with one another, a blanket ethical principle of infinite responsibility provides no basis for discerning who is doing harm, stopping them, and attending to those in need. See Andrew Shepherd, *The Gift of the Other: Levinas, Derrida, and a Theology of Hospitality* (Cambridge: James Clarke, 2014), 40–41. Donald L. Turner and Ford J. Turrell have raised a similar complaint, noting that an effective response to someone can frequently necessitate not attending to someone else. See Donald L. Turner and Ford J. Turrell, "Emmanuel Levinas's Non-existent God," in *Models of God and Alternative Ultimate Realities*, ed. Jeanine Diller and Asa Kasher (Dordrecht, The Netherlands: Springer, 2013), 732.

36 Zak describes such situations as follows: "High stress blocks oxytocin release—in most cases, oxytocin is doubly inappropriate for someone who's being pushed to the edge of survival himself. Oxytocin not only drives empathic concern (compassion)—which might get in the way of fighting for your life—but also damps down the amygdala, the brain structure where anxiety is registered and regulated." Zak, *Moral Molecule*, 64–65.

37 Zak, *Moral Molecule*, 106.

38 Zak, *Moral Molecule*, 192–93.

39 Michael Kasumovic and Keff Kuznekoff, "Study: Low Status Men More Likely to Bully Women Online," *PsyPost*, July 15, 2015, https://www.psypost.org/2015/07/study-low-status-men-who-bad-video-games-likely-bully-women-online-35901.

40 The way Zak describes this phenomenon in relation to US politics is very similar to what happened in Gamergate. "When the humiliation of low social status combines with real economic insecurity, the sense of being squeezed can boil into a rush of oxytocin-impairing DHT. This is probably one of the reasons our political discourse is so polarized these days. Anger and lack of empathy create a negative loop in which it's all too easy to simply lash out and blame 'the other.'" Zak, *Moral Molecule*, 109.

41 This critique is perfectly in line with Levinas' *way* of thinking even if it is not explicitly what he argued. As Benjamin Hutchens notes in his introductory guide to the philosopher, "Levinas's message actually trumpets stridently 'Challenge me, criticize me, above all RESPOND TO ME'. Yet Levinasians have failed to answer this challenge; they are warmed by the seductive whisper, not perturbed by the clarion's call. In this respect, Levinasians satisfied with repetition and exegetical commentary, are the least Levinasian." See Benjamin C. Hutchens, *Levinas: A Guide for the Perplexed* (London: Continuum, 2004), 7.

42 Hutchens, *Levinas*, 147–49; G. J. H. Dumont et al., "Increased Oxytocin Concentrations and Prosocial Feelings in Humans after Ecstasy (3,4-methylenedioxymethamphetamine) Administration," *Social Neuroscience* 4, no. 4 (2009): 359–66.

43 Zak, *Moral Molecule*, 15.

44 Adam L. Penenberg, "Digital Oxytocin: How Trust Keeps Facebook, Twitter Humming," *Fast Company*, July 18, 2011, https://www.fastcompany.com/1767125/digital-oxytocin-how-trust-keeps-facebook-twitter-humming.

45 Zak, *Moral Molecule*, 174.

46 Zak performed the same "soft" social media experiment with a group of Korean reporters and, again, oxytocin levels increased for everyone. *Moral Molecule*, 174–75.

47 Eliza Thompson, "3 Couples Talk About How World of Warcraft Brought Them Together," *Cosmopolitan*, June 9, 2016, https://www.cosmopolitan.com/entertainment/movies/a59553/world-of-warcraft-wedding-stories/.

48 Dacher Keltner, *Born to Be Good: The Science of a Meaningful Life* (New York: Norton, 2009).

49 Mark Wm. Dubin, *How the Brain Works* (Williston, Vt.: Blackwell Science, 2002), 57–70.

50 The caveat that oxytocin and mirror neurons are only part of a holistic understanding of such behavior must be emphasized. Humans are more than just chemicals, but they are also nothing without them. Some bullies might engage in bad behavior because they were abused by a parent or adult figure, but those abusive figures might have had a lack of oxytocin themselves. Human behavior cannot be reduced to electrical impulses and chemical levels, but biology is nonetheless implicated in all explanations of human behavior from the social sciences and humanities.

51 Matthew Nelson Grizzard, "Cooperative Video Game Play and Generosity: Oxytocin Production as a Causal Mechanism Regarding Prosocial Behavior Resulting from Cooperative Video Game Play" (PhD diss., Michigan State University, 2013).

52 Allison Eden, Matthew Grizzard, and Robert J. Lewis, "Moral Psychology and Media Theory: Historical and Emerging Viewpoints," in *Media and the Moral Mind*, ed. Ron Tamborini (New York: Routledge, 2013), 33–82.
53 Carsten K. W. de Dreu et al., "The Neuropeptide Oxytocin Regulates Parochial Altruism in Intergroup Conflict among Humans," *Science* 328, no. 5984 (2010): 1408–11.
54 Nicholas Wade, "Depth of the Kindness Hormone Appears to Know Some Bounds," *New York Times*, January 10, 2011, https://www.nytimes.com/2011/01/11/science/11hormone.html?_r=3&hpw.
55 The inclusion of only thirty-two references, many of which were decades old at the time of publication, also indicates De Dreu's group did not deeply engage cutting-edge evidence in favor of oxytocin's role in promoting prosocial behavior.
56 Sari M. van Anders, James L. Goodson, and Marcy A. Kingsbury, "Beyond 'Oxytocin = Good': Neural Complexities and the Flipside of Social Bonds," *Archives of Sexual Behavior* 42, no. 7 (2013): 1115–18; Xiaole Ma et al., "Oxytocin Increases Liking for a Country's People and National Flag but Not for Other Cultural Symbols or Consumer Products," *Frontiers in Behavioral Neuroscience* 8 (2014): article 266.
57 Burggraeve, "Fraternity, Equality, Freedom," 12.
58 Grizzard, "Cooperative Video Game Play and Generosity."
59 Elizabeth T. Terris et al., "Endogenous Oxytocin Release Eliminates In-group Bias in Monetary Transfers with Perspective-taking," *Frontiers in Behavioral Neuroscience* 12 (2018): article 35.
60 Important evidence in favor of this virtuous cycle as a real possibility would be if oxytocin also increased trust in a zero-sum game, not only in scenarios like trust games in which benefits are shared by all. Preliminary evidence indicates this happens. In ultimatum games the first participant receives a set amount of money, like $10, and can only keep it if they give some of that money to a second participant. The second participant must also agree to the offer from the first or nobody gets any money at all. Experiments in which these win-win parameters must be met and participants were infused with oxytocin have resulted in significant increases in generosity by all participants. Zak, *Moral Molecule*, 46; Paul J. Zak, Angela A. Stanton, and Sheila Ahmadi, "Oxytocin Increases Generosity in Humans," *PLoS ONE* 2, no. 11 (2007): e1128.
61 Oxytocin reduces psychological stress and therefore disinhibits and allows us to take somewhat riskier actions, like trusting a stranger. When oxytocin levels are increased, those chemical levels in turn increase serotonin (lowers anxiety and improves mood) and dopamine (motivation and learning reinforcement) levels. See Lauren J. Pitkow et al., "Facilitation of Affiliation and Pair-Bond Formation by Vasopressin Receptor Gene Transfer into the Ventral Forebrain of a Monogamous Vole," *Journal of Neuroscience* 21, no. 18 (2001): 7392–96; Heather E. Ross et al., "Variation in Oxytocin Receptor Density in the Nucleus Accumbens Has Differential Effects on Affiliative Behaviors in Monogamous and Polygamous Voles," *Journal of Neuroscience* 29, no. 5 (2009): 1312–18; Zoe R. Donaldson and Larry J. Young, "Oxytocin, Vasopressin, and the Neurogenetics of Sociality," *Science* 322, no. 5903 (2008): 900–904; Paul

Zak, "The Physiology of Moral Sentiments," *Journal of Economic Behavior & Organization* 77 (2011): 53–65.

62 Jorge A. Barraza and Paul J. Zak, "Empathy towards Strangers Triggers Oxytocin Release and Subsequent Generosity," *Annals of the New York Academy of Sciences* 1167, no. 1 (2009): 182–89.

63 Zak also had participants play the ultimatum game after watching the emotional video, and those people had the highest increase in oxytocin and gave the most generous offers in that game. These studies are backed up further by what we know about mirror neurons. For more on mirror neurons in relation to this issue, see G. Buccino et al., "Action Observation Activates Premotor and Parietal Areas in a Somatotropic Manner: An fMRI Study," *European Journal of Neuroscience* 13, no. 2 (2001): 400–404; Giacomo Rizzolatti and Luigi Cattaneo, "The Mirror-Neuron System," *Annual Review of Neuroscience* 27 (2004): 169–92.

64 Zak, *Moral Molecule*, 61 (emphasis original).

4 Nontraditional Video Games and LGBTQ+ Others

1 Patricia Hernandez, "*Gone Home*: The Kotaku Review," Kotaku, August 15, 2013, https://kotaku.com/gone-home-the-kotaku-review-1118218265.

2 Nicole Clark, "A Brief History of the 'Walking Simulator,' Gaming's Most Detested Genre," Salon, November 11, 2017, https://www.salon.com/2017/11/11/a-brief-history-of-the-walking-simulator-gamings-most-detested-genre/.

3 The following is only a fraction of games that could be put on such a list: *Firewatch* by Campo Santo; *Dear Esther* by The Chinese Room; *What Remains of Edith Finch* by Giant Sparrow; *ABZÛ* by Giant Squid; *The Stanley Parable* by Davey Wreden.

4 Patricia Hernandez, "Indie Developer Pulls out of PAX, Citing Penny Arcade Controversies," Kotaku, June 21, 2013, https://kotaku.com/indie-developer-pulls-out-of-pax-citing-penny-arcade-c-532336421.

5 Leigh Alexander, "The Story behind Gone Home, and What Makes a 'Great Game,'" Gamasutra, October 24, 2013, https://www.gamasutra.com/view/news/203119/The_story_behind_Gone_Home_and_what_makes_a_great_game.php.

6 Leigh Alexander, "Road to the IGF: The Fullbright Company's Gone Home," Gamasutra, March 20, 2013, https://www.gamasutra.com/view/news/188908/Road_to_the_IGF_The_Fullbright_Companys_Gone_Home.php; Christopher Grant, "Polygon's 2013 Game of the Year: Gone Home," Polygon, January 15, 2014, https://www.polygon.com/2014/1/15/5311568/game-of-the-year-2013-gone-home; David Hinkle, "Gone Home, The Last of Us, Tearaway Top GDC Award Nominations," Engadget, January 9, 2014, https://www.engadget.com/2014-01-09-gone-home-the-last-of-us-tearaway-top-gdc-award-nominations.html; Ludwig Kietzman, "Papers, Please and The Last of Us Honored at GDC Awards Show," Engadget, March 20, 2014, https://www.engadget.com/2014-03-20-papers-please-and-the-last-of-us-honored-at-gdc-awards-show.html.

7 Some of those same tapes are probably still in my parents' house from when I did the same thing.

8   Mike Mahardy, "The Looking Glass Philosophy behind Gone Home," Polygon, April 6, 2015, https://www.polygon.com/features/2015/4/6/8315901/looking-glass-gone-home.
9   Sarkeesian, "Damsel in Distress."
10 Tom Bissell, *Extra Lives: Why Video Games Matter* (New York: Vintage Books, 2011), 126.
11 "About Us," Games for Change, accessed July 2, 2020, http://www.gamesforchange.org/who-we-are/about-us/.
12 Esther Dyson, *Release 2.0: A Design for Living in the Digital Age* (London: Viking Press, 1997); Gordon Graham, *The Internet: A Philosophical Inquiry* (New York: Routledge, 1999); Sherry Turkle, *Life on the Screen: Identity in the Age of the Internet* (New York: Simon & Schuster, 1995).
13 Sherry Turkle, *Alone Together: Why We Expect More from Technology and Less from Each Other* (New York: Basic Books, 2011), 158.
14 Gee and Hayes, *Women and Gaming*, 155.
15 Gee and Hayes, *Women and Gaming*, 159.
16 Mark Dooley, "Nihilism or Salvation? The Challenges of Global Technology for the Humanities," in *Technology and Transcendence*, ed. Michael Breen, Eamonn Conway, and Barry McMillan (Dublin: Columba Press, 2003), 104.
17 Dooley, "Nihilism or Salvation?" 108.
18 For a representative sampling, see Langdon Gilkey, *Maker of Heaven and Earth: The Christian Doctrine of Creation in the Light of Modern Knowledge* (Garden City: Doubleday, 1959); John Polkinghorne, *Science and Providence: God's Interaction with the World* (Boston: Shambhala, 1989); Arthur Peacocke, *God and the New Biology* (London: Dent, 1986); Ian G. Barbour, *Issues in Science and Religion* (Englewood Cliffs, N.J.: Prentice-Hall, 1966).
19 2019 featured a session on the relationship between science-fiction technology and how civic imagination constructs a better future. A 2018 session focused on arguments as to why scientists and scholars of religion should stop debating one another and start better educating the public on the importance of accepting scientific results. A 2017 panel focused on how the religion and science dialogue itself is a sort of technology that is being wielded by politicians to manipulate the public, and another session that same year featured papers on how religion and technology can work together to help vulnerable populations. Further examples are readily available for those who wish to peruse the archives on the AAR website. American Academy of Religion, "Past and Future Annual Meetings," https://www.aarweb.org/AARMBR/Events-and-Networking-/Annual-Meeting-/Past-and-Future-Annual-Meetings.aspx.
20 Jacob Shatzer, *Transhumanism and the Image of God: Today's Technology and the Future of Christian Discipleship* (Downers Grove, Ill.: InterVarsity Press Academic, 2019).
21 Wesley Wildman, "From Grand Dreaming to Problem Solving," *Zygon* 42, no. 2 (2007): 273–76.
22 Deadnaming, the use of a transgender person's given name rather than their chosen name, is not merely a matter of representation. The use of correct names and

pronouns has been linked to lower rates of depression and suicide risk among LGBTQ+ individuals. See Stephen T. Russell, Amanda M. Pollitt, Gu Li, and Arnold H. Grossman, "Chosen Name Use Is Linked to Reduced Depressive Symptoms, Suicidal Ideation, and Suicidal Behavior among Transgender Youth," *Journal of Adolescent Health* 63, no. 4 (2018): 503–5.

23 Gita Jackson, "The Video Games That Made People Question Their Beliefs," Kotaku, July 2, 2019, https://kotaku.com/the-video-games-that-made-people-question-their-beliefs-1836045401.
24 Kosky, *Levinas and the Philosophy of Religion*, 25–46.
25 Tillich, *Theology of Culture*, 34–35.

5 Face to Face with Immigrant Others

1 Javy Gwaltney, "Glory to Arstotzka: Papers, Please and an Interview with Its Creator," CultureMass, April 14, 2013, https://web.archive.org/web/20140111232206/http://culturemass.com/2013/04/14/papers-please-and-an-interview-with-its-creator/; Edge Staff, "The Making of *Papers, Please*," Edge, January 20, 2014, https://web.archive.org/web/20140122052214/http://www.edge-online.com/features/the-making-of-papers-please/.
2 Andrew Webster, "Immigration as a Game: 'Papers, Please' Makes You the Border Guard," The Verge, May 14, 2013, https://www.theverge.com/2013/5/14/4329676/papers-please-a-game-about-an-immigration-inspector.
3 Edge Staff, "Making of *Papers, Please*."
4 Nathan Grayson, "Apple Considered This Video Game Image 'Pornographic,'" Kotaku, December 11, 2014, https://kotaku.com/apple-considered-this-video-game-image-pornographic-1670040744.
5 Gamasutra Staff, "*The Last of Us* Wins Top Honors at Game Developers Choice Awards," Gamasutra, March 19, 2014, https://www.gamasutra.com/view/news/213557/The_Last_Of_Us_wins_top_honors_at_Game_Developers_Choice_Awards.php.
6 Tracey Lien, "Games for Change Awards Go to Papers, Please, Gone Home and The Mission US," Polygon, April 23, 2014, https://www.polygon.com/2014/4/23/5645362/games-for-change-award-winners.
7 Jordan Erica Webber, "This War of Mine: Little Ones—Bringing Children into a War Simulation," *Guardian*, March 4, 2016, https://www.theguardian.com/technology/2016/mar/04/this-war-of-mine-little-ones-children-11-bit-studios.
8 Clint Hocking, "Ludonarrative Dissonance in Bioshock," *Click Nothing* (blog), October 7, 2007, https://clicknothing.typepad.com/click_nothing/2007/10/ludonarrative-d.html. Hocking's blog post about the discrepancy between what players are required to do to play *BioShock* and the meaningful story that the game tries to tell is largely responsible for initiating the current debates about ludonarrative dissonance. For a representative sample of the current status of scholarly debates as to whether gameplay or narrative matters more, see the following: Henry Jenkins, "Game Design as Narrative Architecture," in *First Person: New Media as Story, Performance, and Game*, ed. Noah Wardrip-Fruin and Pat Harrigan, 118–30 (Cambridge, Mass.: MIT Press, 2004);

Jesper Juul, "Games Telling Stories? A Brief Note on Games and Narratives," *Game Studies* 1, no. 1 (2001): www.gamestudies.org/0101/juul-gts; Tim Marsh, "Serious Games Continuum: Between Games for Purpose and Experiential Environments for Purpose," *Entertainment Computing* 2, no. 2 (2011): 61–68; Jan Simmons, "Narrative, Games, and Theory," *Game Studies* 7, no. 1 (2007): http://gamestudies.org/07010701/articles/simons.

9 Peter J. Gomes, introduction to *The Courage to Be* by Paul Tillich (New Haven, Conn.: Yale University Press, 2000), xiii.
10 Gomes, introduction to *Courage to Be*, xvi–xvii.
11 Tillich, *Courage to Be*, 62.
12 Tillich, *Courage to Be*, 155.
13 Tillich, *Courage to Be*, 190.
14 Gomes, introduction to *Courage to Be*, xvii.
15 Tillich, *Love, Power, and Justice*, 78.
16 Tillich, *Shaking of the Foundations*, 162 (emphasis original).
17 Tillich, *Courage to Be*, 3.

6 Other Races and Religions in Protest

1 "Rami Ismail on Muslim Representation," *TheoNerd Podcast*, December 6, 2016, https://www.breaker.audio/theonerd-podcast/e/6212285.
2 Rami Ismail, "We Suck at Inclusivity: How Language Creates the Largest Invisible Minority for Games," *GDC Vault*, 2015, video, 30:09, https://www.gdcvault.com/play/1022362/We-Suck-at-Inclusivity-How.
3 Rami Ismail, "Rami, Ismail, Vlambeer—XOXO Festival," XOXO Festival, 2015, video, 18:43, https://www.youtube.com/watch?v=X1ynZm1wI18&feature=youtu.be.
4 Rami Ismail, (@tha_rami), "This Westworld thing, it's some independent pilot thing that simply cannot afford a single Arab to make sure their Arabic is not this abysmally wrong? It's by small low budget studio called @HBO," Twitter, May 4, 2020, https://twitter.com/tha_rami/status/1257451878432022528.
5 "What Is gamedev.world?" gamedev.world, accessed June 25, 2020, https://gamedev.world/en/.
6 "What Was the GDC Relief Fundraiser?" gamedev.world, accessed July 2, 2020, https://gamedev.world/relief/.
7 Simon Parkin, "A Truly Revolutionary Video Game," *New Yorker*, December 11, 2013, https://www.newyorker.com/tech/annals-of-technology/a-truly-revolutionary-video-game.
8 Horse Volume, "The Sun Also Rises—A Different Kind of War Game," Kickstarter, accessed June 29, 2020, https://www.kickstarter.com/projects/602251016/the-sun-also-rises-a-different-kind-of-war-game.
9 http://horsevolume.com/.
10 http://thesunalsoris.es/.

11 Charles S. Peirce, *The Essential Peirce: Selected Philosophical Writings*, vol. 2, *1893–1913*, ed. Peirce Edition Project (Bloomington: Indiana University Press, 1998), 299, 441.
12 Adams, foreword to Bulman, *Blueprint for Humanity*, 15.
13 Tillich, *Political Expectation*, 173.
14 GameSpot's popularity took a hit when one popular journalist from the site was unjustly fired and several remaining popular figures working for the website quit in solidarity with their colleague. That group eventually founded Giant Bomb, a highly personality-driven website about video games. Eventually the upper management of GameSpot changed, and Giant Bomb accepted an offer from CBS Interactive Entertainment to join their umbrella organization, which includes GameSpot.
15 Tamoor Hussain, Lucy James, Michael Higham, and Jean-Luc Seipke, "GameSpot Play for All Opening and Tim Sweeney and Epic Games Interview," GameSpot, June 1, 2020, video, 1:03:44, https://www.gamespot.com/videos/gamespot-play-for-all-opening-and-tim-sweeney-and-/2300-6452990/.
16 Jordan Ramée, "Black Lives Matter, Black Voices Are Important," GameSpot, June 12, 2020, https://www.gamespot.com/articles/black-lives-matter-black-voices-are-important/1100-6477973/.
17 "Bundle for Racial Justice and Equality," itch.io, last modified June 16, 2020, https://itch.io/b/520/bundle-for-racial-justice-and-equality.
18 Lucas Pope (@dukope), "Papers, Please is $3 for the next 24 hours on Steam and Humble. I'll double all sale proceeds up to $50k and donate everything to the @NAACP, @ACLU, & @eji_org. If you already have the game, don't want it, prefer another charity, etc, please donate on your own #BlackLivesMatter," Twitter, June 6, 2020, https://twitter.com/dukope/status/1269313513027035136.
19 Lucas Pope (@dukope), "Sale done. Final tally: $100k gross + $50k match = $150k total. $50k each to @NAACP, @ACLU, @eji_org. If you're donating, protesting, organizing, lobbying, fighting for equality: THANK YOU. #BlackLivesMatter," Twitter, June 7, 2020, https://twitter.com/dukope/status/1269692529848356864.
20 Chris Kerr, "Canadian Publisher Klei Donates $1 Million to Black Lives Matter Charities," Gamasutra, June 10, 2020, https://www.gamasutra.com/view/news/364515/Canadian_publisher_Klei_donates_1_million_to_Black_Lives_Matter_charities.php.
21 "Black Lives Matter Support Bundle," itch.io, last modified June 18, 2020, https://itch.io/b/513/black-lives-matter-support-bundle.
22 "Black Lives Matter Support Bundle," itch.io.
23 "Fight for Racial Justice Bundle," Humble Bundle, last modified June 23, 2020, https://www.humblebundle.com/fight-for-racial-justice-bundle.
24 "The Adventure Zone: Graduation Ep. 16, 'Give Me A Hand,'" *The Adventure Zone* (podcast), June 11, 2020, https://www.themcelroy.family/2020/6/11/21286940/the-adventure-zone-graduation-ep-16-give-me-a-hand.
25 "What Is The Okra Project?" The Okra Project, accessed July 3, 2020, https://www.theokraproject.com/.

26 Graeme McMillan, "'Adventure Zone' Graphic Novel Tops New York Times' Trade Fiction Best-Seller List," *Hollywood Reporter*, July 26, 2018, https://www.hollywoodreporter.com/heat-vision/adventure-zone-graphic-novel-tops-new-york-times-trade-fiction-bestseller-list-1130198.

27 Annie Branigin, "Two Funds Named for Nina Pop and Tony McDade Will Provide Free Therapy Sessions for Black Transgender Folks," The Root, June 2, 2020, https://www.theroot.com/two-funds-named-for-nina-pop-and-tony-mcdade-will-provi-1843861377.

28 Ben Bayliss, "10 Hour Animal Crossing: New Horizons Stream Brings in Over $150,000 in Support of Black Lives Matter," DualShockers, June 3, 2020, https://www.dualshockers.com/i-need-diverse-games-director-raises-150-000-for-bail-project-streaming-animal-crossing/.

7 Economic and Social Polarities

1 Tilghman and Ernst, "Plugging into the Video Game Market"; "Global Games Market Report Free Version 2019."

2 Mark Daniels, "Kraft Family Pledges $1 Million to Social Justice Causes," *Providence Journal*, June 5, 2020, https://www.providencejournal.com/sports/20200605/kraft-family-pledges-1-million-to-social-justice-causes.

3 Amazon, "Amazon Donates $10 Million to Organizations Supporting Justice and Equity," *The Amazon Blog*, June 3, 2020, https://blog.aboutamazon.com/policy/amazon-donates-10-million-to-organizations-supporting-justice-and-equity.

4 Klei Entertainment (@klei), "We stand with the Black community, and Klei is donating a $1 million to ACLU and the NAACP legal defense fund. More Information:" Twitter, June 9, 2020, https://twitter.com/klei/status/1270498738578919424.

5 Mike Fahey, "How Much Money Did Game Developers Make in 2010?" Kotaku, April 27, 2010, https://kotaku.com/how-much-money-did-game-developers-make-in-2010-5796166.

6 Evan Narcisse, "How Much Game Makers Get Paid," Kotaku, July 22, 2014, https://kotaku.com/how-much-game-makers-get-paid-1608955400.

7 Dan Starkey, "Total Cost of Publishing One Indie Game," Kotaku, August 8, 2014, https://kotaku.com/total-cost-of-publishing-an-indie-game-last-week-sixty-1618376285.

8 Lucas Pope (@dukope), "Papers Please is 3 years old today. 1.8 million units sold across all platforms/bundles/sales. Thank you all!" Twitter, August 8, 2016, https://twitter.com/dukope/status/762851441719390208.

9 Dave Lee, "Papers, Please: The 'Boring' Game that Became a Smash Hit," BBC News, March 12, 2014, https://www.bbc.com/news/technology-26527109.

10 Graham Smith, "Cart Life No Longer on Steam, Now Open Source," Rock Paper Shotgun, March 21, 2014, https://www.rockpapershotgun.com/2014/03/21/cart-life-no-longer-on-steam-now-open-source/.

11 Niebuhr, translator's preface to *Religious Situation*, 11–15.

12 Tillich, *Protestant Era*, 34–38; *Systematic Theology*, 3:353–54.

13 Such a view is compatible with noting that there is also progress throughout history, different periods realizing what is possible at a time while also learning from what came before. But such a "yes" to every historical moment also comes with a "no" that rejects the possibility of standing outside of time's flow and pointing to some objective achievement as the one that will be forever decisive of all history. No historical fact, movement, or person has the final say, but that does not mean that they are all failures. Rather, the fact that nothing concrete can exclusively be lifted up as the absolute solution to existence should result in driving deeper into concrete history. See Tillich, *Protestant Era*, 41–42.
14 Tillich, *Protestant Era*, 42.
15 Tillich, *Protestant Era*, 45.
16 Tillich, *Protestant Era*, 33.
17 Tillich, *Protestant Era*, 49.
18 Tillich, *Christianity and the Encounter of World Religions*, 11.
19 Tillich, *Religious Situation*, 198–200.
20 Purcell, *Levinas and Theology*, 103.
21 Purcell, "Is Theology Fundamental?" 133.
22 Tillich, *New Being*, 23 (emphasis original).
23 Levinas, *Difficult Freedom*, 121.
24 Tillich, *Courage to Be*, 87–88.
25 DiCenso, "Anxiety, Risk and Transformation," 56.
26 Tillich, *Courage to Be*, 179.
27 Tillich, *Courage to Be*, 3.
28 McLuhan, *Understanding Media*, 5
29 See Mark Dery, "Flame Wars," in *Flame Wars: The Discourse of Cyberculture*, ed. Mark Dery (Durham, N.C.: Duke University Press, 1994), 1–10, for another perspective that has not aged well.
30 Adams, "Foreword," in *A Blueprint for Humanity*, 20.
31 Shira Chess, *Ready Player Two: Women Gamers and Designed Identity* (Minneapolis: University of Minnesota Press, 2017).
32 Adrienne Shaw, *Gaming at the Edge: Sexuality and Gender at the Margins of Gamer Culture* (Minneapolis: University of Minnesota Press, 2014), 147–99.

Remaining Missions

1 Bissell, *Extra Lives*, xiii.
2 Jackson, "Video Games That Made People Question Their Beliefs."
3 Russell Heimlich, "Civic-Minded Teen Video Gamers," Pew Research Center, June 1, 2009, https://www.pewresearch.org/fact-tank/2009/06/01/civic-minded-teen-video-gamers/.
4 Vít Šisler, "Palestine in Pixels: The Holy Land, Arab-Israeli Conflict, and Reality Construction in Video Games," *Middle East Journal of Culture and Communication* 2 (2009): 275–92.

5. The "Highway of Death" mission in the game blames Russians for what occurred, but the highway is a real place where US and French forces killed hundreds of retreating Iraqi soldiers and captured thousands more during the Gulf War. Charlie Hall, "*Call of Duty: Modern Warfare*'s Highway of Death Controversy, Explained," Polygon, October 30, 2019, https://www.polygon.com/2019/10/30/20938550/call-of-duty-modern-warfare-highway-of-death-controversy.

6. "Review bombing" is when people give incredibly low user reviews on various online platforms as a punitive measure against games. In the case of *The Last of Us Part II*, a game that takes dozens of hours to complete, it had a user-review average of barely above zero from thousands of reviews just minutes after the game was released. Paul Tassi, "'The Last Of Us Part 2' Is Getting Predictably User Score Bombed On Metacritic," *Forbes*, June 21, 2020, https://www.forbes.com/sites/paultassi/2020/06/21/the-last-of-us-part-2-is-getting-predictably-user-score-bombed-on-metacritic/?sh=16fbcfc85c25.

7. Maddy Myers, "The Cost of Being a Woman Who Covers Video Games," Kotaku, January 3, 2020, https://kotaku.com/the-cost-of-being-a-woman-who-covers-video-games-1840793836.

8. Jason Schreier, "Video Game Industry Rocked by Outpouring of Sexual Misconduct Allegations," Bloomberg, June 24, 2020, https://www.bloomberg.com/news/articles/2020-06-24/video-game-industry-rocked-by-outpouring-of-sexual-misconduct-allegations.

9. Ethan Gatch, "Multiple Women Accuse Games Writer Chris Avellone of Sexual Misconduct," Kotaku, June 23, 2020, https://kotaku.com/multiple-women-accuse-games-writer-chris-avellone-of-se-1844135498.

10. Nathan Grayson, "A Wave of Sexual Abuse Stories Is Causing a Reckoning in the Twitch Streaming World," Kotaku, June 24, 2020, https://kotaku.com/a-wave-of-sexual-abuse-stories-is-causing-a-reckoning-i-1844122735.

11. The original *Final Fantasy VII* contained a scene in which the lead male character wore a dress, and in-game dialogue from other characters made a transphobic joke about the situation. However, *Final Fantasy VII Remake*, released twenty-three years after the original, learned from criticism and modified the scene into a celebration of gender fluidity.

12. Robertson Allen, *America's Digital Army: Games at Work and War* (Lincoln: University of Nebraska Press, 2017); Cecilia D'Anastasio, "The U.S. Army Has a New Plan to Recruit Gamers," Kotaku, December 4, 2018, https://kotaku.com/the-u-s-army-has-a-new-plan-to-recruit-gamers-1830850297.

13. Corey Mead, *War Play: Video Games and the Future of Armed Conflict* (Boston: Houghton Mifflin Harcourt, 2013).

14. Bissell, *Extra Lives*, 132.

15. Luke Plunkett, "EA Won't Be Paying for Real Guns in Video Games Anymore," Kotaku, May 7, 2013, https://kotaku.com/ea-wont-be-paying-for-real-guns-in-video-games-anymore-494940003.

16. John Anderson, "Who Really Invented the Video Game?" *Creative Computing Video & Arcade Games* 1, no. 1 (1983): 8.

17. Christian Beekman, "The History of Video Games and the Military," Task & Purpose, November 17, 2014, https://taskandpurpose.com/entertainment/us-militarys-close-history-video-games; Defense Advanced Research Projects Agency, "DARPA: 60 Years 1958–2018," accessed July 1, 2020, https://www.darpa.mil/attachments/DARAPA60_publication-no-ads.pdf.
18. Bissell, *Extra Lives*, 133.
19. Imran Khan, "Video Games Have to Reckon with How They Depict the Police," Kotaku, June 12, 2020, https://kotaku.com/video-games-have-to-reckon-with-how-they-depict-the-pol-1844013471.
20. Bissell, *Extra Lives*, 155.
21. Larry Irving, et al., "Origin of the Term Digital Divide" (emails collected off Benton Foundation's digitaldividelist listserv) (2000), http://www.rtpnet.org/lists/rtpnettact/msg00080.html. See also David J. Gunkel, "Second Thoughts: Toward a Critique of the Digital Divide," *New Media & Society* 5, no. 4 (2003): 501–5.
22. Hamish McRae, "Unleashing the Digital Divide: The Changes in Television Will Change Global Society as We Lose Something that Unifies a Nation," *Independent*, November 17, 1998, https://www.independent.co.uk/arts-entertainment/unleashing-the-digital-divide-1185423.html.
23. Julia Angwin and Laura Castaneda, "The Digital Divide: High-Tech Boom a Bust for Blacks, Latinos," *San Francisco Chronicle*, May 4, 1998, https://www.sfgate.com/news/article/The-Digital-Divide-High-tech-boom-a-bust-for-3007911.php.
24. Benjamin M. Compaine, ed., *The Digital Divide: Facing a Crisis or Creating a Myth?* (Cambridge, Mass.: MIT Press, 2001).
25. Joseph Kahne, Ellen Middaugh and Chris Evans, *The Civic Potential of Video Games* (Cambridge, Mass.: MIT Press, 2009).
26. Tanya Basu, "AOC's Among Us Livestream Hints at Twitch's Political Power," *MIT Technology Review*, October 21, 2020, https://www.technologyreview.com/2020/10/21/1011038/aocs-among-us-livestream-hints-at-twitchs-political-power/.
27. James Paul Gee, *Situated Language and Learning: A Critique of Traditional Schooling* (New York: Routledge, 2004).
28. Henry Jenkins, *Convergence Culture: Where Old and New Media Collide* (New York: New York University Press, 2006), 3.
29. Pew Research Center, "Teen Content Creators and Consumers," November 2, 2005, https://www.pewresearch.org/internet/2005/11/02/teen-content-creators-and-consumers/.
30. Daniel Goleman, *Emotional Intelligence: Why It Can Matter More than IQ* (New York: Bantam Books, 1995).
31. Daniel Goleman, *Social Intelligence: The New Science of Human Relationships* (New York: Bantam Books, 2006).
32. For a representative sampling, see the contributions in Stephanie N. Arel and Shelly Rambo, eds., *Post-Traumatic Public Theology* (Cham, Switzerland: Palgrave Macmillan, 2016), and Shelly Rambo, *Resurrecting Wounds: Living in the Aftermath of Trauma* (Waco, Tex.: Baylor University Press, 2017).

33 John W. Auxier, "*That Dragon, Cancer* Goes to Seminary: Using a Serious Video Game in Pastoral Training," *Christian Education Journal: Research on Educational Ministry* 15, no. 1 (2018): 105–17.
34 Owen Good, "*Papo y Yo* Is a Bittersweet Allegory of Growing Up with a Drug User," Kotaku, June 3, 2011, https://kotaku.com/papo-yo-is-a-bittersweet-allegory-of-growing-up-with-5808495.
35 Asi Burak and Laura Parker, *Power Play: How Video Games Can Save the World* (New York: St. Martin's Press, 2017); Sivilia Ascarelli, "Opinion: Why Your Doctor May Soon Have You Playing Video Games," MarketWatch, December 5, 2017, https://www.marketwatch.com/story/neuroscientists-could-soon-have-you-playing-video-games-2017-10-24.
36 Zack Zwiezen, "A Video Game Developed to Detect Alzheimer's Disease Seems to Be Working," Kotaku, April 27, 2019, https://kotaku.com/a-video-game-developed-to-detect-alzheimer-s-disease-se-1834331632.
37 Wesley Wildman, *Effing the Ineffable: Existential Mumblings at the Limits of Language* (Albany: SUNY Press, 2018), 141–213.
38 Albert Borgmann, *Technology and the Character of Contemporary Life* (Chicago: University of Chicago Press, 1984), 14.
39 Thomas P. Hughes, *American Genesis: A Century of Invention and Technological Enthusiasm, 1870–1970* (Chicago: University of Chicago Press, 2004), xvii.
40 Marshall McLuhan, *The Gutenberg Galaxy: The Making of Typographic Man* (Toronto: University of Toronto Press, 1962), lxii.
41 Mark C. Taylor, *Nots* (Chicago: University of Chicago Press, 1993), 186.
42 Tom Beaudoin, *Virtual Faith: The Irreverent Spiritual Quest of Generation X* (San Francisco: Jossey-Bass, 1998), 109.
43 Beaudoin, *Virtual Faith*, 117.
44 Levinas, *Levinas Reader*, 291–92.
45 Deut 10:17-18 (NRSV).
46 Tillich, *Courage to Be*, 146.
47 Tillich, *Courage to Be*, 147.
48 Wildman, *Effing the Ineffable*, 39–42, 45–60.
49 Tillich, *Systematic Theology*, 1:3.
50 Jacques Ellul, *The Technological Society*, trans. John Wilkinson (Toronto: Vintage Books, 1964). Ellul argued in favor of a pessimistic view of technology in 1964, and developments like Gamergate since then indicate the problem has arguably gotten worse.
51 Christopher W. Boerl and Katie Donbavand, *A God More Powerful Than Yours: American Evangelicals, Politics, and the Internet Age* (Newcastle upon Tyne: Cambridge Scholars Publishing, 2015).
52 Michael Heim, *The Metaphysics of Virtual Reality* (Oxford: Oxford University Press, 1993), 87–92.
53 "Center for Open & Relational Theology," Northwind Seminary, accessed July 4, 2020, https://www.northwindseminary.org/center-for-open-relational-theology.

54 Tripp Fuller, "Community." Homebrewed Christianity, accessed June 25, 2020, https://trippfuller.com/community/.
55 Tillich, *Courage to Be*, 62.
56 Tillich, *Religious Situation*, 129–30.

Credits

Bibliography

Adams, James Luther. Foreword to *A Blueprint for Humanity: Paul Tillich's Theology of Culture*, by Raymond F. Bulman, 11–23. Lewisburg, Penn.: Bucknell University Press, 1981.

———. Introduction to *Political Expectation*, by Paul Tillich, vi–xx. New York: Harper & Row, 1971.

———. *Paul Tillich's Philosophy of Culture, Science, and Religion*. Washington, D.C.: University Press of America, 1982.

"The Adventure Zone: Graduation Ep. 16, 'Give Me A Hand.'" *The Adventure Zone* (podcast). June 11, 2020. https://www.themcelroy.family/2020/6/11/21286940/the-adventure-zone-graduation-ep-16-give-me-a-hand.

Alexander, Leigh. "'Diversity Lounge'? PAX Has a Lot of Work to Do." Gamasutra, December 19, 2013. https://www.gamasutra.com/view/news/207402/Diversity_Lounge_PAX_has_a_lot_of_work_to_do.php.

———. "Road to the IGF: The Fullbright Company's Gone Home." Gamasutra, March 20, 2013. https://www.gamasutra.com/view/news/188908/Road_to_the_IGF_The_Fullbright_Companys_Gone_Home.php.

———. "The Story behind Gone Home, and What Makes a 'Great Game.'" Gamasutra, October 24, 2013. https://www.gamasutra.com/view/news/203119/The_story_behind_Gone_Home_and_what_makes_a_great_game.php.

Allaway, Jennifer. "#Gamergate Trolls Aren't Ethics Crusaders; They're a Hate Group." Jezebel, October 13, 2014. https://jezebel.com/gamergate-trolls-arent-ethics-crusaders-theyre-a-hate-1644984010.

Allen, Robertson. *America's Digital Army: Games at Work and War*. Lincoln: University of Nebraska Press, 2017.

Amazon. "Amazon Donates $10 Million to Organizations Supporting Justice and Equity." *The Amazon Blog*, June 3, 2020. https://blog.aboutamazon.com/policy/amazon-donates-10-million-to-organizations-supporting-justice-and-equity.

American Academy of Religion. "Past and Future Annual Meetings." Accessed January 11, 2021. https://www.aarweb.org/AARMBR/Events-and-Networking-/Annual-Meeting-/Past-and-Future-Annual-Meetings.aspx.

American Psychological Association's Society for Media Psychology and Technology. "News Media, Public Education and Public Policy Committee." *The Amplifier Magazine*, June 12, 2017. https://div46amplifier.com/2017/06/12/news-media-public-education-and-public-policy-committee.

American Psychological Association Task Force on Violent Media. "Technical Report on the Review of the Violent Video Game Literature." 2015. https://www.apa.org/pi/families/review-video-games.pdf.

Anderson, John. "Who Really Invented the Video Game?" *Creative Computing Video & Arcade Games* 1, no. 1 (1983): 8.

Anderson, Monica. "A Majority of Teens Have Experienced Some Form of Cyberbullying." Pew Research Center, September 27, 2018. https://www.pewresearch.org/internet/2018/09/27/a-majority-of-teens-have-experienced-some-form-of-cyberbullying/.

Angwin, Julia, and Laura Castaneda. "The Digital Divide: High-Tech Boom a Bust for Blacks, Latinos." *San Francisco Chronicle*, May 4, 1998, https://www.sfgate.com/news/article/The-Digital-Divide-High-tech-boom-a-bust-for-3007911.php.

Arel, Stephanie N., and Shelly Rambo, eds. *Post-Traumatic Public Theology*. Cham, Switzerland: Palgrave Macmillan, 2016.

Arisia Inc. "About Arisia." Accessed June 25, 2020. https://www.arisia.org/AboutArisia.

———. "Arisia Settles Cancellation Fees with Westin and Aloft Hotels." Last modified December 30, 2019. http://corp.arisia.org/Arisia-settles-cancellation-fees.

———. "Code of Conduct." Accessed June 25, 2020. https://www.arisia.org/Code-of-Conduct.

Ascarelli, Sivilia. "Opinion: Why Your Doctor May Soon Have You Playing Video Games." *Market Watch*, December 5, 2017. https://www.marketwatch.com/story/neuroscientists-could-soon-have-you-playing-video-games-2017-10-24.

Auxier, John W. "That Dragon, Cancer Goes to Seminary: Using a Serious Video Game in Pastoral Training." *Christian Education Journal: Research on Educational Ministry* 15, no. 1 (2018): 105–17.

Barbour, Ian G. *Issues in Science and Religion*. Englewood Cliffs, N.J.: Prentice-Hall, 1966.

Barraza, Jorge A., and Paul J. Zak. "Empathy towards Strangers Triggers Oxytocin Release and Subsequent Generosity." *Annals of the New York Academy of Sciences* 1167, no. 1 (2009): 182–89.

Basu, Tanya. "AOC's Among Us Livestream Hints at Twitch's Political Power." *MIT Technology Review*, October 21, 2020. https://www.technologyreview.com/2020/10/21/1011038/aocs-among-us-livestream-hints-at-twitchs-political-power/.

Bayliss, Ben. "10 Hour Animal Crossing: New Horizons Stream Brings in Over $150,000 in Support of Black Lives Matter." DualShockers, June 3, 2020. https://www.dualshockers.com/i-need-diverse-games-director-raises-150-000-for-bail-project-streaming-animal-crossing/.

Beaudoin, Tom. *Virtual Faith: The Irreverent Spiritual Quest of Generation X*. San Francisco: Jossey-Bass, 1998.

Beekman, Christian. "The History of Video Games and the Military." Task & Purpose, November 17, 2014. https://taskandpurpose.com/entertainment/us-militarys-close-history-video-games.

Benedikt, Michael. "Introduction." In *Cyberspace: First Steps*, edited by Michael Benedikt, 1–25. Cambridge, Mass.: MIT Press, 1991.

Bird, Michael. "Film as Hierophany." In *Religion in Film*, edited by John R. May and Michael Bird, 3–22. Knoxville: University of Tennessee Press, 1982.

Bissell, Tom. *Extra Lives: Why Video Games Matter*. New York: Vintage Books, 2011.

Blumberg, Fran C. *Learning by Playing: Video Gaming in Education*. New York: Oxford University Press, 2014.

Boerl, Christopher W., and Katie Donbavand. *A God More Powerful Than Yours: American Evangelicals, Politics, and the Internet Age*. Newcastle upon Tyne: Cambridge Scholars Publishing, 2015.

Borchers, Callum, and Dennis Keohane. "Citing Threats, Game Maker Pulls Her Company from PAX East Fest." *Boston Globe*, February 24, 2015. https://www.bostonglobe.com/business/2015/02/24/pax-east-withdrawal-reveals-sexist-side-video-game-culture/SiRAzMnuI6iea0woo9ob6I/story.html.

Borgmann, Albert. *Technology and the Character of Contemporary Life*. Chicago: University of Chicago Press, 1984.

Bosman, Frank G. *Gaming and the Divine: A New Systematic Theology of Video Games*. London: Routledge, 2019.

Branigin, Annie. "Two Funds Named for Nina Pop and Tony McDade Will Provide Free Therapy Sessions for Black Transgender Folks." The Root, June 2, 2020. https://www.theroot.com/two-funds-named-for-nina-pop-and-tony-mcdade-will-provi-1843861377.

Brant, Jonathan. *Paul Tillich and the Possibility of Revelation through Film*. New York: Oxford University Press, 2012.

Brown, Anna. "Younger Men Play Video Games, but So Do a Diverse Group of Other Americans." Pew Research Center, September 11, 2017. https://www.pewresearch.org/fact-tank/2017/09/11/younger-men-play-video-games-but-so-do-a-diverse-group-of-other-americans/.

Brown, Harry J. *Videogames and Education*. London: Routledge, 2015.

Buccino, G., F. Binkofski, G. R. Fink, L. Fadiga, L. Fogassi, V. Gallese, R. J. Seitz, K. Zilles, G. Rizzolatti, and H. J. Freund. "Action Observation Activates Premotor and Parietal Areas in a Somatropic Manner: An fMRI Study." *European Journal of Neuroscience* 13, no. 2 (2001): 400–404.

Bulman, Raymond F. *A Blueprint for Humanity: Paul Tillich's Theology of Culture*. Lewisburg, Penn.: Bucknell University Press, 1981.

Burak, Asi, and Laura Parker. *Power Play: How Video Games Can Save the World*. New York: St. Martin's Press, 2017.

Burggraeve, Roger. "'Fraternity, Equality, Freedom': On the Soul and the Extent of Our Responsibility." In *Responsibility, God and Society: Theological Ethics in Dialogue*, edited by Johan de Tavernier, Joseph Selling, Johan Verstraeten, and Paul Schotsmans, 1–22. Leuven: Uitgeverij Peeters, 2008.

Burnham, Terence C. "High-Testosterone Men Reject Low Ultimatum Game Offers." *Proceedings of the Royal Society: Biological Sciences* 274, no. 1623 (2007): 2327–30.

Calcutt, Andrew. *White Noise: An A-Z of the Contradictions of Cyberculture*. New York: Saint Martin's Press, 1999.

Campbell, Heidi A., and Gregory Price Grieve. *Playing with Religion in Video Games*. Bloomington: Indiana University Press, 2014.

Campbell, Heidi A., Rachel Wagner, Shanny Luft, Rabia Gregory, Gregory Price Grieve, and Xenia Zeiler. "Gaming Religionworlds: Why Religious Studies Should Pay Attention to Religion in Gaming." *Journal of the American Academy of Religion* 84, no. 3 (2016): 641–64.

Chess, Shira. *Ready Player Two: Women Gamers and Designed Identity*. Minneapolis: University of Minnesota Press, 2017.

Chicka, Benjamin J., and Andrew Tripp. "The Science of Online Bullying: A Lesson in Diversity." Filmed March 8, 2015, at PAX East, Boston, Mass. Video, 1:15:09. https://www.youtube.com/watch?v=Dh9z_A5Td2k.

Clark, Nicole. "A Brief History of the 'Walking Simulator,' Gaming's Most Detested Genre." Salon, November 11, 2017. https://www.salon.com/2017/11/11/a-brief-history-of-the-walking-simulator-gamings-most-detested-genre/.

Cobb, Jennifer J. *Cybergrace: The Search for God in the Digital World*. New York: Crown Publishers, 1998.

Cobb, Kelton. *The Blackwell Guide to Theology and Popular Culture*. Malden, Mass.: Blackwell, 2005.

———. "Reconsidering the Status of Popular Culture in Tillich's Theology of Culture." *Journal of the American Academy of Religion* 63, no. 1 (1995): 53–84.

Cohen, Richard. *Elevations: The Height of the Good in Rosenzweig and Levinas*. Chicago: University of Chicago Press, 1994.

Compaine, Benjamin M., ed. *The Digital Divide: Facing a Crisis or Creating a Myth?* Cambridge, Mass.: MIT Press, 2001.

Conditt, Jessica. "Fighting Depression in the Video Game World, One AFK at a Time." Engadget, March 25, 2016. https://www.engadget.com/2016-03-25-mental-illness-video-games-take-this-please-knock.html.

D'Anastasio, Cecilia. "The U.S. Army Has a New Plan to Recruit Gamers." Kotaku, December 4, 2018. https://kotaku.com/the-u-s-army-has-a-new-plan-to-recruit-gamers-1830850297.

Daniels, Mark. "Kraft Family Pledges $1 Million to Social Justice Causes." *Providence Journal*, June 5, 2020. https://www.providencejournal.com/sports/20200605/kraft-family-pledges-1-million-to-social-justice-causes.

Davis, Erik. *TechGnosis: Myth, Magic, and Mysticism in the Age of Information*. Berkeley, Calif.: North Atlantic Books, 2015.

De Dreu, Carsten K. W., Lindred L. Greer, Michel J. J. Handgraaf, Shaul Shalvi, Gerben A. Van Kleef, Matthijs Baas, Femke S. Ten Velden, Eric Van Dijk, and Sander W. W.

Feith. "The Neuropeptide Oxytocin Regulates Parochial Altruism in Intergroup Conflict among Humans." *Science* 328, no. 5984 (2010): 1408–11.

Defense Advanced Research Projects Agency. "DARPA: 60 Years 1958–2018." Accessed July 1, 2020. https://www.darpa.mil/attachments/DARAPA60_publication-no-ads.pdf.

Derrida, Jacques. *The Work of Mourning*. Edited by Pascale-Anne Brault and Michael Naas. Chicago: University of Chicago Press, 2001.

Dery, Mark. "Flame Wars." In *Flame Wars: The Discourse of Cyberculture*, edited by Mark Dery, 1–10. Durham, N.C.: Duke University Press, 1994.

Detweiler, Craig. *iGods: How Technology Shapes our Spiritual and Social Lives*. Grand Rapids: Brazos, 2013.

DiCenso, James J. "Anxiety, Risk and Transformation: Re-Visiting Tillich with Lacan." In *Secular Theology: American Radical Theological Thought*, edited by Clayton Crockett, 51–72. London: Routledge, 2001.

Dickman, Nathan Eric. "Anxiety and the Face of the Other: Tillich and Levinas on the Origin of Questioning." *Sophia* 48, no. 3 (2009): 267–79.

Donaldson, Zoe R., and Larry J. Young, "Oxytocin, Vasopressin, and the Neurogenetics of Sociality." *Science* 322, no. 5903 (2008): 900–904.

Dooley, Mark. "Nihilism or Salvation? The Challenges of Global Technology for the Humanities." In *Technology and Transcendence*, edited by Michael Breen, Eamonn Conway, and Barry McMillan, 103–13. Dublin: Columba Press, 2003.

Dowd, Nancy E., Dorothy G. Singer, and Robin Fretwell Wilson, eds. *Handbook of Children, Culture, and Violence*. Thousand Oaks, Calif.: Sage Publications, 2006.

Dubin, Mark Wm. *How the Brain Works*. Williston, Vt.: Blackwell Science, 2002.

Duggan, Maeve. "Gaming and Gamers." Pew Research Center, December 15, 2015. https://www.pewresearch.org/internet/2015/12/15/gaming-and-gamers/.

Dumont, G. J., F. C. G. J. Sweep, R. van der Steen, R. Hermsen, A. R. T. Donders, D. J. Touw, J. M. A. van Gerven, J. K. Buitelaar, and R. J. Verkes. "Increased Oxytocin Concentrations and Prosocial Feelings in Humans after Ecstasy (3,4-methylenedioxymethamphetamine) Administration." *Social Neuroscience* 4, no. 4 (2009): 359–66.

Dyson, Esther. *Release 2.0: A Design for Living in the Digital Age*. London: Viking Press, 1997.

Eaglestone, Robert. "Levinas and the Holocaust." In *The Oxford Handbook of Levinas*, edited by Michael L. Morgan, 35–52. New York: Oxford University Press, 2019.

Eden, Allison, Matthew Grizzard, and Robert J. Lewis. "Moral Psychology and Media Theory: Historical and Emerging Viewpoints." In *Media and the Moral Mind*, edited by Ron Tamborini, 33–82. New York: Routledge, 2013.

Edge Staff. "The Making of *Papers, Please*." Edge, January 20, 2014. https://web.archive.org/web/20140122052214/http://www.edge-online.com/features/the-making-of-papers-please/.

Ehrenreich, Barbara. *Nickel and Dimed: On (Not) Getting By in America*. New York: Henry Holt, 2001.

Ellul, Jacques. *The Technological Society*. Translated by John Wilkinson. Toronto: Vintage Books, 1964.

Elwell, J. Sage. *Crisis of Transcendence: A Theology of Digital Art and Culture*. Lanham, Md.: Lexington Books, 2011.

Fahey, Mike. "How Much Money Did Game Developers Make in 2010?" Kotaku, April 27, 2010. https://kotaku.com/how-much-money-did-game-developers-make-in-2010-5796166.

Feshbach, Seymour. "The Catharsis Hypothesis of Interaction with Aggressive and Neutral Play Objects." *Journal of Personality* 24 (1956): 449–62.

Fishman, Andrew. "Blame Game: Violent Video Games Do Not Cause Violence." *Psychology Today*, July 16, 2019. https://www.psychologytoday.com/us/blog/video-game-health/201907/blame-game-violent-video-games-do-not-cause-violence.

Fukuyama, Francis. *Our Posthuman Future: Consequences of the Biotechnology Revolution*. New York: Farrar, Straus and Giroux, 2002.

Fuller, Tripp. "Community." Homebrewed Christianity. Accessed June 25, 2020. https://trippfuller.com/community/.

Gamasutra Staff. "*The Last Of Us* wins top honors at Game Developers Choice Awards." Gamasutra, March 19, 2014. https://www.gamasutra.com/view/news/213557/The_Last_Of_Us_wins_top_honors_at_Game_Developers_Choice_Awards.php.

gamedev.world. "What Is gamedev.world?" Accessed June 25, 2020. https://gamedev.world/en/.

———. "What was the GDC Relief Fundraiser?" Accessed July 2, 2020. https://gamedev.world/relief/.

Games for Change. "About Us." Accessed July 2, 2020. http://www.gamesforchange.org/who-we-are/about-us/.

Gatch, Ethan. "Multiple Women Accuse Games Writer Chris Avellone of Sexual Misconduct." Kotaku, June 23, 2020. https://kotaku.com/multiple-women-accuse-games-writer-chris-avellone-of-se-1844135498.

Gee, James Paul. *Situated Language and Learning: A Critique of Traditional Schooling*. New York: Routledge, 2004.

Gee, James Paul, and Elisabeth R. Hayes. *Women and Gaming: "The Sims" and 21st Century Learning*. New York: Palgrave Macmillan, 2010.

Geraci, Robert M. *Virtually Sacred: Myth and Meaning in "World of Warcraft" and "Second Life."* New York: Oxford University Press, 2014.

Gilkey, Langdon. *Maker of Heaven and Earth: The Christian Doctrine of Creation in the Light of Modern Knowledge*. Garden City: Doubleday, 1959.

Goleman, Daniel. *Emotional Intelligence: Why It Can Matter More than IQ*. New York: Bantam Books, 1995.

———. *Social Intelligence: The New Science of Human Relationships*. New York: Bantam Books, 2006.

Golub, Alex. "Being in the World (of Warcraft): Raiding, Realism, and Knowledge Production in a Massively Multiplayer Online Game." *Anthropological Quarterly* 83, no. 1 (2010): 17–46.

Gomes, Peter J. Introduction to *The Courage to Be*, by Paul Tillich, xi–xxxiii. New Haven, Conn.: Yale University Press, 2000.

Good, Owen. "*Papo y Yo* Is a Bittersweet Allegory of Growing Up with a Drug User." Kotaku, June 3, 2011. https://kotaku.com/papo-yo-is-a-bittersweet-allegory-of-growing-up-with-5808495.

Graham, David John. "Uses of Film in Theology." In *Explorations in Theology and Film: Movies and Meaning*, edited by Clive Marsh and Gaye Ortiz, 35–43. Oxford: Blackwell, 1997.

Graham, Gordon. *The Internet: A Philosophical Inquiry*. New York: Routledge, 1999.

Grant, Christopher. "Polygon's 2013 Game of the Year: Gone Home." Polygon, January 15, 2014. https://www.polygon.com/2014/1/15/5311568/game-of-the-year-2013-gone-home.

Grayson, Nathan. "Apple Considered This Video Game Image 'Pornographic.'" Kotaku, December 11, 2014. https://kotaku.com/apple-considered-this-video-game-image-pornographic-1670040744.

———. "The Indie Game Reality TV Show That Went to Hell." Kotaku, March 31, 2014. https://kotaku.com/the-indie-game-reality-tv-show-that-went-to-hell-1555599284.

———. "Was PAX East's Diversity Lounge a Success? I Asked People Who Went." Kotaku, April 21, 2014. https://kotaku.com/was-pax-easts-diversity-lounge-a-success-i-asked-peopl-1564499083.

———. "A Wave of Sexual Abuse Stories Is Causing a Reckoning in the Twitch Streaming World." Kotaku, June 24, 2020. https://kotaku.com/a-wave-of-sexual-abuse-stories-is-causing-a-reckoning-i-1844122735.

Grizzard, Matthew Nelson. "Cooperative Video Game Play and Generosity: Oxytocin Production as a Causal Mechanism Regarding Prosocial Behavior Resulting from Cooperative Video Game Play." PhD diss., Michigan State University, 2013.

Grossman, Vasily. *Life and Fate*. Translated by Robert Chandler. London: Harvill Press, 1995.

Gunkel, David J. "Second Thoughts: Toward a Critique of the Digital Divide." *New Media & Society* 5, no. 4 (2003): 499–522.

———. *Thinking Otherwise: Philosophy, Communication, Technology*. West Lafayette, Ind.: Purdue University Press, 2007.

Gunter, Barrie. "Psychological Effects of Video Games." In *Handbook of Computer Games Studies*, edited by Joost Raessens and Jeffrey Goldstein, 145–60. Cambridge, Mass.: MIT Press, 2005.

Gwaltney, Javy. "Glory to Arstotzka: Papers, Please and an Interview with Its Creator." *CultureMass*, April 14, 2013. https://web.archive.org/web/20140111232206/http://culturemass.com/2013/04/14/papers-please-and-an-interview-with-its-creator/.

Hall, Charlie. "*Call of Duty: Modern Warfare*'s Highway of Death Controversy, Explained." Polygon, October 30, 2019. https://www.polygon.com/2019/10/30/20938550/call-of-duty-modern-warfare-highway-of-death-controversy.

Hamman, Jaco J. *Growing Down: Theology and Human Nature in the Virtual Age*. Waco, Tex.: Baylor University Press, 2017.

Hart, Kevin. *The Trespass of the Sign: Deconstruction, Theology, and Philosophy*. New York: Fordham University Press, 2000.

Hayles, N. Katherine. *How We Became Posthuman: Virtual Bodies in Cybernetics, Literature, and Informatics*. Chicago: Chicago University Press, 1999.

Heim, Michael. *The Metaphysics of Virtual Reality*. Oxford: Oxford University Press, 1993.

———. *Virtual Realism*. Oxford: Oxford University Press, 1998.

Heimlich, Russell. "Civic-Minded Teen Video Gamers." Pew Research Center, June 1, 2009. https://www.pewresearch.org/fact-tank/2009/06/01/civic-minded-teen-video-gamers/.

Hernandez, Patricia. "*Gone Home*: The Kotaku Review." Kotaku, August 15, 2013. https://kotaku.com/gone-home-the-kotaku-review-1118218265.

———. "Indie Developer Pulls out of PAX, Citing Penny Arcade Controversies." Kotaku, June 21, 2013. https://kotaku.com/indie-developer-pulls-out-of-pax-citing-penny-arcade-c-532336421.

Hinkle, David. "Gone Home, The Last of Us, Tearaway Top GDC Award Nominations." Engadget, January 9, 2014. https://www.engadget.com/2014-01-09-gone-home-the-last-of-us-tearaway-top-gdc-award-nominations.html.

Hocking, Clint. "Ludonarrative Dissonance in Bioshock." *Click Nothing* (blog), October 7, 2007. https://clicknothing.typepad.com/click_nothing/2007/10/ludonarrative-d.html.

Horse Volume. "The Sun Also Rises—A Different Kind of War Game." Kickstarter. Accessed June 29, 2020. https://www.kickstarter.com/projects/602251016/the-sun-also-rises-a-different-kind-of-war-game.

Huff, Crystal. "Why I'm Not at Arisia Anymore: My Rapist is President. Again." Accessed June 12, 2018. http://www.jimchines.com/2018/10/arisia-rapist/.

Hughes, Thomas P. *American Genesis: A Century of Invention and Technological Enthusiasm, 1870–1970*. Chicago: University of Chicago Press, 2004.

Humble Bundle. "Fight for Racial Justice Bundle." Last modified June 23, 2020. https://www.humblebundle.com/fight-for-racial-justice-bundle.

Hussain, Tamoor, Lucy James, Michael Higham, and Jean-Luc Seipke. "GameSpot Play for All Opening and Tim Sweeney and Epic Games Interview." GameSpot, June 1, 2020. Video, 1:03:44. https://www.gamespot.com/videos/gamespot-play-for-all-opening-and-tim-sweeney-and-/2300-6452990/.

Hutchens, Benjamin C. *Levinas: A Guide for the Perplexed*. London: Continuum, 2004.

Irving, Larry, A. Carvin, S. Myrland, and J. Hallman. "Origin of the Term Digital Divide." Emails collected off Benton Foundation's digitaldividelist listserv. 2000. http://www.rtpnet.org/lists/rtpnettact/msg00080.html.

Ismail, Rami. "Rami, Ismail, Vlambeer—XOXO Festival." XOXO Festival, 2015. Video, 18:43. https://www.youtube.com/watch?v=X1ynZm1wI18&feature=youtu.be.

———. "We Suck at Inclusivity: How Language Creates the Largest Invisible Minority for Games." *GDC Vault*, 2015. Video, 30:09. https://www.gdcvault.com/play/1022362/We-Suck-at-Inclusivity-How.

itch.io. "Black Lives Matter Support Bundle." Last modified June 18, 2020. https://itch.io/b/513/black-lives-matter-support-bundle.

———. "Bundle for Racial Justice and Equality." Last modified June 16, 2020. https://itch.io/b/520/bundle-for-racial-justice-and-equality.

Jackson, Gita. "The Video Games That Made People Question Their Beliefs." Kotaku, July 2, 2019. https://kotaku.com/the-video-games-that-made-people-question-their-beliefs-1836045401.

James, William. *Sciousness*. Edited by Jonathan Bricklin. Guilford, Conn.: Eirini Press, 2006.

Jenkins, David. "PAX East Attendance Figures Up by 17,000." gamesindustry.biz, March 15, 2011. https://www.gamesindustry.biz/articles/2011-03-15-pax-east-attendance-figures-up-by-17-000.

Jenkins, Henry. *Confronting the Challenges of Participatory Culture: Media Education for the 21st Century*. Cambridge, Mass.: MIT Press, 2009.

———. *Convergence Culture: Where Old and New Media Collide*. New York: New York University Press, 2006.

———. "Game Design as Narrative Architecture." In *First Person: New Media as Story, Performance, and Game*, edited by Noah Wardrip-Fruin and Pat Harrigan, 118–30. Cambridge, Mass.: MIT Press, 2004.

Jilani, Zaid. "Gamergate's Fickle Hero: The Dark Opportunism of Breitbart's Milo Yiannopoulos." Salon, October 29, 2014. https://www.salon.com/2014/10/28/gamergates_fickle_hero_the_dark_opportunism_of_breitbarts_milo_yiannopoulos/.

Juul, Jesper. "Games Telling Stories? A Brief Note on Games and Narratives." *Game Studies* 1, no. 1 (2001): www.gamestudies.org/0101/juul-gts.

———. *Half-Real: Video Games between Real Rules and Fictional Worlds*. Cambridge, Mass.: MIT Press, 2005.

Kahne, Joseph, Ellen Middaugh, and Chris Evans. *The Civic Potential of Video Games*. Cambridge, Mass.: MIT Press, 2009.

Kasumovic, Michael, and Keff Kuznekoff. "Study: Low Status Men More Likely to Bully Women Online." PsyPost, July 15, 2015. https://www.psypost.org/2015/07/study-low-status-men-who-bad-video-games-likely-bully-women-online-35901.

Keltner, Dacher. *Born to Be Good: The Science of a Meaningful Life*. New York: Norton, 2009.

Kerr, Chris. "Canadian Publisher Klei Donates $1 Million to Black Lives Matter Charities." Gamasutra, June 10, 2020. https://www.gamasutra.com/view/news/364515/Canadian_publisher_Klei_donates_1_million_to_Black_Lives_Matter_charities.php.

Khan, Imran. "Video Games Have to Reckon with How They Depict the Police." Kotaku, June 12, 2020. https://kotaku.com/video-games-have-to-reckon-with-how-they-depict-the-pol-1844013471.

Kietzman, Ludwig. "Papers, Please and The Last of Us Honored at GDC Awards Show." Engadget, March 20, 2014. https://www.engadget.com/2014-03-20-papers-please-and-the-last-of-us-honored-at-gdc-awards-show.html.

Kosky, Jeffrey L. *Levinas and the Philosophy of Religion*. Bloomington: Indiana University Press, 2001.

Kutner, Lawrence, and Cheryl K. Olson. *Grand Theft Childhood: The Surprising Truth about Violent Video Games and What Parents Can Do*. New York: Simon & Schuster, 2009.

Lanier, Jaron. *You Are Not a Gadget: A Manifesto*. New York: Vintage Books, 2011.

Lee, Dave. "Papers, Please: The 'Boring' Game that Became a Smash Hit." *BBC News*, March 12, 2014. https://www.bbc.com/news/technology-26527109.

Levinas, Emmanuel. *Alterity and Transcendence*. New York: Columbia University Press, 1999.

———. *Beyond the Verse: Talmudic Readings and Lectures*. Bloomington: Indiana University Press, 1994.

———. *Collected Philosophical Papers*. Translated by Alphonso Lingis. Pittsburgh: Duquesne University Press, 1998.

———. *Difficult Freedom: Essays on Judaism*. Translated by Seán Hand. Baltimore: Johns Hopkins University Press, 1990.

———. *Emmanuel Levinas: Basic Philosophical Writings*. Edited by Adriaan T. Peperzak, Simon Critchley, and Robert Bernasconi. Bloomington: Indiana University Press, 1996.

———. *Entre Nous: Thinking-of-the-Other*. Translated by Michael B. Smith and Barbara Harshav. New York: Columbia University Press, 1998.

———. *Ethics and Infinity: Conversations with Philippe Nemo*. Pittsburgh: Duquesne University Press, 1985.

———. *Existence and Existents*. Pittsburgh: Duquesne University Press, 2001.

———. *God, Death, and Time*. Translated by Bettina Bergo. Stanford, Calif.: Stanford University Press, 2000.

———. *The Levinas Reader*. Edited by Seán Hand. Oxford: Basil Blackwell, 1989.

———. *Nine Talmudic Readings*. Translated by Annette Aronowicz. Bloomington: Indiana University Press, 1990.

———. *Of God Who Comes to Mind*. Stanford, Calif.: Stanford University Press, 1998.

———. *Otherwise Than Being or Beyond Essence*. Boston: Martinus Nijhoff, 1981.

———. *Time and the Other*. Translated by Richard A. Cohen. Pittsburgh: Duquesne University Press, 1987.

———. *Totality and Infinity: An Essay on Exteriority*. Pittsburgh: Duquesne University Press, 1969.

Lien, Tracey. "Games for Change Awards Go to Papers, Please, Gone Home and The Mission US." Polygon, April 23, 2014. https://www.polygon.com/2014/4/23/5645362/games-for-change-award-winners.

Lynch, Gordon. *Understanding Theology and Popular Culture*. Oxford: Blackwell, 2005.

Ma, Xiaole, Lizhu Luo, Yayuan Geng, Weihua Zhao, Qiong Zhang, and Keith M. Kendrick. "Oxytocin Increases Liking for a Country's People and National Flag but Not for Other Cultural Symbols or Consumer Products." *Frontiers in Behavioral Neuroscience* 8 (2014): article 266.

Mahardy, Mike. "The Looking Glass Philosophy behind Gone Home." Polygon, April 6, 2015. https://www.polygon.com/features/2015/4/6/8315901/looking-glass-gone-home.

Manning, Russell Re. *Theology at the End of Culture: Paul Tillich's Theology of Culture and Art*. Leuven, Belgium: Peeters, 2005.

———. "Tillich's Theology of Art." In *The Cambridge Companion to Paul Tillich*, edited by Russell Re Manning, 152–72. Cambridge: Cambridge University Press, 2009.

Marsh, Clive, and Gaye Ortiz. Introduction to *Explorations in Theology and Film: An Introduction*, edited by Clive Marsh and Gaye Ortiz, 1–6. Malden, Mass.: Blackwell, 1997.

Marsh, Tim. "Serious Games Continuum: Between Games for Purpose and Experiential Environments for Purpose." *Entertainment Computing* 2, no. 2 (2011): 61–68.

McLuhan, Marshall. *The Gutenberg Galaxy: The Making of Typographic Man*. Toronto: University of Toronto Press, 1962.

———. *Understanding Media: The Extensions of Man*. Cambridge, Mass.: MIT Press, 1994.

McMillan, Graeme. "'Adventure Zone' Graphic Novel Tops New York Times' Trade Fiction Best-Seller List." *Hollywood Reporter*, July 26, 2018. https://www.hollywoodreporter.com/heat-vision/adventure-zone-graphic-novel-tops-new-york-times-trade-fiction-bestseller-list-1130198.

McRae, Hamish. "Unleashing the Digital Divide: The Changes in Television Will Change Global Society as We Lose Something that Unifies a Nation." *Independent*, November 17, 1998.

Mead, Corey. *War Play: Video Games and the Future of Armed Conflict*. Boston: Houghton Mifflin Harcourt, 2013.

Merton, Thomas. *The Seven Storey Mountain*. San Diego: Harcourt Brace, 1999.

Morgan, Michael L. *The Cambridge Introduction to Emmanuel Levinas*. Cambridge: Cambridge University Press, 2011.

———. *Discovering Levinas*. Cambridge: Cambridge University Press, 2007.

Morhenn, Vera, Laura E. Beavin, and Paul J. Zak. "Massage Increases Oxytocin and Reduces Adrenocorticotropin Hormone in Humans." *Alternative Therapies in Health and Medicine* 18, no. 6 (2012): 11–18.

Murray, Stephen Butler, and Aimee Upjohn Light, eds. *God and Popular Culture: A Behind-the-Scenes Look at the Entertainment Industry's Most Influential Figure*. 2 vols. Santa Barbara, Calif.: Praeger, 2015.

Myers, Maddy. "The Cost of Being a Woman Who Covers Video Games." Kotaku, January 3, 2020. https://kotaku.com/the-cost-of-being-a-woman-who-covers-video-games-1840793836.

Narcisse, Evan. "How Much Game Makers Get Paid." Kotaku, July 22, 2014. https://kotaku.com/how-much-game-makers-get-paid-1608955400.

Neville, Robert Cummings. *Metaphysics of Goodness: Harmony and Form, Beauty and Art, Obligation and Personhood, Flourishing and Civilization*. Albany: SUNY Press, 2019.

———. *On the Scope and Truth of Theology: Theology as Symbolic Engagement*. New York: T&T Clark, 2006.

Newzoo. "Global Games Market Report Free Version 2019." Newzoo. Accessed June 24, 2020. https://newzoo.com/insights/trend-reports/newzoo-global-games-market-report-2019-light-version/.

Niebuhr, H. Richard. Translator's preface to Paul Tillich, *The Religious Situation*, translated by H. Richard Niebuhr, 9–24. Cleveland: Meridian Books, 1956.

Noble, David F. *The Religion of Technology: The Divinity of Man and the Spirit of Invention*. New York: Penguin Books, 1999.

Northwind Seminary. "Center for Open & Relational Theology." Accessed July 4, 2020. https://www.northwindseminary.org/center-for-open-relational-theology.

Nuovo, Victor. "Tillich's Theory of Art and the Possibility of a Theology of Culture." In *Religion et Culture: Actes du Colloque International du Centenaire Paul Tillich, Université*

Laval, Québec 18–22 août 1986, edited by Michel Despland, Jean-Claude Petit, and Jean Richard, 393–404. Laval, Quebec: Presses de l'Université Laval/Éditions du Cerf, 1987.

The Okra Project. "What Is The Okra Project?" Accessed July 3, 2020. https://www.theokraproject.com/.

Owen, Phil. "4 Video Games That Help You Understand and Deal with Your Depression." Kotaku, April 19, 2013. https://kotaku.com/4-video-games-that-help-you-understand-and-deal-with-yo-473476131.

———. "WTF is Wrong with Video Games?" Polygon, September 28, 2015. https://www.polygon.com/2015/9/28/9370821/wtf-is-wrong-with-video-games-excerpt.

Paeth, Scott R. "The Moral Complexity of Video Games: Virtual Good and Evil." *Christian Century* 129, no. 6 (2012): 22–25.

Parkin, Simon. "A Truly Revolutionary Video Game." *New Yorker*, December 11, 2013. https://www.newyorker.com/tech/annals-of-technology/a-truly-revolutionary-video-game.

Pattison, George. *Thinking about God in an Age of Technology*. New York: Oxford University Press, 2005.

Paul, Kari. "GamerGaters Are Targeting People Who Were Victims of the Patreon Hack." Vice, October 14, 2015. https://www.vice.com/en_us/article/4x3k8n/gamergaters-are-targeting-people-who-were-victims-of-the-patreon-hack.

Peacocke, Arthur. *God and the New Biology*. London: Dent, 1986.

Pedersen, Cort. "How Love Evolved from Sex and Gave Birth to Intelligence and Human Nature." *Journal of Bioeconomics* 6, no. 1 (2004): 39–63.

Peirce, Charles S. *The Essential Peirce: Selected Philosophical Writings*. Vol. 2, *1893–1913*. Edited by the Peirce Edition Project. Bloomington: Indiana University Press, 1998.

Penenberg, Adam L. "Digital Oxytocin: How Trust Keeps Facebook, Twitter Humming." *Fast Company*, July 18, 2011. https://www.fastcompany.com/1767125/digital-oxytocin-how-trust-keeps-facebook-twitter-humming.

Peperzak, Adriaan T. *Ethics as First Philosophy: The Significance of Emmanuel Levinas for Philosophy, Literature, and Religion*. New York: Routledge, 1995.

———. Preface to *Emmanuel Levinas: Basic Philosophical Writings*, edited by Adriaan T. Peperzak, Simon Critchley, and Robert Bernasconi, vi–xv. Bloomington: Indiana University Press, 1996.

Pew Research Center. "Teen Content Creators and Consumers." November 2, 2005. https://www.pewresearch.org/internet/2005/11/02/teen-content-creators-and-consumers/.

Pitkow, Lauren J., Catherine A. Sharer, Xianglin Ren, Thomas R. Insel, Ernest F. Terwilliger, and Larry J. Young. "Facilitation of Affiliation and Pair-Bond Formation by Vasopressin Receptor Gene Transfer into the Ventral Forebrain of a Monogamous Vole." *Journal of Neuroscience* 21, no. 18 (2001): 7392–96.

Plant, Robert. "Levinas, Philosophy, and Biography." In *The Oxford Handbook of Levinas*, edited by Michael L. Morgan, 789–814. New York: Oxford University Press, 2019.

Plate, S. Brent. "Religion is Playing Games: Playing Video Gods, Playing to Play." *Religious Studies and Theology* 29, no. 2 (2010): 215–30.

Plato. *Phaedrus*. Translated by James H. Nichols Jr. Ithaca, N.Y.: Cornell University Press, 1998.

Plunkett, Luke. "EA Won't Be Paying for Real Guns in Video Games Anymore." *Kotaku*, May 7, 2013. https://kotaku.com/ea-wont-be-paying-for-real-guns-in-video-games-anymore-494940003.

Polkinghorne, John. *Science and Providence: God's Interaction with the World*. Boston: Shambhala, 1989.

Postman, Neil. *Technopoly: The Surrender of Culture to Technology*. New York: Alfred A. Knopf, 1992.

Purcell, Michael. "Is Theology Fundamental? The Scope and Limits of Doing Theology with Levinas." In *Responsibility, God and Society: Theological Ethics in Dialogue*, edited by Johan De Tavernier, Joseph Selling, Johan Verstraeten, and Paul Schotsmans, 123–41. Leuven: Uitgeverij Peeters, 2008.

———. *Levinas and Theology*. Cambridge: Cambridge University Press, 2006.

Rambo, Shelly. *Resurrecting Wounds: Living in the Aftermath of Trauma*. Waco, Tex.: Baylor University Press, 2017.

Ramée, Jordan. "Black Lives Matter, Black Voices Are Important." *GameSpot*, June 12, 2020. https://www.gamespot.com/articles/black-lives-matter-black-voices-are-important/1100-6477973/.

"Rami Ismail on Muslim Representation." *TheoNerd Podcast*, December 6, 2016. https://www.breaker.audio/theonerd-podcast/e/6212285.

Rizzolatti, Giacomo and Luigi Cattaneo. "The Mirror-Neuron System." *Annual Review of Neuroscience* 27 (2004): 169–92.

Root, Andrew. "A Screen-Based World: Finding the Real in the Hyper-Real." *Word & World* 32, no. 3 (2012): 237–44.

Ross, Heather E., Sara M. Freeman, Lauren L. Spiegel, Xianghui Ren, Ernest F. Terwilliger, and Larry J. Young. "Variation in Oxytocin Receptor Density in the Nucleus Accumbens Has Differential Effects on Affiliative Behaviors in Monogamous and Polygamous Voles." *Journal of Neuroscience* 29, no. 5 (2009): 1312–18.

Russell, Stephen T., Amanda M. Pollitt, Gu Li, and Arnold H. Grossman. "Chosen Name Use Is Linked to Reduced Depressive Symptoms, Suicidal Ideation, and Suicidal Behavior among Transgender Youth." *Journal of Adolescent Health* 63, no. 4 (2018): 503–5.

Sarkeesian, Anita. "Damsel in Distress (Part 1) Tropes vs Women." *Feminist Frequency*, March 7, 2013. Video, 23:34. https://feministfrequency.com/video/damsel-in-distress-part-1/.

———. "Lingerie Is Not Armor." *Feminist Frequency*, June 6, 2016. Video, 16:41. https://feministfrequency.com/video/lingerie-is-not-armor/.

Scharlemann, Robert P. *Reflection and Doubt in the Thought of Paul Tillich*. New Haven, Conn.: Yale University Press, 1969.

Schrag, Calvin O. "The Problem of Being and the Question about God." *International Journal for Philosophy of Religion* 45, no. 1 (1999): 67–81.

Schreier, Jason. "Video Game Industry Rocked by Outpouring of Sexual Misconduct Allegations." *Bloomberg*, June 24, 2020. https://www.bloomberg.com/news/articles/2020-06-24/video-game-industry-rocked-by-outpouring-of-sexual-misconduct-allegations.

———. "Why Most Video Game 'Aggression' Studies Are Nonsense." *Kotaku*, August 14, 2015. https://kotaku.com/why-most-video-game-aggression-studies-are-nonsense-1724116744.

Schrijvers, Joeri. *Ontotheological Turnings? The Decentering of the Modern Subject in Recent French Phenomenology*. Albany: SUNY Press, 2011.

Schut, Kevin. *Of Games and God: A Christian Exploration of Video Games*. Grand Rapids: Brazos, 2013.

Shapiro, Andrew L. *The Control Revolution: How the Internet Is Putting Individuals in Charge and Changing the World We Know*. New York: Century Foundation, 1999.

Shatzer, Jacob. *Transhumanism and the Image of God: Today's Technology and the Future of Christian Discipleship*. Downers Grove: InterVarsity Press Academic, 2019.

Shaw, Adrienne. *Gaming at the Edge: Sexuality and Gender at the Margins of Gamer Culture*. Minneapolis: University of Minnesota Press, 2014.

Shepherd, Andrew. *The Gift of the Other: Levinas, Derrida, and a Theology of Hospitality*. Cambridge: James Clarke, 2014.

Simmons, Jan. "Narrative, Games, and Theory." *Game Studies* 7, no. 1 (2007): http://gamestudies.org/07010701/articles/simons.

Šisler, Vít. "Palestine in Pixels: The Holy Land, Arab-Israeli Conflict, and Reality Construction in Video Games." *Middle East Journal of Culture and Communication* 2 (2009): 275–92.

Šisler, Vít, Kerstin Radde-Antweiler, and Xenia Zeiler, eds. *Methods for Studying Video Games and Religion*. New York: Routledge, 2018.

Skrade, Carl. "Theology and Films." In *Celluloid and Symbols*, edited by John C. Cooper and Carl Skrade, 1–24. Philadelphia: Fortress, 1970.

Slouka, Mark. *War of the Worlds: Cyberspace and the High-Tech Assault on Reality*. New York: Basic Books, 1995.

Smid, Robert. "The Metaphysics of Relative Goodness: Or, Recovery of the Axiological Measure." *The Pluralist* 15, no. 3 (2020): 27–37.

Smith, Graham. "Cart Life No Longer on Steam, Now Open Source." *Rock Paper Shotgun*, March 21, 2014. https://www.rockpapershotgun.com/2014/03/21/cart-life-no-longer-on-steam-now-open-source/.

Stanovsky, Derek. "Virtual Reality." In *The Blackwell Guide to the Philosophy of Computing and Information*, edited by Luciano Floridi, 167–77. Malden, Mass.: Blackwell, 2004.

Starkey, Dan. "Total Cost of Publishing One Indie Game." *Kotaku*, August 8, 2014. https://kotaku.com/total-cost-of-publishing-an-indie-game-last-week-sixty-1618376285.

Steinkuehler, Constance, Kurt Squire, and Sasha Barab, eds. *Games, Learning, and Society: Learning and Meaning in the Digital Age*. Cambridge: Cambridge University Press, 2012.

Tassi, Paul. "'The Last Of Us Part 2' Is Getting Predictably User Score Bombed On Metacritic." *Forbes*, June 21, 2020. https://www.forbes.com/sites/paultassi/2020/06/21/the-last-of-us-part-2-is-getting-predictably-user-score-bombed-on-metacritic/?sh=16fbcfc85c25.

Taylor, Mark C. *Nots*. Chicago: University of Chicago Press, 1993.

Taylor, Mark C., and Esa Saarinen. *Imagologies: Media Philosophy*. New York: Routledge, 1994.

Taylor, Mark Lewis. "Tillich's Ethics: Between Politics and Ontology." In *The Cambridge Companion to Paul Tillich*, edited by Russell Re Manning, 189–207. Cambridge: Cambridge University Press, 2009.

Terris, Elizabeth T., Laura E. Beavin, Jorge A. Barraza, Jeff Schloss, and Paul J. Zak. "Endogenous Oxytocin Release Eliminates In-group Bias in Monetary Transfers with Perspective-taking." *Frontiers in Behavioral Neuroscience* 12 (2018): article 35.

"Thomas Merton." PBS Religion and Ethics Newsweekly, June 4, 2009. Video, 10:54. https://www.pbs.org/video/religion-and-ethics-newsweekly-thomas-merton/.

Thompson, Eliza. "3 Couples Talk About How World of Warcraft Brought Them Together." *Cosmopolitan*, June 9, 2016. https://www.cosmopolitan.com/entertainment/movies/a59553/world-of-warcraft-wedding-stories/.

Thweatt-Bates, Jeanine. *Cyborg Selves: A Theological Anthropology of the Posthuman*. Burlington, Vt.: Ashgate, 2012.

Tilghman, Scott, and Daniel Ernst. "Plugging into the Video Game Market: Trends, Challenges and Opportunities in the Interactive Entertainment Market." *Hudson Square Research Report*, October 2009. https://nanopdf.com/download/presentation-5afdbf8055284_pdf.

Tillich, Paul. *Biblical Religion and the Search for Ultimate Reality*. Chicago: University of Chicago Press, 1955.

———. *The Boundaries of Our Being*. London: Collins, 1973.

———. *The Courage to Be*. New Haven, Conn.: Yale University Press, 2000.

———. *Dynamics of Faith*. New York: HarperCollins, 2001.

———. *Gesammelte Werke*. 14 vols. Edited by Renate Albrecht. Stuttgart: Evangelisches Verlagswerk, 1959–1975.

———. *The Interpretation of History*. Translated by N. A. Resetzki and Elsa L. Talmey. New York: Charles Scribner's Sons, 1936.

———. *The Irrelevance and Relevance of the Christian Message*. Cleveland: Pilgrim Press, 1996.

———. *Love, Power, and Justice: Ontological Analyses and Ethical Applications*. New York: Oxford University Press, 1954.

———. *Main Works/Hauptwerke*. 6 vols. Edited by Carl Heinz Ratschow. Berlin: Walter de Gruyter, 1987–1992.

———. *Morality and Beyond*. New York: Harper & Row, 1963.

———. *My Search for Absolutes*. New York: Simon and Schuster, 1967.

———. *My Travel Diary: 1936: Between Two Worlds*. Edited by Jerald C. Brauer. Translated by Maria Pelikan. New York: Harper & Row, 1970.

———. *The New Being*. New York: Charles Scribner's Sons, 1955.

———. *On Art and Architecture*. Edited by John Dillenberger and Joan Dillenberger. Translated by Robert P. Scharlemann. New York: Crossroad, 1987.

———. "On the Idea of a Theology of Culture." In *Visionary Science: A Translation of Tillich's "On the Idea of a Theology of Culture" with an Interpretative Essay*, trans. Victor Nuovo, 17–39. Detroit: Wayne State University Press, 1987.

———. *Political Expectation*. New York: Harper & Row, 1971.

———. *The Protestant Era*. Chicago: University of Chicago Press, 1948.

———. "Relation of Metaphysics and Theology." *The Review of Metaphysics* 10, no. 1 (1956): 57–63.

———. *The Religious Situation*. Translated by H. Richard Niebuhr. Cleveland: Meridian Books, 1956.

———. *The Shaking of the Foundations*. New York: Charles Scribner's Sons, 1948.

———. *The Socialist Decision*. Translated by Franklin Sherman. New York: Harper & Row, 1977.

———. *The System of the Sciences according to Objects and Methods*. Translated by Paul Wiebe. Lewisburg, Penn.: Bucknell University Press, 1981.

———. *Systematic Theology*. Vol. 1, *Reason and Revelation; Being and God*. Chicago: University of Chicago Press, 1951.

———. *Systematic Theology*. Vol. 2, *Existence and the Christ*. Chicago: University of Chicago Press, 1957.

———. *Systematic Theology*. Vol. 3, *Life and the Spirit; History and the Kingdom of God*. Chicago: University of Chicago Press, 1963.

———. "Die Theologie des Kairos und die gegenwärtige geistige Lage: Offener Brief an Emanuel Hirsch." *Theologische Blätter* XIII, no. 11(1934): 305–28.

———. *Theology of Culture*. Edited by Robert C. Kimball. New York: Oxford University Press, 1959.

———. *What Is Religion?* Translated with introduction by James Luther Adams. New York: Harper & Row, 1969.

Turkle, Sherry. *Alone Together: Why We Expect More from Technology and Less from Each Other*. New York: Basic Books, 2011.

———. *Life on the Screen: Identity in the Age of the Internet*. New York: Simon & Schuster, 1995.

Turner, Donald L., and Ford J. Turrell. "Emmanuel Levinas's Non-existent God." In *Models of God and Alternative Ultimate Realities*, edited by Jeanine Diller and Asa Kasher, 727–33. Dordrecht, The Netherlands: Springer, 2013.

van Anders, Sari M., James L. Goodson, and Marcy A. Kingsbury. "Beyond 'Oxytocin = Good': Neural Complexities and the Flipside of Social Bonds." *Archives of Sexual Behavior* 42, no. 7 (2013): 1115–18.

Wade, Nicholas. "Depth of the Kindness Hormone Appears to Know Some Bounds." *New York Times*, January 10, 2011. https://www.nytimes.com/2011/01/11/science/11hormone.html?_r=3&hpw.

Wagner, Kyle. "The Future of the Culture Wars Is Here, and It's Gamergate." Deadspin, October 14, 2014. https://deadspin.com/the-future-of-the-culture-wars-is-here-and-its-gamerga-1646145844.

Wagner, Rachel. *Godwired: Religion, Ritual and Virtual Reality*. Abingdon, UK: Routledge, 2012.

Wardrip-Fruin, Noah, and Pat Harrigan, eds. *First Person: New Media as Story, Performance, and Game*. Cambridge, Mass.: MIT Press, 2004.

Warschauer, Mark. *Technology and Social Inclusion: Rethinking the Digital Divide*. Cambridge, Mass.: MIT Press, 2003.

Webber, Jordan Erica. "This War of Mine: Little Ones—Bringing Children into a War Simulation." *Guardian*, March 4, 2016. https://www.theguardian.com/technology/2016/mar/04/this-war-of-mine-little-ones-children-11-bit-studios.

Webster, Andrew. "Immigration as a Game: 'Papers, Please' Makes You the Border Guard." The Verge, May 14, 2013. https://www.theverge.com/2013/5/14/4329676/papers-please-a-game-about-an-immigration-inspector.

Weed, Eric A. *The Religion of White Supremacy in the United States*. Lanham, Md.: Lexington Books, 2017.

Wertheim, Margaret. *The Pearly Gates of Cyberspace: A History of Space from Dante to the Internet*. New York: W. W. Norton & Company, 1999.

Westphal, Merold. "Thinking about God and God-Talk with Levinas." In *The Exorbitant: Emmanuel Levinas Between Jews and Christians*, edited by Kevin Hart and Michael A. Signer, 216–29. New York: Fordham University Press, 2010.

Whitby, Blay. "The Virtual Sky Is Not the Limit: Ethics in Virtual Reality." *Intelligent Tutoring Media* 4, no. 1 (1993): 23–28.

Wildman, Wesley J. *Effing the Ineffable: Existential Mumblings at the Limits of Language*. Albany: SUNY Press, 2018.

———. "From Grand Dreaming to Problem Solving." *Zygon* 42, no. 2 (2007): 273–76.

———. *Religious Philosophy as Multidisciplinary Comparative Inquiry: Envisioning a Future for the Philosophy of Religion*. Albany: SUNY Press, 2010.

Women in Games. "About." Accessed June 23, 2020. http://www.womeningames.org/about/.

Zak, Paul J. *The Moral Molecule: The Source of Love and Prosperity*. New York: Dutton, 2012.

———. "The Neurobiology of Trust." *Scientific American* 298, no. 6 (2008): 88–92, 95.

———. "The Physiology of Moral Sentiments." *Journal of Economic Behavior & Organization* 77 (2011): 53–65.

Zak, Paul J., Angela A. Stanton, and Sheila Ahmadi. "Oxytocin Increases Generosity in Humans." *PLoS ONE* 2, no. 11 (2007): e1128.

Zak, Paul J., Karla Borja, William Matzner, and Robert Kurzban. "The Neuroeconomics of Distrust: Sex Differences in Behavior and Physiology." *American Economic Review Papers and Proceedings* 95, no. 2 (2005): 360–63.

Zak, Paul J., Robert Kurzban, Sheila Ahmadi, Ronald S. Swerdloff, Jang Park, Levan Efremidze, Karen Redwine, Karla Morgan, and William Matzner. "Testosterone Administration Decreases Generosity in the Ultimatum Game." *PLoS ONE* 4, no. 12 (2009): 1–7.

Zak, Paul J., Robert Kurzban, and William T. Matzner. "Oxytocin Is Associated with Human Trustworthiness." *Hormones and Behavior* 48, no. 5 (2005): 522–27.

Zwiezen, Zack. "A Video Game Developed to Detect Alzheimer's Disease Seems to Be Working." Kotaku, April 27, 2019. https://kotaku.com/a-video-game-developed-to-detect-alzheimer-s-disease-se-1834331632.

Video Games Referenced

1979 Revolution: Black Friday. iNK Stories: iNK Stories, 2016. Windows, macOS, Android, PlayStation 4, Nintendo Switch, Xbox One.

A Mortician's Tale. Laundry Bear Games: Laundry Bear Games, 2017. Windows, macOS, iOS.

ABZÛ. Giant Squid Studios: 505 Games, 2016. Windows, PlayStation 4, Nintendo Switch, Xbox One.

Animal Crossing: New Horizons. Nintendo: Nintendo, 2020. Nintendo Switch.

ARMA. Franchise. Bohemia Interactive: Bohemia Interactive, 2006–2013. Windows, Linux, Android, iOS, Xbox.

Battlefield 3. EA Dice: Electronic Arts, 2011. Windows, PlayStation 3, Xbox 360.

Battlezone. Atari: Atari, 1980. Arcade. Atari, 1983. Atari 2600.

BioShock. Franchise. 2K Boston, 2K Marin, Irrational Games: 2K Games, 2007–2014.

Bound. Plastic Studios: Sony Interactive Entertainment, 2016. PlayStation 4.

Brothers: A Tale of Two Sons. Starbreeze Studios: 505 Games, 2013. Windows, Xbox 360, PlayStation 3.

Bury Me, My Love. The Pixel Hunt, Figs, and ARTE France: Dear Villagers, 2017. Windows, Android, iOS, Nintendo Switch.

Call of Duty. Franchise. Infinity Ward, Treyarch, and Sledgehammer Gamers: Activision, 2003–2019. Various platforms.

Cart Life. Richard Hofmeier: Richard Hofmeier, 2010. Windows.

Civilization. Franchise. MicroProse, Activision, and Firaxis Games: MicroProse, Activision, Hasbro Interactive, Infogrames, and 3K Games, 1991–2019. Various platforms.

Coming Out Simulator. Nicky Case: Nicky Case, 2014. Web browsers, Windows.

Counter-Strike. Franchise. Valve, Turtle Rock Studios: Valve, Sierra Entertainment, 2000–2012. Various platforms.

CURTAIN. DREAMFEEL: DREAMFEEL, 2014. Windows, Linux, macOS.

Dear Esther. The Chinese Room: The Chinese Room and Curve Digital, 2012. Windows, macOS, PlayStation 4, Xbox One.

Depression Quest. Zoë Quinn: The Quinnspiracy, 2013. Web browsers, Windows, Linux, macOS.

Diaries of a Spaceport Janitor. Sundae Month: TinyBuild Games, 2016. Windows, macOS.

Doom. Franchise. id Software, Midway Games: GT Interactive Software, id Software, Midway Games, Activision, Bethesda Softworks, 1993–2020. Various platforms.

Dragon Age: Inquisition. BioWare: Electronic Arts, 2014. Windows, PlayStation 3, PlayStation 4, Xbox 360, Xbox One.

Dream Daddy: A Dad Dating Simulator. Game Grumps: Game Grumps, 2017. Windows, Linux, macOS, PlayStation 4, Nintendo Switch.

Final Fantasy VII. Square: Sony Interactive Entertainment, 1997. PlayStation.

Final Fantasy VII Remake. Square Enix: Square Enix, 2020. PlayStation 4.

Firewatch. Campo Santo: Panic, 2016. Windows, Linux, macOS, PlayStation 4, Nintendo Switch, Xbox One.

Flower. Thatgamecompany: Sony Interactive Entertainment, 2009. Windows, PlayStation 3, PlayStation 4, PlayStation Vita.

Gone Home. The Fullbright Company: The Fullbright Company, Majesco Entertainment, and Annapurna Interactive, 2013. Windows, Linux, macOS, PlayStation 4, Nintendo Switch, Xbox One.

Grand Theft Auto. Franchise. Rockstar North, Digital Eclipse, Rockstar Leeds: Rockstar Games, 1997–2013. Various Platforms.

If Found . . . DREAMFEEL: Annapurna Interactive, 2020. Windows, macOS.

Journey. Thatgamecompany: Sony Interactive Entertainment, 2012. Windows, PlaySation 3, PlayStation 4.

Mass Effect. Franchise. BioWare: Electronic Arts, 2007–2017. Windows, PlayStation 3, PlayStation 4, Wii U, Xbox 360, Xbox One.

Medal of Honor. Franchise. DreamWorks Interactive, 2015 Inc., EA Los Angeles, Danger Close Games: Electronic Arts, 1999–2012.

Minecraft. Mojang: Mojang, Microsoft Studios, Sony Interactive Entertainment, 2011. Various platforms.

Mortal Kombat. Franchise. Midway Games, NetherRealm Studios: Midway Games, Williams Entertainment, and Warner Bros. Interactive Entertainment, 1992–2019. Various platforms.

Papers, Please. Lucas Pope: 3909 LLC, 2013. Windows, Linux, macOS, PlayStation Vita.

Papo y Yo. Minority Media: Minority Media, 2012. Windows, Linux, macOS, PlayStation 3.

Sea Hero Quest. Glitchers: Alzheimer's Research UK, University College London, University of East Anglia, Deutsche Telekom, 2016. iOS, Android.

Second Life. Linden Lab: Linden Lab, 2003. Windows, Linux, macOS.

Super Mario Bros. Nintendo: Nintendo, 1985. Nintendo Entertainment System.

Tennis for Two. William Higinbotham: William Higinbotham, 1958. Analog computer.

That Dragon, Cancer. Numinous Games: Numinous Games, 2016. Windows, macOS, Android, Ouya.

The Last of Us. Naughty Dog: Sony Interactive Entertainment, 2013. PlayStation 3, PlayStation 4.

The Last of Us Part II. Naughty Dog: Sony Interactive Entertainment, 2020. PlayStation 4.

The Stanley Parable. Galactic Cafe: Galactic Cafe, 2011. Windows, Linux, macOS.

This War of Mine. 11 bit studios: 11 bit studios, 2014. Windows, Linux, macOS, Android, PlayStation 4, Nintendo Switch, Xbox One.

Uncharted. Franchise. Naughty Dog: Sony Interactive Entertainment, 2007–2017.

What Remains of Edith Finch. Giant Sparrow: Annapurna Interactive, 2017. Windows, PlayStation 4, Nintendo Switch, Xbox One.

World of Warcraft. Blizzard Entertainment: Blizzard Entertainment, 2004. Windows, macOS.

Fast Travel

Page numbers in *italics* refer to figures.

AAA games, 14, 15, 147, 153
abduction, 116
AbleGamers Charity, 7, 147
absence. *See* illeity
absolute truth, 67
access to information, 147–48
ACLU, donations to, 122
Adams, James Luther, 23, 24, 25, 27–28, 36, 117
ADHD, 150
Adventure Zone, The, 122–23
AFK (away from keyboard) rooms, 6, 38
Alzheimer's disease, 150
Amazon, 128
American Academy of Religion, 90
Animal Crossing: New Horizons, 123
anxiety, 2, 27, 37, 68, 104–5, 106, 153, 157
Apple, 96–97
Arbery, Ahmaud, 120
Arisia, 8–9, 10
ARMA franchise, 145
asymmetrical dependence, 65
Atari 2600, 5
atheism, 55, 58, 59, 92
autonomy, 21, 22, 25, 26, 135, 140–41, 159; cultural, 26, 28; form and, 34; senses of, for Levinas and Tillich, 49; theonomy and, 28, 138
Auxier, John W., 149–50
Avellone, Chris, 145

Bail Project, donations to, 122, 123
Barth, Karl, 20–21, 26, 29

Battlefield franchise, 145
Battlefield 3, 110–11, 113, 117, 144
Battlezone, 146
Beaudoin, Tom, 152–53
being itself, 22, 24, 54, 64
Benedikt, Michael, 11–12
Biblical Religion and the Search for Ultimate Reality (Tillich), 174n10
Biden, Joe, 148
binary, 27, 76, 143
BioShock, 181–82n8
Bissell, Tom, 143, 146; *Extra Lives*, 85
Black Americans: player demographics, 5; police murders of, 109, 120; transgender, support for, 122–23; in video game industry, 121
Black Lives Matter movement, 109, 122, 146, 154, 157
Blackwell Guide to Theology and Popular Culture, The, 168n44
Bosman, Frank G., *Gaming and the Divine*, 18, 166n52
Boston Gameloop, 118–19
Bound, 150
Bowman, Donna, 156
Brant, Jonathan, *Paul Tillich and the Possibility of Revelation through Film*, 168n44
Brexit, 155
bullying, 5, 74, 177n50
Bulman, Raymond, 26
bundles, for racial justice fundraising, 121–22, 128, 129
Burggraeve, Roger, 50, 71–72, 76
Bury Me, My Love, 101–2, 106

Caballero, Vander, 150
Calcutt, Andrew, 11
Call of Duty, 144, 145, 186n5
capitalism, 105, 131, 134, 157
Cart Life, 32, 129–31, *132*, 147; courage in, 130, 131; emotional effect of, 36, 130, 131; gameplay of, 130–31; learning potential of, 32, 131, 149
Case, Nicky, 87
catharsis hypothesis, 11
censorship, 96
Center for Open and Relational Theology, 156
centered person, 138
characters: choice of, 9–10, 88; dress of, 4; LGBTQ+, 81, 82, 85–88, 91, 103–4, 140, 144; marginalized group representation, 2, 3, 9–10, 99, 103–4, 112, 113, 123, 140
charity, 120, 129
China, 145
Civilization series, 149
Cobb, Kelton, 34
Coming Out Simulator, 87–88
community, of game players, 7–9, 15, 38, 74, 77, 118–19, 148, 158; ethics of, 123–24; marginalized members of, 119, 123, 141, 149, 153; as pluralistic, 142
Community Bail Fund, donations to, 121
content, 31, 32, 33, 34
Contigo Games, 122
Control Revolution, The (Shapiro), 148
cortisol, 72
Counter-Strike, 145
courage, 37–38, 65, 105–7, 108, 118, 138–39, 153–54
Courage to Be, The (Gomes), 104
COVID-19 pandemic, 111, 120, 129, 156
Craig, Kate, 80
Crisis of Transcendence (Elwell), 17–18
culture: autonomous, 26–27; distortions of, 158; as form of religion, 3, 26, 28, 29; participatory, 148; rejection of, 21; relation of God to, 24–25, 27, 136; religious aspects of, 117
culture war, 2, 6, 29, 76, 139, 158
Curtain, 86

D&D. See *Dungeons and Dragons*
dark web, 3
dating simulators, 87

Davis, Erik, *TechGnosis*, 139
De Dreu, Carsten, 75–76, 178n55
demonic distortions, 20, 29, 36, 37, 111, 116, 138; video games and, 139–40
DePass, Tanya, 123
Depression Quest, 3–4
Derrida, Jacques, 169n1
Deuteronomy, book of, 154
DHT. *See* dihydrotestosterone
Diaries of a Spaceport Janitor, 132–33
DiCenso, James J., 138, 173–74n4
Dickman, Nathan, 65–66
difference, 45, 75, 76, 153–54
digital divide, 147–48
dihydrotestosterone (DHT), 70, 73, 76
Discovering Levinas (Morgan), 43
disruption, 35, 38, 92, 111, 117, 119, 125, 151
distrust, 69, 75
divine depths, 22, 23, 25, 29, 31, 37, 68, 106, 153
Doom, 145
Dragon Age series, 86, 140
Dream Daddy, 87, 140
DREAMFEEL, 86
Dungeons and Dragons (D&D), 9–10

Eaglestone, Robert, 170n8
Ehrenreich, Barbara, *Nickle and Dimed*, 149
8chan, 3, 4
Electronic Arts, 110
Electronic Entertainment Expo (E3), 120
Ellul, Jacques, 188n50
Elwell, J. Sage, *Crisis of Transcendence*, 17–18
emotional intelligence, 149
empathy, 14, 44, 74, 77, 115–16, 149, 153
Epic Games, 120
epinephrine, 72
Equal Justice Initiative, donations to, 122
essence, 64, 65, 67, 68, 69, 92
estrangement, 2, 22, 26, 27–28, 35, 67, 153–54; in societies, 29
eternal now, 152
ethics, 13, 14, 140, 149; in game scenarios, 101, 106–7; Gamergate and, 4, 7, 29, 134; vs. ontology, 45; philosophy of, 41, 44, 50, 52–53, 54, 58, 66–67, 137–38, 162n2; risk and, 153; theological, 117, 123, 140; utilitarian, 75

ethnocentrism, 75
E3. *See* Electronic Entertainment Expo
Explorations in Theology and Film (Marsh and Ortiz), 168n44
Extra Lives (Bissell), 85

Fells, Dominique, 122
Feminist Frequency, 4
FemShep, 9
Feshbach, Seymour, 11
Final Fantasy, 186n11
firearm industry, 145
first-person shooters, 32, 145
Flower, 32–33
Floyd, George, 120
forgiveness, 52–53
form, 31, 32, 33, 34, 67, 69, 155; autonomy and, 34
4chan, 3, 4
Fullbright Company, The, 80
Fuller, Tripp, 157; *Homebrewed Christianity*, 156–57
fundraising, 9, 121–23, 124, 127–29

Game Developers Conference (GDC), 110–11
gamedev.world, 111
Gamergate, 2–5, 22, 27, 36, 37, 72–73, 74, 134, 144–45, 148, 151; anxiety and, 157; compared to other tragedies, 42–44, 165n41; culture war and, 2, 6, 29, 139; difference and, 45, 105; as end of an era, 157–58; heteronomy and, 29, 38, 139; polarization and, 28, 37; positive developments after, 3, 5–6, 43, 80, 109, 140, 141, 158–59; responses to, 6, 14, 36, 38, 109, 159
Games for Change, 86
Gamesforchange.org, 149
Gamesforhealth.org, 149
GameSpot, 120–21, 183n14
Gaming and the Divine (Bosman), 18
Gardner, Wendi, 73
Gaynor, Steve, 80, 82
GDC. *See* Game Developers Conference
Gee, James Paul, 32, 89
Gehalt, 32, 33
Generation X, 152–53
Gjoni, Eron, 3, 4
God: as encountered through games, 1, 2, 93, 152; experienced in the other, 65, 134; as ground-of-being, 1, 22, 23, 24, 26, 27, 66, 69, 92, 118, 134, 135–36, 152; as not a being, 2, 23, 24, 56–57, 58, 64; otherness of, 65; presence of, 134, 139, 150; prophets and, 30; relation to human culture, 24–25, 27, 136, 140; supernatural, 21, 22, 53, 59, 155; transcendence of, 13, 53, 55, 57–58, 59, 93; as ultimate meaning, 24, 27; ultimate reality and, 1, 24; as unconditioned, 23, 25, 59, 64, 66, 69, 94, 137, 138
Godwired (Wagner), 17
Gomes, Peter, *The Courage to Be*, 104
Gone Home, 13, 36, 80–83, 83, 84, 91–92, 94, 103, 124; emotional effect of, 84–85, 103; gameplay of, 79, 81, 82; learning potential of, 146; release of, 32, 79; success of, 80; tropes in, 82, 83, 140
goodness, 50, 59, 66–67
Gore, Al, 147
Grand Theft Auto, 10, 11, 112
Grayson, Nathan, 3–4
Grossman, Vasily, *Life and Fate*, 50
ground-of-being, 1, 22, 24, 26, 27, 38, 69; connection to, 25, 28; essence and, 64, 69, 92; estrangement and, 27; transcendence and, 65, 118
Growing Down (Hamman), 18
Gunkel, David, *Thinking Otherwise*, 59

Hamman, Jaco J., *Growing Down*, 18
Hart, Kevin, 174n19
Hayes, Elisabeth, 32, 89
HBO, 111
Heidegger, Martin, 44–45, 53, 64, 89–90, 90
Heim, Michael, 11; *The Metaphysics of Virtual Reality*, 155
heteronomy, 25, 111, 135, 159; dangers of, 38, 107; estrangement and, 28; in societies, 29
Heyer, Heather Danielle, 51
Hispanics, player demographics, 5
Hitler, Adolf, 19, 20
Hocking, Clint, 181–82n8
Hofmeier, Richard, 130, 131
Holocaust, 13, 42, 43, 50, 52, 59, 165n41, 170n8
homophobia, 5, 61
Horse Volume, 115
Hughes, Thomas, 151

Humble Bundle, 122, 129
Hutchens, Benjamin, 177n41

I Need Diverse Games, 123
identity, 46, 67, 93; difference and, 45; exploring of, 9; God found in, 92; playing with, 88–89
idolatry, 23, 26, 137, 138
If Found. . . , 86–87, 91, 92–93, 94, 124
illeity, 59–60
immigration, 99, 105, 106; in games, 97–102, 105–6, 123
import, 31–32; theonomy and, 34
inattentiveness, 153
independent games, 14–15, 95, 121, 151
indifference, 51, 52–53
iNK Stories, 112
inversion of intentionality, 46
Iran, 108, 112–13, 140
irreligion, 152
Islam, 112–13, 140
Ismail, Rami, 109–12, 116, 117, 118, 119, 123, 141, 151
itch.io, 121–22, 128

James, William, 48
justice, 52, 68; racial, 120, 148, 152

kairos, 20, 36, 39, 135, 136, 152, 158
Khonsari, Navid, 112, 113
Kickstarter, 116
Klei Entertainment, 122, 128
Kosky, Jeffrey, 46, 47, 54, 55, 60–61, 92
Kotaku, 3–4, 79
Kraft, Robert, 127, 128

Lanier, Jaron, 167n34
Last of Us Part II, The, 144, 186n6
Levinas, Emmanuel, 1, 140, 171n49, 172n66; autonomy and, 49; first philosophy of, 13–14, 44, 162n2; on goodness, 50, 59; heteronomy and, 48–49; individual and, 48, 55, 137; limitations of, 61, 71, 73, 74, 76; on mythical elements, 137; ontology and, 45, 47, 64, 175n20; *Otherwise Than Being*, 43; philosophy of applied to video games, 59–62, 69, 77–78, 103, 123, 124; power and, 52–53, 154; responsibility to others and, 2, 13–14, 44, 45–46, 47, 49–50, 52, 53, 58, 60–62, 65, 71, 76, 77–78, 94, 106, 138; similarities to Tillich, 2, 56–58, 63, 64–69, 106–7, 137–38, 151–52, 153–54, 165n41; on transcendence, 13, 54–58, 92, 93; World War I and, 41; World War II and, 13, 42, 50, 170n8
Lewis, A. David, 7
Lewis, C. S., 158
LGBTQ+ people, 5, 10, 89, 93–94; rights of, 119, 140; in video game industry, 80. *See also* characters: LGBTQ+; transgender people
Life and Fate (Grossman), 50
losing, 14, 44, 79
ludonarrative dissonance, 102–3
Luther, Martin, 21

marginalized groups, 2, 3, 141; acceptance of, 89; harassment of, 5, 153; privileged by Levinas, 53, 59, 107; representation of, 76–77, 124–25, 141–42, 149; support for, 38, 119, 124, 134, 141
Marsh, Clive, *Explorations in Theology and Film*, 168n44
masculinity, toxic, 4, 142
Mass Effect, 9, 85–86, 88, 140
Massively Multiplayer Online games (MMOs), 10, 12, 17
Maximum Fun Podcast Network, 122
McDade, Tony, 122
McElroy brothers, 122–23
McGee, Llaura, 86
McLuhan, Marshall, 61, 139, 151
Me Too movement, 109
Medal of Honor franchise, 145
mental health, 131
Merton, Thomas, 42
Metaphysics of Virtual Reality, The (Heim), 155
military, 145–46
millennials, 38, 152
Milton, Riah, 122
Minecraft, 148
mirror neurons, 35–36, 74, 169n67, 177n50, 179n63
MMOs. *See* Massively Multiplayer Online games
morality, 26, 70, 76; justice and, 68; measurement of, 70; physiology and, 74
Morgan, Michael, 42, 49–50, 51, 52, 54–58; *Discovering Levinas*, 43, 172n66
Mortal Kombat, 10

Mortician's Tale, A, 103–4, 133–34
Muslims, 109–10, 111, 117, 119, 140, 144; in games, 113, 115, 116, 123
My Search for Absolutes (Tillich), 20
mysticism, 93

NAACP, donations to, 121, 122
National Bail Fund Network, donations to, 122
National Public Radio, 157
National Telecommunications and Information Administration (NTIA), 147
Naughty Dog, 95
needs, 47
neuroscience, 2
Neville, Robert, x–xi, 66–67, 161–62n5, 174n15
Nickle and Dimed (Ehrenreich), 149
Niebuhr, H. Richard, 134
Nietzsche, Friedrich, 54
9/11 terrorist attacks, 65
1979 Revolution: Black Friday, 112–13, *114, 115*, 118, 147; courage in, 112; emotional effect of, 36, 112–13; learning potential of, 36, 112, 113, *114*; Muslims in, 112–13, *115*, 119, 147
Noble, David, *The Religion of Technology*, 139
nominalism, 175n25
nontraditional games, 14–15, 43–44, 69, 96, 144, 151, 153; controversy over, 32; as religious experience, 140
Nordhagen, Johnnemann, 80
Northwind Theological Seminary, 156
Nour's Choice, 102
NTIA. *See* National Telecommunications and Information Administration

Ocasio-Cortez, Alexandria, 148, 157
Of Games and God (Schut), 17
Okra Project, 122–23
omnipotence, 25
ontology, 45, 47, 60, 66, 68, 153
Oord, Thomas Jay, 156, 157
Ortiz, Gaye, *Explorations in Theology and Film*, 168n44
other, the: call of, 45, 46, 48, 49, 52, 55, 69, 94, 124; encountered in games, 1, 2, 3, 10, 13, 14, 36, 44, 60–61, 62, 69, 77, 78, 92, 103, 124; ethical demands of, 56, 66, 67, 137–38, 153; face of, 44, 45, 48, 49,

55–56, 60–62, 69; God as, 27; inviolability of, 62; playing games as, 3, 9, 10, 151; responsibility to (*see* responsibility to others)
Otherwise Than Being (Levinas), 43
oxytocin, 70, 72, 73–74, 75, 76, 77, 78, 175–76n26, 176n30, 176n36, 177n40, 177n46, 177n50, 178n55, 178n60, 178–79n61, 179n63

Papers, Please, 95–101, *100*, 103, 105, 153; emotional effect of, 97, 99; gameplay of, 97–99, 102–3; learning potential of, 146–47; success of, 101, 128–29; tropes in, 140–41
Papo y Yo, 150
Pattison, George, *Thinking about God in an Age of Technology*, 18
Paul Tillich and the Possibility of Revelation through Film (Brant), 168n44
PAX. *See* Penny Arcade Expo
Pearly Gates of Cyberspace, The (Wertheim), 139
Peirce, Charles S., xi, 116
Penny Arcade Expo (PAX), 6, 15, 80
people with disabilities, 7, 147
Phaedrus (Plato), 12
philosophical theology. *See* theology: philosophical
Plant, Robert, 170n8
Plato, 12, 155
Playdius, 101
polarization, 2, 27, 35, 37, 107, 117, 154, 155, 158
police, in games, 146
police brutality, 22, 53, 108, 124; responses to, 109, 121, 123
policy, setting of, 141–42
political pressure, 141
politics: conservative Christians and, 155; Gamergate and, 3, 29, 134, 155; as polarized, 2, 177n40; power and, 51, 67–68; separated from theology, 37; violent games and, 10–11
Pollock, Jackson, 117
Pop, Nina, 122
Pope, Lucas, 95–96, 101, 121–22, 128–29
popular culture, xi, 30, 31, 36; Tillich's neglect of, 34
Postman, Neil, *Technopoly*, 12
poverty, in games, 130, 131, 149

power balance/imbalance, 50–51, 52–53, 107, 154
power of being, 22, 24, 27, 117
protests, 108, 119–20, 141; in games, 112, 113
Pugh, Jeffrey, 156
Purcell, Michael, 43, 47–48, 55, 137, 172n70

questioning, 66, 68
Quinn, Zoë, 3–4, 6, 79, 105

Race Forward, donations to, 122
racism, 61, 124
Re Manning, Russell, 34–35
realism, 21
ReedPop, 6
religion: estrangement and, 28; personal aspects of, 29–30; responsibility and, 54; as substance of culture, 3, 24, 26, 28, 29, 117; supernatural forms of, 25
Religion of Technology, The (Noble), 139
Religious Situation, The (Tillich), 134
remaking, 89
Republia Times, The, 96
responsibility to others: difference and, 45; as divine manifestation, 1–2, 59; ethics and, 47, 51, 52–53, 59–60, 69, 91–92, 103, 124, 152, 153, 158; impediments to, 74–76, 78; justice and, 52, 107; limitations and, 71–72; as particular and historical, 137; video games as reinforcing, 94. *See also under* Levinas, Emmanuel
retroduction, 116
revelation, 29–30
Rockstar Games, 112
Russell, Bertrand, 35

Sanders, Bernie, 157
Sarkeesian, Anita, 4, 83
Scharlemann, Robert, 66
Schelling, Friedrich Wilhelm Joseph, 20, 27
Schleiermacher, Friedrich, 20
Schut, Kevin, *Of Games and God*, 17
science fiction, 8
Second Life, 89
Seriousgamessource.com, 149
sexism, 4, 145
Shapiro, Andrew, *The Control Revolution*, 148
Shaw, Carol, 5

Shepherd, Andrew, 176n35
Slouka, Mark, 12
Smid, Robert, 174n15
social intelligence, 149
social media, 72, 73, 74, 139, 145
Socialist Decision, The (Tillich), 173n2
Stanovsky, Derek, 11
stress, 72–73, 176n36
Sun Also Rises, The, 115–18
Super Mario Bros. franchise, 82
supernaturalism, 13
suspicion. *See* distrust
Sweeney, Tim, 120
symbols, 24, 27, 38
Systematic Theology (Tillich), 20, 155

TakeThis.org, 6
Taylor, Breonna, 120
Taylor, Mark C., 152
Taylor, Mark Lewis, 173n2
TechGnosis (Davis), 139
technology, 36, 147, 151; concerns about, 18, 35, 61, 188n50; control and, 150–51; as democratizing, 148; Heidegger and, 89–90; optimism about, 139; promises and perils of, 11–12, 155; theology and, 90–91
Technopoly (Postman), 12
Tennis for Two, 145
testosterone, 70–71, 72, 77
That Dragon Cancer, 149–50
TheoCon, 156
theology: apophatic, 23, 57–58, 68; conservative, 153; cultural engagement and, x, xi, 29, 30, 33, 36–37, 69; of culture, 1, 110, 118; film and, 156; liberal, 153, 155; narrative, x–xi; philosophical, x–xi, 16, 54, 66–67, 175n21, 175n25; supernatural, 21, 29; trauma and, 149–50
Theology of Culture (Tillich), 30
TheoNerd Podcast, 7
theonomy, 21–22, 26–28, 49, 137, 138, 159; embodied in culture, 33, 111; in societies, 29, 113, 123
Thinking about God in an Age of Technology (Pattison), 18
Thinking Otherwise (Gunkel), 59
This War of Mine, 102, 106–7
Tillich, Paul, 3, 47, 56, 125; on anxiety, 105, 106, 155, 157; arts and, 2, 30–31, 33–35, 154; on autonomy, 21; *Biblical*

Religion and the Search for Ultimate Reality, 174n10; on courage, 37–38, 105, 106, 108, 118, 124, 138–39, 154; cultural engagement and, x, 1, 21, 30–31, 36–37, 65, 106, 117; estrangement and, 67; heteronomy rejected by, 21, 29, 49, 107; on history, 20, 21, 38, 105, 135, 136, 140, 155, 157, 185n13; idolatry and, 64–65; *kairos* and, 38–39; limitations of, 34–35; *My Search for Absolutes*, 20; ontology and, 2, 66, 153; political engagement and, 119, 134, 135, 138, 158; on power, 51; power and, 52; on revelation, 29–30; similarities to Levinas, 2, 51–52, 56–58, 63, 64–69, 106–7, 136, 137–38, 151–52, 153–54, 165n41; *The Socialist Decision*, 173n2; supernatural God rejected by, 20, 21, 22, 64; *Systematic Theology*, 20, 155; technology and, 35, 36, 37; terms for God, 22, 24, 27, 56, 92; theism and, 64; theology of applied to video games, 22, 31, 32, 36, 37, 124; *Theology of Culture*, 30; theonomy and, 49, 107, 137; on transcendence, 13, 56, 92, 93; unconditional God and, 23, 25, 59, 64, 66, 69, 93, 94, 138; World War I and, 13, 19, 20, 22, 29, 37; World War II and, 13, 19, 20, 22, 29, 34
totalization, 44
tragedy, 13–14, 20, 38, 42, 43, 65, 68; existence of God and, 22, 59; redemption after, 38, 119
transcendence, 26, 54–56, 69, 92; of God, 13, 57–58, 59, 92, 93; of human beings, 138
transgender people, 10, 28, 92, 93, 103–4, 122–23, 180–81n22
transparency, 25
Trinity Western University, 149
Tripp, Andrew, 6, 7
trolley problem, 75
Tropes vs. Women in Video Games, 4
Trump, Donald, 37, 51, 155
trust, 69, 73
trust games, 70, 73, 178n60
Turkle, Sherry, 88
Turner, Donald L., 176n35
Turrell, Ford J., 176n35
Twitch.tv, 123, 145

ultimate meaning, 23, 24, 27; conveyance of, 32, 35
ultimate reality, 1, 2, 22, 27
ultimate truth, 21, 22
ultimatum games, 178n60, 179n63
Uncharted franchise, 95

validation, 140
video game industry: dark side of, 144–46, 151; diversity in, 3, 118; income of, ix–x, 14, 127, 128–29; marginalized members of, 119, 141; maturing of, x, 143; racial justice and, 109; real-world issues and, 119–24, 148, 152, 157, 158; theonomous approach to, 28; women in, 5–6, 141, 145
video games: accessibility of, 146–48, 156; as art form, 1, 2; as cultural form, 151–52, 158; diversity in, 3, 10, 76; interactivity of, 14, 15, 33, 44, 124, 143–44, 146, 156; learning potential of, 10, 12, 146–49, 156; military use of, 145–46; nontraditional (*see* nontraditional games); player demographics, x, 5; reasons for popularity of, ix; religious studies and, 16–18; theological growth and, 155–56, 157, 159; therapeutic potential of, 150; transformative potential of, 144; tropes of, 4, 82–83, 118, 140–41, 159; violence in, 10–11, 28, 145–46; what counts as, 32, 33, 79, 80
violence, 45; police (*see* police brutality); threats of, 4, 62; in video games, 10–11, 28, 145–46, 146
Vlambeer, 109

Wagner, Rachel, *Godwired*, 17
walking simulators, 32, 33, 79, 80, 150
war, in games, 102, 106–7, 115–16, 145–46
Weisbecker, Joyce, 5
Wertheim, Margaret, *The Pearly Gates of Cyberspace*, 139
Westphal, Merold, 68
What Remains of Edith Finch, 150
Whitby, Blay, 11
white nationalism, 2, 4, 45
white supremacists, 51
Wildman, Wesley, 68, 91, 150, 154, 175n21, 175n25
winning, 14

women: blamed for destroying "real" games, 4, 79; harassment of, 4, 5, 62, 83, 145; player demographics, 5; in video game industry, 5–6, 80, 141, 145
Women in Games, 7–8, 118
World of Warcraft, 17, 148
World War I, 13, 19, 20, 41, 146
World War II, 13, 19, 20, 52

Wu, Brianna, 4, 79, 105

Yiannopoulos, Milo, 2–3

Zak, Paul, 69–70, 72, 73, 74, 77, 176n36, 177n40, 177n46, 179n63
zero-sum games, 178n60
Zimonja, Karla, 80